Research-Based Unit and Lesson Planning

Research-Based Unit and Lesson Planning

Maximizing Student Achievement

Marie Menna Pagliaro

ROWMAN & LITTLEFIELD EDUCATION
A division of
ROWMAN & LITTLEFIELD PUBLISHERS, INC.
Lanham • New York • Toronto • Plymouth, UK

Published by Rowman & Littlefield Education
A division of Rowman & Littlefield Publishers, Inc.
A wholly owned subsidary of The Rowman & Littlefield Publishing Group, Inc.
4501 Forbes Boulevard, Suite 200, Lanham, Maryland 20706
http://www.rowmaneducation.com

Estover Road, Plymouth PL6 7PY, United Kingdom

British Library Cataloguing in Publication Information Available

Library of Congress Cataloging-in-Publication Data

Pagliaro, Marie Menna, 1934–
    Research-based unit and lesson planning : maximizing student achievement / Marie Menna Pagliaro.
        p. cm.
    Includes bibliographical references.
    ISBN 978-1-61048-453-4 (cloth : alk. paper)—ISBN 978-1-61048-454-1 (pbk. : alk. paper)—ISBN 978-1-61048-455-8 (ebook)
    1. Lesson planning. 2. Academic achievement. I. Title.
    LB1027.4.P35 2012
    371.3028—dc23   2011039053

⊗™ The paper used in this publication meets the minimum requirements of American National Standard for Information Sciences—Permanence of Paper for Printed Library Materials, ANSI/NISO Z39.48-1992.

Printed in the United States of America

Contents

Introduction   vii

Chapter 1   Learning Theory: A Foundation for   1
                 Implementing All Curriculum and
                 Instruction

Chapter 2   Implementing Curriculum and Instructional   29
                 Planning Skills

Chapter 3   Assessment/Evaluation of Learning   41

Chapter 4   Reviewing Unit and Lesson Planning Basics   91

Chapter 5   Maximizing Unit Planning for Student   117
                 Achievement

Chapter 6   Differentiating Instruction   157

Chapter 7   Designing Optimal Lesson Plans   173

References   209

About the Author   225

Introduction

As a teacher or prospective teacher, you are a very important person, for it has been well documented that what teachers know and can do is the single largest factor affecting student growth. This teacher factor holds true regardless of class size; school location (rural, urban, suburban); student ethnicity; amount of expenditure per student; homogeneous or heterogeneous grouping of students; or percentage of students eligible for free lunch (National Commission on Teaching and America's Future, NCTAF, 1996; Sanders and Rivers 1996; Wright, Horn, and Sanders 1997; Haycock 1998; Pipho 1998; Joyce and Showers 2002).

If, as indicated, teacher performance is the key to student achievement, it is imperative for teachers to know the nature of that performance and how to develop and constantly improve that performance.

Teaching is extremely complex and is no small task. After extensive research on teacher effectiveness, Marzano (2003, 2007) has concluded that there are three comprehensive skills needed by teachers: *classroom management, use of instructional strategies,* and *classroom curriculum design.* Uplift Education of Dallas, Texas confirmed Marzano's conclusions by using predictive research to recommend the hiring of teachers who would likely be most effective. Of the 29 effective teacher attributes Uplift Education identified, one of the most important was the ability to offer *detailed instructional planning* (Pappano 2011). It is this attribute, classroom curriculum design (detailed unit and lesson planning), that the content of this book addresses.

By integrating the best of current research and practice in curriculum planning (Marzano 2003, 2007; Wiggins 2005; Wiggins and McTighe 2005, 2011; Lavoie 2005a and 2005b); Stiggins 2005; Tomlinson and McTighe 2006; Silver, Strong, and Perini 2007; Popham 2008, 2011), this book presents that comprehensive topic in a manageable form. Examples throughout are representative of different grade levels and subject areas. It should be understood at the outset that the content offered for curriculum planning is not a rigid prescriptive formula but a careful and purposeful thought process that must be considered to obtain optimal results.

In addition to developing knowledge about curriculum and instructional planning (what teachers should know), this book offers an innovative method for translating that knowledge into performance (what teachers are able to do). Knowledge is implemented by the use of coaching rubrics, sets of criteria for developing performance. Though readers will receive a thorough background in the planning process just from the content itself, its potential will be fully realized when readers also use the coaching rubrics.

We in the Teacher Education Division at Dominican College did not have the ingenuity to come up with the idea of coaching rubrics. They originated from our students who were searching for a way to make the quantum leap from knowing *that* to knowing *how*.

Outlines of teaching skills were not enough, nor were scoring rubrics. Our students felt that getting a numerical score did not actually tell them enough about their teaching performance, nor did a check mark, or using words such as "Yes" or "Satisfied". After wrestling with the problem for quite a while, the students came up with the idea of stating actual examples of the criteria performed. Thus was the birth of the coaching rubric.

Coaching rubrics for numerous teaching skills and strategies were eventually designed collaboratively by professors in the division, students, and school district teachers and administrators in our Teacher Education Division Advisory Council. After the coaching rubrics were constructed, they were used in student teaching in place of the usual checklist forms.

Cooperating teachers immediately joined our effort, stating that the coaching rubrics provided an objective means for discussing the performance of student teachers. These cooperating teachers reported that they were better able to reflect on their own teaching practice and to model excellent performance for their student teachers by using the coaching rubrics. Teachers in our Teacher Education Division Advisory Council also gave us positive feedback on the coaching rubrics after introducing them in their school districts, with many teachers indicating that they wished they had had such instruments in their teacher education programs.

Relevant coaching rubrics are placed strategically throughout the book. These rubrics assist readers in summarizing important information as well as in enhancing their practice.

Teachers are professionals rather than technicians. As professionals, teachers must understand the theory upon which their methodology is built.

Therefore, Chapter 1 reviews past and current learning principles (theory), providing a context and basis for the curriculum planning and instruction chapters that eventually follow.

Chapter 2 introduces a method for acquiring and developing teaching skills along with a corresponding field-tested tool, the coaching rubric. An explanation regarding how to use coaching rubrics with an accompanying example helps the reader gain a firm understanding of the process.

Since it is current practice to plan the assessment before instruction, Chapter 3 offers a comprehensive presentation of assessment and evaluation which includes traditional and contemporary methods.

Chapter 4 ensures that teachers have a thorough understanding of the basics of unit and lesson planning; in particular, standards, benchmarks, goals, objectives, and objective domains.

After acquiring this foundation, a detailed description of the unit planning process is presented in Chapter 5. Unit planning is presented first because it is the overall framework into which lesson planning fits.

Before lesson planning is actually reviewed, a discussion of differentiated instruction is offered in Chapter 6, emphasizing the need to consider the differentiation *before* planning daily lessons. This chapter also discusses the Universal Design for Learning (UDL).

Chapter 7 covers lesson planning components from both traditional and constructivist perspectives along with a discussion of grouping for instruction.

A recent study has indicated that when the skills of some teachers improve, other teachers follow. In other words, there is a "spillover effect" (Viadero 2009). The fact that you are reading this book already indicates that you are interested in improving your own knowledge and performance, which will subsequently have a growth effect on your colleagues. Good luck in your venture.

Marie Menna Pagliaro

Chapter 1

Learning Theory

A Foundation for Implementing All Curriculum and Instruction

Since the focus in education is currently more on students than on schools, there has now been a corresponding shift from an emphasis on methods of teaching to how every student can learn well (Stansbury 2008). The best way to develop your skills as an effective teacher is to concentrate on how students learn. To ensure that your instruction is as effective and efficient as possible, it is imperative that you be thoroughly familiar with the basic learning principles. These principles should be integrated into all aspects of your planning for instruction.

As you review this chapter, you will note that much of the same content is presented in different ways and might seem repetitive, but it is done so deliberately. Viewing this information from various perspectives will help you understand it better and remember it longer. Also, the different presentations should help clarify your personal beliefs regarding how meaningful learning should take place.

The information on learning principles is presented historically, beginning with traditional theories that originate from behavioral and cognitive psychology and are part of the teacher effectiveness research of the 1970s. You will note that almost all of the references in the first section are at least twenty years old.

As you proceed through the chapter, you will examine more current learning principles based on constructivism and on recent research on the brain. Try to concentrate on similarities and differences between the traditional and current principles. Reading through the evolution of these principles will give you a better sense of how the educational literature has progressed and how this progression changes the way teachers practice.

TRADITIONAL LEARNING PRINCIPLES

Motivation. *Motivation* is a psychological state that stimulates, directs, and sustains behavior. Motivation is the key to all learning. A motivated person learns better and faster, and will overcome many obstacles to achieve a goal s/he is interested in and thinks worthy. The more a person desires to learn, the greater the probability that s/he will.

There are basically two types of motivation: intrinsic and extrinsic. *Intrinsic motivation* is the inner desire or natural tendency to do something. It is performing an activity for the sake of the activity, especially when the activity is not required. Intrinsic motivation is self-sustaining (Deci and Ryan 1985). *Extrinsic motivation* is that which comes from outside factors such as incentives (rewards) or punishments. The reward is not in performing the task itself but in the what's-in-it-for-me attitude. A task is performed because a reward will result for task completion, or punishment for non-completion.

Though many students come to school with the inner desire to learn (the ideal), the reality is that many others do not. It is then incumbent upon the teacher to create the motivation that supports learning by capturing and maintaining students' interest (Brophy 1988). Interest can be aroused by introducing a little frustration (stress, tension) which throws students off balance just enough to make them want to come back into a state of equilibrium.

The science of teaching tells the teacher that the right amount of frustration should be introduced. The art of teaching determines how much frustration is just right. Too little frustration leads to boredom; too much frustration turns students off. Initiating frustration is like giving someone a vaccine. If too much of the dead or weakened agent is injected, a patient could become seriously ill by possibly actually developing the disease. If the amount of dead or weakened agent is too little, the vaccine will probably not immunize the patient. But if just the right amount is injected, the patient will become resistant to the disease.

Goal-directed activities. How many times have you been in a classroom when you asked yourself, "What is the point?" "What is this leading to?" or "What am I doing here?" How did you react to not knowing where the lesson (class) was going?

An overwhelming amount of research shows that students who are aware of goals and objectives of instruction are highly likely to achieve them. When there is a purpose in learning something, especially when the goal is personally important to learners, they are likely to become ego-involved and thus succeed. Goals and objectives should be made clear to students in every lesson unless the objective itself is to discover the objective.

Success. An old adage states, "Nothing succeeds like success." When you were a student, consider your own learning experiences. Which were successful? What did success do to your attitude toward learning? If you were like most students, you probably wanted to achieve even more.

Learning tends to improve as an individual experiences success. Students should be provided successful opportunities, and the sooner the better. Make sure that the first activities you provide are those which will lead to success.

You can do this by introducing at the beginning of school some content with which the students are already familiar, and new content in small segments after which the students experience satisfaction and gain the confidence to continue. You should be particularly sensitive to providing initial successful experiences for less able, emotionally challenged, and second language learners to give them encouragement.

Feedback. Feedback means knowledge of results. When were you particularly interested in knowing how well you performed on a test? Probably immediately after taking the test. Several days or a week later you were likely to have lost interest.

Students need to be constantly informed of their progress, especially knowing where their errors are. Quick knowledge of results allows students to correct errors before they become consistent (Elawar and Corno 1985). You should note that students would rather know their answer was incorrect (receive negative feedback) than have no knowledge of results at all.

Realistic and positive level of expectation. Think about the following quote.

> If you treat people the way they are, they will stay the way they are. If you treat them the way they could and ought to be, they will become what they could and ought to be.
>
> —Johann von Goethe

You should always treat students in a way that can assist them in reaching their potential. Of course you must be realistic in what you expect the student to achieve and provide instruction supporting that expectation. Conveying the attitude, "You can do it," is likely to produce the possibility that the student will be able to "do it."

A student who expects to fail probably will; a student who expects to succeed probably will (Rosenthal and Jacobson 1968). A positive expectation on your part applies not only to academic work but to behavior as well.

What do you think would be behavior likely to result from the following statements of Ms. Davis and Ms. Higgins?

Ms. Davis: "Class, we are about to leave on our field trip. If you don't behave properly, we will turn this bus around and come back."

Ms. Higgins: "Class, I know that on this field trip you will be shining examples of good behavior and will make me and our chaperones proud of all of you and of our school."

In the first statement Ms. Davis conveys the expectation through the power of suggestion that the misbehavior will occur, making it more likely that it will.

In the second statement Ms. Higgins conveys the expectation that the students would display exemplary positive behavior and the chances are better that the students will behave that way.

Active involvement. The more actively engaged students are in the learning process, the better they will learn. Active learning is more efficient than passive learning and is more likely to promote long-term retention. The Chinese proverb (source unknown) states, "I hear I forget, I see I remember, I do I understand."

Use of senses. Concurrent with active involvement is the use of senses. The more senses employed in a learning activity, the better will be the learning. For example, some people who live in the Midwest may have never seen an ocean. They may have read or heard about one, and/or have seen pictures or videos. But unless the Midwesterners have been in an ocean, smelled the salt air, been thrust about by the waves, felt the undertow, felt their feet sinking in the sand, heard the waves crashing against the shore, tasted the salt water, their knowledge of an ocean is incomplete.

Whenever possible, provide experiences that involve as many senses as possible. More senses will be involved if you provide direct experiences, rather than indirect experiences, with indirect experiences still better than vicarious experiences. Actually dissecting a frog (a direct experience) is more effective than viewing a picture or video of the parts of a frog (an indirect experience), and both of these are more effective than just reading about the parts of a frog (a vicarious experience).

Discovery learning. Students learn more efficiently when they are allowed to discover relationships for themselves (Bruner 1966). Try the following:

Write the first answer that comes to mind to the question, "What is the formula for the circumference of a circle?" Stop reading and write your answer now.

It is highly likely that you wrote C = πr, and if you did, it should tell you that you do not know the difference between linear and surface measurement. This is probably NOT your fault. Think of how you likely learned about circumference. Was it more like the way it was presented by Mr. Kravitt or by Mr. Pastor?

> Mr. Kravitt: Today we are going to learn how to find the circumference of a circle. The circumference is the distance around the circle. The formula for the circumference of a circle is C = πd. (He writes this formula on the board.) Open your books to page 73 and let's do the first problem. This problem is followed by several more problems performed in class, some providing the length of the radius instead of the diameter. Additional problems are assigned for homework. The next day Mr. Kravitt checks the homework and moves on to the perimeter of a different plane figure.

If you "learned" the formula for the circumference of a circle the way it was presented by Mr. Kravitt, it is probable that you forgot the formula because you learned it by rote and it had little meaning for you.

Now consider the presentation of Mr. Pastor.

> Mr. Pastor: Today we are going to discover the formula for the circumference of a circle.
> What does circumference mean? (Pause) Frank.
> Frank: The distance around a circle.
> Mr. Pastor: Good, Frank. (Mr. Pastor writes the definition on the board and then distributes to everyone in the class a packet containing different-sized colored circles, a tape measure, and a structured chart. He encourages students to place any personal items with circular shapes they may have on the desk.) Now measure the circumference and diameter of each circle and write the measurements on the chart in your packet. (He has already reproduced the chart on a whiteboard in the front of the room.)
>
> (When all students have completed the measurements, Mr. Pastor asks five of the students to place one of their results on the whiteboard.) Take a few moments to see if you can find a pattern in the measurements regardless of the circle sizes. (Pause.) Jeanette.

Table 1.1.   Circumference of a Circle

Circumference	Diameter

Jeanette: The diameter is 1/3 the size of the circumference.

Mr. Pastor: Excellent, Jeanette. Can anyone state that in another way? (Pause) Paul.

Paul: I was thinking the circumference is three times the diameter.

Mr. Pastor: Exactly three times in all the examples, Paul?

Paul: Uh, uh, no, it's, it's almost or approximately three times.

Mr. Pastor: Let's see if Paul is right. Check the measurements of all your circles and personal objects to see if they all follow the same pattern. (After the students check the measurements and decide that all the circles follow the same pattern, Mr. Pastor writes on the whiteboard, "The circumference of a circle is approximately three times its diameter.") So you were right, Paul. There is a mathematical name for something that means approximately but not exactly three times, and that is the Greek letter, pi (π). It is the irrational number, 3.1416 . . . or 22/7. You've just reviewed irrational numbers, so who can remind us of what they are? (Pause.) Elly.

Elly: One that can't be expressed as a decimal with a repeating pattern, and can't be expressed as the quotient of two integers.

Mr. Pastor: Great memory, Elly. Do 3.1416 . . . and 22/7 meet those criteria? (Elly and the rest of the students look for a moment and then nod in agreement.) If the circumference is approximately three times the diameter no matter how large or small the circle, how can this sentence on the board be expressed in terms of π? (Pause) Jim.

Jim: Circumference is π times d.

Mr. Pastor: How can π times d be expressed mathematically, Jim?

Jim: $\pi \times d$ or πd.

                (Mr. Pastor writes under the sentence defining circumference he has already written on the whiteboard the equation, $C = \pi \times d = \pi d$.)

Mr. Pastor: O.K., Jim, what is the relationship between the diameter and the radius of a circle?

Jim: The diameter's twice the radius.

Mr. Pastor: Since the diameter is twice the radius, Jim, how can we express the formula in terms of r?

Jim: (Thinks for a moment) $C = \pi 2r$ or $2\pi r$.

Mr. Pastor: Excellent. What law allows us to change the order of the three factors in a multiplication problem without changing the product? (Pause) Olga.

Olga: The commutative . . . uh, no, the associative law of multiplication.

                (Mr. Pastor adds $C = 2\pi r$ next to the circumference equations already written on the whiteboard. He then has one of the students transfer the information to a poster that is displayed in the front of the room for reinforcement and future reference.)

By using the discovery approach, Mr. Pastor gives the students a better chance to understand the formula by giving it *meaning*. If they forget the formula, they can reconstruct the experience they had in discovering the formula (measuring the diameters and circumferences of the different circles to find the pattern) to help recall it.

Many teachers complain that discovery takes too much time. However, discovery learning is more efficient in that it leads to understanding (meaning) and, therefore, long-term retention.

Meaningful materials. Materials related to the experiences of the learner are more successful in promoting learning (Gagne 1977). In the 1970s, a teacher in New York's Harlem community, frustrated that her students had such difficulty reading, discarded the Sally, Dick, and Jane series the students were using as basal readers.

Most of her students had not been farther than a mile radius from their homes. The students could not relate to living in suburban houses with white picket fences, to running around the yard with a dog named Spot, or having fathers with attaché cases driving station wagons to and from the train station. Instead the teacher substituted the local Harlem newspaper as the basic reader where her students were able to read about events, places, and people they knew. In addition to increasing student motivation, the teacher was able to increase reading scores considerably within a short period of time.

Readiness. Have you ever read a book you did not like, then picked it up several years later and found it to be great? One student reported hating *Lord of the Flies* when reading it in the 8th grade but loving it when reading it as a college sophomore.

Perhaps you saw a movie you did not like and many years afterward saw the movie again and found it to be excellent. In your first exposure to the book or movie, you might not have been ready for the experience. Most of the content the book or movie was trying to convey may have gone over your head.

Readiness means that students have the experiential background with which to connect the new learning. A student who has never been to a zoo to see exotic animals will not connect to a story about these animals in the same way as a student who has had that experience. Teachers will often say that their students will be more motivated to read after a rich experience with that topic.

Students may not be developmentally ready for certain experiences. A student who cannot discriminate between C (an open symbol) and O (a closed one) is not ready to learn to read. This student will need more experiences discriminating different shapes and figures.

Sequence. Even if a student is ready for an experience, some topics must follow a sequence in order to be understood. A student who knows what a noun is has a better chance of learning what a pronoun is in a meaningful connected way. A student must know *two* before s/he can learn about *three*. But *z* can be taught before *t,* and similar independent topics can be taught before others that generally precede them. You have to constantly ask yourself if the order of the learning makes a real difference.

Transfer. Learning has more meaning and is more efficient when it is applied to new situations and contexts (Salomon and Perkins 1989). Learners must be able to recognize how new knowledge is used or transferred to different settings. A student who learns the formula for the area of a rectangle will be inclined to forget that formula if it is studied in isolation but will tend to understand the formula better if used to measure rectangles for the purpose of buying carpeting for the classroom or covering counters with Formica, tile, or granite.

Related topics from different subject areas should be connected with each other. When studying the Korean War in social studies, students should read novels from that time period in English classes. Internet research studied in computer classes should be applied for the purpose of finding information in all classes.

Part vs. whole learning. In general it is better to learn a subject or activity as a whole first and then see how the parts fit into the whole, rather than learn the parts separately before putting them together (Ausubel 1963). For example, it is more effective to read a chapter summary first before beginning the chapter. Then you can see how the different sections are related.

A coach who first shows his/her team the overall strategy makes them understand how each movement contributes to the accomplishment of the goal. When learning to play a clarinet sonata, it is more effective to listen to the entire sonata before practicing each movement.

Part and whole are relative terms. What is the part in one situation can be the whole in another, depending on the developmental and cognitive level of the student. For a student who is first learning to read words, the word is the whole and the letters are the part. When reading a sentence, the sentence is the whole and the words are the part. The sentence is a part when reading a whole paragraph; the paragraph is a part when reading a whole chapter. Can you think of other examples?

Early review. If you have taken a course in general psychology, you will probably recall studying the forgetting curve. It demonstrates that most new learning is forgotten within the first 24 hours. Therefore, in order that the new information be retained, it should be reviewed (reinforced) once within the first day after the learning. The learning is reinforced by any consequence that strengthens the learning.

If a student spends a short time reviewing notes taken within the first 24 hours after a class, s/he will learn the material better and remember it longer. Some ways early review can be employed in the classroom include these: summarizing the main points of the lesson at the end; assigning meaningful homework (not busy work) relevant to the lesson; applying the new content; and reviewing the main content of the previous lesson before introducing the next one. These methods reinforce (strengthen) the learning.

Law of distributed practice. Short practice periods distributed over a long period of time are more learning efficient than one long practice session (Mumford et al. 1994). Cramming for exams is a typical example of inefficient learning. Studying a subject a few minutes each day will yield better results than cramming that subject the night before an exam. A student may do well on the exam but will not retain the information as s/he would through shorter review (practice) periods.

The same applies when learning a skill, whether it is related to sports or to playing a musical instrument. Practicing a piece of music only ten minutes a day every day for a week will lead to greater achievement than practicing an hour once just before the next lesson.

Recitation. *Recitation* means reading a certain amount of material, then saying what was read out loud without referring back to the text. Recitation has a greater effect on understanding and retention than re-reading. Knowing in advance that you will have to recite after reading is more motivational because this knowledge makes you more inclined to concentrate on the reading. Reciting out loud gives you immediate feedback that helps you determine whether or not you have understood the material before continuing reading.

Interference. When two topics are similar, they should be studied separately, with time in between to make the processing more effective. Studying two foreign languages at the same time may cause confusion with vocabulary words and spelling in those languages.

Examples:

The word "cheese" is fromage in French, and formaggio in Italian. Students often confuse the spelling of the first three letters, *fro* and *for,* and the fact that in French the word is spelled with one g, while in Italian with two.

Since the letters *b* and *d* are similar in appearance, they can be confused by children first learning the alphabet and phonics. Teachers should, therefore, not teach *b* and *d* within close proximity but teach other letters in between. The lower case letters *p* and *q* are also similar in appearance and should be taught separately with enough time lapsing. What other topics with which you have worked, if taught in close proximity, might cause confusion?

Nature of original learning. The way new material is learned (encoded) is critical to how it is processed. When new material is "processed" in a confused or incorrect manner, the student does not have the option of pressing a delete button, but must "unprocess" the material.

There are ways to assist students with learning the original material more effectively. These include the following:

Vividness. Learning is understood better and remembered longer if the original experience with the content is vivid. Vivid experiences gain attention and have a greater impact on the learner. They include color, loudness, music, or physical activity to convey a message.

A student who jumps over the numerals on a brightly-colored and decorated number line placed on the classroom floor while simultaneously stating the jumps, "Two jumps plus three jumps equals five jumps," can learn and remember addition facts more effectively than by completing worksheets. If six students are given one card to hold up, each with a letter in the word *cannot*, and they line up in that spelling order, and then if an additional student is given an *apostrophe* card, this student can physically (but gently) push away the students who are holding the second *n* and the *o* before the *t* (in *cannot*) and replace them to form *can't*.

Contrast. The more strongly one part of a situation contrasts with another, the more likely a student is to remember it. Students understand and remember situations that are different, those that are exceptions or that stand out. For example, the only word in the English language that ends in *–sede* is *supersede*. Knowing this makes it easier *not* to spell *–cede* words, such as *accede* or *secede*, with a *–sede* ending or *supersede* as *supercede*, which is commonly done.

If females are in class with only one male student, ten years later they will probably remember that male student better than they would their female classmates. While addressing an audience where everyone is wearing uniforms and one person is in regular clothing, the speaker will likely notice the person in regular clothing. When teaching the spelling rule that, in forming the past tense of some verbs that end in a consonant, you double the consonant and add *ed*, the students will remember the rule better if the letters involved in the change are enlarged and colored.

Present Tense	**Past Tense**
stop	sto$\mathbf{PP}$ed

Frequency. The more often students come in contact with the content, the better the chance they will learn it. Did you ever watch a TV show and note with impatience that at every break, the commercial was the same? This was no programming error, but a deliberate attempt to have you encode the commercial's message. In school, review (reinforcement) makes it possible for students to have more frequent contact with content; however, it is more effective if this review occurs in *different* ways.

Emotional environment. In order for students to be free to learn, they must feel emotionally safe (Covington and Omelich 1987). Too much stress does not allow a student to focus on the learning but on distracting factors such as, "Will I make a jerk of myself in front of my friends if I try to answer this question?"

Varying activities. Learners have limited attention spans. Sedentary activities over too long a time period can make students restless and take their attention away from learning. Instruction should alternate sedentary with active learning.

Summary of Traditional Learning Principles
Motivation
Goal-directed activities
Success
Feedback
Realistic and positive level of expectation
Active involvement
Use of senses
Discovery learning
Meaningful materials
Readiness
Sequence
Transfer
Part vs. whole learning
Early review
Law of distributed practice
Recitation
Avoiding interference
Nature of the original learning
Tension-free environment
Varying activities

CONTEMPORARY LEARNING PRINCIPLES

Brandt (1998) offered ten principles of learning. They are summarized below.

As you read through them, note any connection his principles may have with the traditional principles cited above.

People learn well when

- what they learn is personally meaningful.
- what they learn is challenging and they accept the challenge.
- what they learn is appropriate for their developmental level.
- what they learn is learned in their own way and they have some degree of choice and control.
- they use what they already know as they construct new knowledge.
- they have opportunities for social interaction.
- they get helpful feedback.
- they acquire and use strategies.
- they experience a positive emotional climate.
- the learning environment supports the intended learning.

Constructivism

Constructivism is concerned with how students make meaning of the world.

> Constructivism is based on the premise that the learner constructs all knowledge from previously acquired knowledge, personally, socially, or in combination, and therefore, learning is a more subjective affair than one might imagine (Bransford, Brown, and Cocking 2000). No two people can or should construct the same knowledge (although it might be quite similar) because each of us has our own unique experience, our own schema or knowledge structure, our own learning styles, and our own particular motivation to learn. Because this is so . . . it is more appropriate to expose learners to broad ideas than to particularistic skills. The former permits individual accommodation, while the latter assumes that everyone (at least within a group) needs the same thing. And that same thing is a *reductionist* approach to learning as opposed to a *holistic* approach to learning (Ellis 2001, 130).

Differing ideas about constructivism come from psychological (Phillips 1997), social (Palincsar 1998), and sociological (Gergen 1985, 1994) viewpoints of how students actually make meaning of the world. Exactly how this knowledge is constructed is a source of debate among the proponents of the various viewpoints. Is knowledge made meaningful through external world realities, through Piagetian internal processes, or both?

Irrespective of the persistent controversies surrounding constructivism, there is common agreement regarding classroom planning and implementation. The constructivists believe that

- instruction should be student-centered.
- students should be provided with complex problems that replicate those encountered in the real world, those requiring many interacting components, multiple solutions, and solutions that give rise to new problems.
- support for these problems should come from authentic situations faced outside of school. The teacher's role is to support the students in their problem exploration with resources, progress monitoring, task assistance in problem structuring, refining, and analysis.
- social negotiation in which students are provided opportunities to construct meaning through collaboration in reaching goals should be used. This process relies on skills of listening, communicating, negotiating, and respecting the positions of other students.
- content should be represented in many ways. This variety may be implemented by using different examples, analogies, applications, and contexts for the same content. Content learned in one grade can be expanded in another by examining it with different perspectives, contexts, or applications.
- students should be taught to understand the processes involved in constructing their knowledge. How do different experiences and assumptions shape their thinking and the thinking of others?

Airasian and Walsh (1997) warned those who want to jump aboard the constructivist bandwagon " . . . that constructivism is not an instructional approach; it is a theory about how learners come to know" (p. 62). And even that theory is still being debated between those who believe in a traditional (developmental) approach to constructing meaning and those who believe in a social-contextual approach.

While the debate continues, Foote, Vermette, and Battaglia (2001) identified connections between constructivism and current innovations. These innovations include using multiple intelligences; journal writing; portfolio assessment; cooperative learning; curriculum mapping; higher-order thinking and discussions; and the Hunter Model—one with a structured lesson that emphasizes deep thinking (pp. 72–75).

LEARNING IMPLICATIONS OF BRAIN RESEARCH

Most of the research on the brain began in the 1990s, which was designated as the decade of the brain. This research was made possible by advances in technology. Before this technology was developed, brains could be studied only through autopsies.

But with the subsequent arrival of sophisticated scanning through Positron Emission Tomography, PET, and Magnetic Resonance Imaging, MRI, scientists were able to examine how living brains grow, change, learn, and remember. During the 1990s neuroscientists were also able to identify more than 60 chemicals in the brain and counting. Many of these chemicals have a direct effect on learning.

The brain is a complex organ. To be a competent brain-informed teacher, you must familiarize yourself with the structure of the brain so that you can better understand the application of brain research.

Given space limitations, you should remember for the purposes of this section that the brain cells with which this chapter is concerned are called neurons. It is not so much how many neurons a person possesses, but the number of dendrites (branches) the neuron contains. More dendrites on a neuron allow more connections between neurons. It is the connections that determine learning and enable us to perform higher-level thinking.

With all the advances the decade of the 1990s has produced in our knowledge of the brain, less than one percent of this knowledge is related to education (Jensen 1998). In fact, most of what was learned about the brain only provided the biological proof, the *hard science,* that verified the research about teaching and learning already conducted through traditional research methodology from the *soft sciences* of psychology and sociology, which advanced the principles you read at the beginning of this chapter.

Brain research has helped explain why the traditional theories "worked." As you read the next section regarding the major findings brain research has produced, try to identify which traditional principles of learning and those offered by Brandt (1998) already presented in this chapter are reinforced by this research.

Neuroscientists have concluded that the only way we know that learning has taken place is through memory, and the only way we can get to memory is through attention. The brain is always paying attention to something. Our survival depends on it (Jensen 1998). When teachers say that a student is not paying attention, what they really mean is that the student is paying attention to something but not to the lesson. Though students can process information peripherally without direct attention (Caine and Caine 1994), this processing does not lead to higher levels of understanding.

The student's attention can be gained through the emotions. The emotions are powerful attention-getters. The best way to reach a student emotionally is by making the learning personal. How can you capitalize on students' personal interests? How can you make learning *personal* to them, their families, or to their neighborhoods? It must be made clear to students what the content means to them personally and how it can be applied.

Emotions ⟶ ⟶ ⟶ Attention ⟶ ⟶ ⟶ Memory

Learning can also be made personal by using students' names during the lesson such as in math problems or in stories. There are now available computerized books that have the recipient's name inserted as the hero, and names of his/her friends or relatives as characters. What person would not want to read a story about him/herself?

Many teachers keep learning personal (and emotional) by displaying pictures of the students doing work or involved in special projects. Teachers who show their personal excitement for the lesson also have a better chance of getting their students personally excited.

Attention can be solicited by priming the brain. This means that students will note something if their attention is directed to it. A teacher who says, "Today you are going to find out how to begin to use the Internet for research," or "In the video, note in particular how the blood flows through the heart," or who, before reading, asks the students several questions to look for in a story, primes (focuses) the students to pay particular attention to that content. This attention gives the student an outstanding opportunity to learn that content.

Neuroscientists inform us that the brain is not designed to give continuous attention. Brain-savvy teachers who want to maintain students' attention keep involving them personally by making the learning more student-centered. These teachers offer choices in instruction and even in assessment, and vary the activities by introducing something new (novel), whether it is new materials with which to work or a new methodology. Brain-informed teachers provide breaks at appropriate times for students to reflect upon and process new information.

In order to gain and maintain attention, the appropriate amount of stress must be provided. Too much stress (frustration, tension) and too little stress (boredom) both tend to shut down the brain. Think of stress as the tension on a violin or guitar string. When the string is loose, it has no tension. If in the no-tension state the string is bowed, plucked, or strummed, there is no sound, and, therefore, no music. But if the string is tightened too much, there is too much tension on it, and the string will break when bowed or plucked.

It has been suggested that too much stress, whether it be at home, in the neighborhood, or in school, may be the single greatest impediment to attention, and therefore, to learning (Sylwester 2000). High levels of stress produce chemical reactions in the brain that interfere with memory. Also, too much stress can lead to illness, which affects attendance and can lead to violent and aggressive behavior.

To introduce the appropriate or moderate amount of stress, teachers must determine what the students already know so that new learning can be connected to prior knowledge. Did you ever experience a high level of frustration when a teacher tried to teach you something from "out of the blue," information that had no connection to what you already knew, and therefore, had no meaning for you?

According to Sousa (2006), the appropriate amount of stress can be applied when teachers balance *novelty* (introducing something new), with *rituals* (routines). New activities offer challenge, and routines provide a comfort level that keeps students from experiencing a stress level that is too high.

Novelty can be introduced through enriched environments. Research reported by Diamond and Hopson (1998) has demonstrated that rats placed in rich environments—those with sensory stimulation such as bells, interactive toys, colorful materials, and ladders—developed larger, heavier brains with greater connections from one brain cell to another than rats placed in impoverished environments. Increased cell connections increase learning.

Moreover, Diamond (1997) reported that rats who simply watched the other rats interacting in the enriched environments, but who had no interaction themselves, showed no increase in cell connections. It is clear that learning is not a spectator sport. The rats had to be *active participants* to grow their brains.

Note that Diamond (1997) did not enrich environments of rats from normal environments and make those rats superintelligent. She enriched the environments of rats from impoverished environments and increased brain growth.

Jensen (1998) asserted that the hands are the most important "organ" of the brain, with the sense of touch creating important pathways to the brain. This is the reason that interactive "hands-on" learning is highly effective.

Arts. The arts include music, the visual arts, and movement. Franklin (2005) described a heart and circulatory system lesson taught by an elementary school teacher who took students to the gym, gave them red and blue ribbons, and had the students form lines that moved in the same path in which blood flowed through the body. Memory was strengthened because the students performed the activity physically.

In addition to offering a higher quality of life, the arts aid and support human development by fostering the growth of cognitive, emotional, and psychomotor pathways in the brain. In particular, the arts develop eight competencies identified by Eisner (1998) and reported by Sousa (2001).

These competencies are as follows:

The perception of relationships . . .
An attention to nuance . . .
The perspective that problems can have multiple solutions . . .
The ability to shift goals in process . . .
The permission to make decisions in the absence of a rule . . .
The use of imagination as the source of content . . .
The acceptance of operating within constraints . . .
The ability to see the world from an aesthetic perspective (pp. 217–218).

Another educational implication of brain research is the critical importance of understanding the difference between *procedural* and *semantic* knowledge. Procedural knowledge is *knowing how* to do something such as divide fractions or clean a carburetor—it is knowledge in action.

Procedural knowledge must be demonstrated. When faced with a fraction to divide, the student must divide correctly. Students demonstrate procedural knowledge when they translate a passage into Spanish, correctly categorize a geometric shape, or craft a coherent paragraph (Woolfolk 2008, 280). Typing, making a bed, taking a shower, playing a musical instrument, and driving a car are also examples of procedural knowledge.

Rote rehearsal (practicing the same way over and over again) is appropriate for most types of procedural knowledge. Most of school learning, however, does not cover procedural but concerns semantic knowledge, that which involves meaning.

Because procedural knowledge can be taught by rote, many non brain-informed teachers make the consistent error of teaching semantic knowledge also by rote. A typical example of learning by rote is evidenced by completing a course and several weeks later remembering very little. Unfortunately, this is a very common experience. To encode and retrieve semantic knowledge, however, a student should learn it through elaborative rehearsal.

In order to understand elaborative rehearsal, think of how you learned vocabulary. The purpose was to have you understand what the words mean (semantic knowledge). It is likely that you were provided with a list of vocabulary words, were required to look them up in the dictionary, and write a sentence for each. Perhaps you had a test on this vocabulary shortly afterward. You subsequently probably forgot most of the meanings.

Wolfe (2001a) informed us that we are competing with a brain that was designed for survival, a brain that has kept us safe from predators. Schoolwork, though important for cultural survival, is not important to the brain for physical protection.

LeDoux (1996) has demonstrated that with a brain that is programmed to forget what is not critical to survival, namely, the content we learn in school, we are at the mercy of our elaborations. Therefore, if we do not elaboratively rehearse, we will forget. Elaborative rehearsal makes learning meaningful, especially personally meaningful, by creating connections to what we already know, and reinforcing the information in several different ways.

Example:

> Give each student a different word; have the students look up the word in the dictionary; write a dictionary definition; write a definition that makes sense to the student (put it into his/her own words); create a visual (picture, diagram, chart) of what that word means to the student personally; put all of the above on a vocabulary poster; have each student present and discuss his/her poster in class; and hang all the students' posters around the room. It was demonstrated that using this method increased vocabulary retention 200 percent! (Wolfe 2001b). Methods *do* make a difference in learning.

Marzano (2003) described a current way of looking at memory. There is working memory and permanent memory. Working memory is involved in what you are reading now, and you are probably understanding what you are reading now. But the content will not get into your permanent memory unless you DO something with it—encode the information in different ways (elaboratively rehearse). Research conducted at Vanderbilt University and reported by Breaden (2008) has indicated that a 30 percent gain on a reasoning test was achieved by students who explained academic concepts either to their parents/guardians or who explained them out loud to themselves.

Other ways to provide connections (pathways) in the brain are through *mnemonics*, techniques to improve memory. One such technique is using an acronym, a word formed by the first letters of terms involved in a series. Common examples of acronyms are the names of the spaces in succession on the G-clef (FACE), and the names of the Great Lakes (Huron, Ontario, Michigan, Erie, Superior)—HOMES).

Besides acronyms, sentences can be used to help recall information. You are probably already familiar with the sentence or some variation of it used to remember the planets in order of distance from the sun, "My very excellent mother just started unwrapping neat packages," corresponding to Mercury, Venus, Earth, Mars, Jupiter, Saturn, Uranus, Neptune, and Pluto, as well as the sentence to recall the lines on the G-clef, "Every good boy deserves fudge (or fun)," for EGBDF.

Jingles, music, and rhymes can also be employed. Multiplication Rock was designed to help students remember single digit multiplication. To remember the number of days in each month you probably learned a variation of

Thirty days has September,
April, June and November.
All the rest have 31 except February
Which alone has 28 and one day more
When leap year comes one year in four.

Any connection that can be made between new material and what students already know will increase understanding, and therefore, memory. For example, in remembering how to spell *whippoorwill*, it will help students to know that the word can be put together by combining three words with which they are already familiar—*whip*, *poor*, and *will*.

The types of associations commonly connected in order to distinguish between *principal* and *principle* and between *hear* and *here* are that the principal (a person) is your pal and that you hear with your ear. The difference between *desert* and *dessert* is remembered by associating the double *s* in dessert with *strawberry shortcake*. Students who have difficulty remembering whether to spell the word as *seperate* or *separate* should remember the correct spelling by knowing that there is *a rat* in separate.

Also, it is a good suggestion to teach students how they learn and how their brains work (Jensen 2005). Thus, students can apply this knowledge in making learning more efficient.

To recapitulate, in order for learning to be brain compatible, learning must shift from passive to active; memorizing to constructing meaning; listening to responding; telling to discovery; and using textbooks and worksheets to using primary sources (Jensen 1998).

Before concluding this section it should be noted that both constructivism and brain-compatible learning can be misinterpreted if their applications lead teachers to believe that they should avoid structuring content and corresponding activities to promote the construction of meaning (Marzano 2003).

- Use novelty balanced with routines to maintain interest and ensure moderate stress levels
- Employ music and art to trigger pathways
- Make learning student-centered by using learners' interests and experiences in lessons and by capitalizing on learners' emotions
- Provide intermittent breaks in learning and use varieties of activities such as debates, role playing, simulations, drama, and challenging problem solving
- Use visuals (time lines, pictures, charts, advance organizers, diagrams, graphic organizers, semantic webs)
- Tie in lessons with other areas of the curriculum
- Introduce many hands-on activities with multisensory stimulation
- Prime the brain by ensuring that learners know the lesson objective
- Employ discovery approaches to learning
- Use elaborative rehearsal, when appropriate, by avoiding an emphasis on rote learning
- Introduce patterns and provide options
- Add rhymes, rhythms, and other mnemonics, when applicable
- Use other learners
- Emphasize depth rather than breadth of learning
- Ensure that learners (not you) are doing most of the work
- Have learners apply what they are learning
- Assess understanding
- Teach students how their brains work

Can the learner say the material in his/her own words?
Can the learner put the material in writing?
Can the learner successfully teach the content to another learner?

Figure 1.1.   Guidelines For Being A Brain-Informed, Meaning-Maker Teacher

OTHER LEARNING CONSIDERATIONS

Learning Styles

When considering how students learn, it is worthy to consider the fact that students (and teachers) have different learning style preferences. These include cognitive learning styles and modalities.

Cognitive styles. Students' cognitive styles determine the way they perceive and process information (Riding and Raynor 1998; Green 1999; Cruickshank, Jenkins, and Metcalf 2003). Some students are field-dependent. They are more global in their learning, tending to perceive concepts and materials as a whole, thereby developing a general overview of content.

As a result, these students are likely to have problems selecting details, focusing on a particular aspect of a problem, analyzing the overall content into parts, or regulating their own strategies in learning and problem solution. These students are inclined to be extrinsically motivated, work better in small groups, enjoy cooperation, social activities, and people-oriented subjects such as history and literature. They may need more structured learning, with the teacher providing detailed, sequential instruction.

On the other hand, field-independent students are more analytic, tending to perceive individual parts of the whole and capable of analyzing content into different parts. Field-independent students are more likely to be intrinsically motivated and pursue their own goals. There is less need for field-independent students to be socially involved. They generally like to work alone and prefer subjects such as science and math.

Learning Modalities. Another style preference is according to learning modalities. Some students are visual learners. They need materials that include pictures, diagrams, charts, videos, graphic organizers, concept maps, or timelines to help them learn and organize information.

Some students are auditory learners. They learn best through listening. They enjoy lectures, audiotapes, and being told the information.

Another group of students demonstrates tactile-kinesthetic preferences. These students like to learn through movement and enjoy hands-on activities where they can manipulate objects.

Multiple Intelligences

Read the following question and answer it before reading the question that follows.

How smart are you?

If, and only if you have answered the above question, read the next question and answer it.

How are you smart?

Gardner (1995) emphasized that it is not how smart you are but how you are smart that counts. In the past, IQ was considered something that was fixed, could be exhibited by only verbal and mathematical ability, was

Table 1.2. Teaching to Different Modalities

Visual	Auditory	Tactile/Kinesthetic
Shapes	Lectures	Manipulating objects
Diagrams	Audiotapes	Body movements
Pictures	Rhythms	Gestures
Patterns	Songs	Pantomimes
Colors	Stating orally	
Videos		

quantifiable numerically, and could predict student success. Teachers always had the instinct that there was something much more to intelligence.

Gardner expanded the way intelligence was viewed by exploring " . . . the way in which particular cultures value individuals and the way individuals create different products or serve their cultures in various capacities" (Silver, Strong, and Perini 2000, 6). As a result, Gardner defined intelligence as the ability to solve real-life situations, identify new problems for solution, and create a product or service one's culture values. He proposed that there were multiple intelligences, at least eight different kinds related to the classroom and possibly more. So far, Gardner has identified the following:

Verbal/linguistic. Ability to manipulate language through sensitivity to the meaning and function of words.
Logical/mathematical. Ability to test ideas, discern patterns, identify sequence, identify cause and effect relationships, conduct controlled experiments.
Visual/spatial. Ability to manipulate space and create pictures and images.
Musical. Sensitivity to tone and pitch and the ability to produce melody and rhythm.
Bodily/kinesthetic. Ability to control the body and objects with skill.
Interpersonal. Ability to work with people by being sensitive to their temperaments, attitudes, and needs and respond to them accordingly.
Intrapersonal. Sensitivity to one's own emotions and feelings.
Naturalist. Identifying and using resources in the natural environment to classify living and non-living things and/or to create products or solve problems.

In addition, Gardner (1999) has considered Existential intelligence, the ability to consider questions about the meaning of life. Gardner described this intelligence as " . . . the capacity to locate oneself with respect to such existential features of the human condition as the significance of life, the meaning of death, the ultimate fate of the physical and the psychological worlds, and such profound experiences as love of another person or total immersion in a work of art" (p. 60).

Gardner (1999) has also struggled with the possibility of coming up with a consensual definition of a final intelligence, Moral intelligence. He describes this as " . . . a concern with those rules, behaviors and attitudes that govern the sanctity of life—in particular, the sanctity of human life, and, in many cases, the sanctity of any other living creatures and the world they inhabit" (p. 70).

In terms of classroom applications of the multiple intelligence theory, Armstrong (2000, 40–43) has suggested the activities in Figure 1.2 for eight of the different intelligences.

Linguistic	—	brainstorming, storytelling, journal keeping, tape recording one's own words, publishing
Logical-mathematical	—	Socratic questioning, quantifications and calculations, scientific thinking, classifications
Spatial	—	picture metaphors, visualization, idea sketching, graphic symbols, color cues
Bodily-kinesthetic	—	hands-on thinking, classroom theater, body maps, kinesthetic concepts, body answers
Musical	—	musical concepts, mood music, super-memory music, discographies, rhythms, songs, raps, chants
Interpersonal	—	cooperative groups, board games, peer sharing, simulations, people sculpting
Intrapersonal	—	goal-setting sessions, choice time, personal connections, one-minute reflection periods, feeling-tones moments
Naturalist	—	nature walks, pet-in-the-classroom, ecostudy, plants as props, windows onto learning

Figure 1.2. Activities for Different Intelligences

Silver, Strong, and Perini (2000) presented a broader interpretation of multiple intelligences applications. They encourage

Targeting the development of specific intelligences
Differentiating instruction through use of all the intelligences
Diversifying the content to be intelligence-rich and intelligence-fair
Offering students choices of learning activities and assessments
Supporting student learning in one specific intelligence by allowing students to use another more developed intelligence to enhance understanding
Using intelligences as pathways to understanding broad topics (pp. 13–18).

In an interview with Checkley (1997), Gardner clarified his theory.

. . . I am not arguing that kids shouldn't learn the literacies . . . nor that kids shouldn't learn the disciplines. I'm a tremendous champion of the disciplines. What I argue against is the notion that there's only one way to learn how to read, only one way to learn how to compute, only one way to learn about biology. I think that such contentions are nonsense. It's equally nonsensical to say that everything should be taught seven or eight ways. That's not the point of the MI theory (italics mine).The point is to realize that any topic of importance, from any discipline, can be taught in more than one way. There are things people need to know, and educators have to be extraordinarily imaginative and persistent in helping students understand things better (p. 10).

Gardner (1998) also cautioned about carrying implications of multiple intelligences theory too far. According to Gardner's own suggestions, the greatest implications are for

- personalizing instruction,
- cultivating the skills the community and the larger society value, and
- approaching a subject in depth by implementing and assessing instruction in varieties of ways.

Process Intelligence

While Gardner was interested in intelligence as different abilities, Sternberg (1990) developed the idea of intelligence as a process that may be common to all learners. He proposed the *triarchic* theory of intelligence, one that has three elements: analytic, creative, and practical.

Analytic intelligence is the ability to apply thinking strategies, from basic ones such as solving analogies or developing vocabulary, to strategies that are more complex, such as planning, selecting strategies, and monitoring performance.

Creative intelligence is the ability to deal with new situations and demonstrate consistently proficiency in making new solutions to problems, such as diagnosing a problem with your computer, or locating resources for unit planning.

Practical intelligence is the ability to adapt to an ever-changing environment and continually shape or reshape the environment for success, such as taking a course in an area you feel you need for success but are deficient.

Teachers who are interested in further exploring applications of process intelligence should find the strategies Sternberg and Kaufman (1998) developed for writing, reading, test-taking, and homework based on the theory of triarchic intelligence useful in the classroom.

WHAT IS NEW IN LEARNING THEORY?

What is new in learning theory is what is old, but with a new twist. The theories presented in the beginning of this chapter, though over thirty years old, have been validated by subsequent research (Marzano 2003). What is new in these theories is some of the ways they are interpreted and applied. For instance, you already know that motivation is important for learning. Whereas in the past it was the teacher's role to motivate, now there is more emphasis on student self-motivation.

Dweck (2010) conducted research in which 400 New York City 5th graders were given a simple short test. Almost all did well. They were then divided into two groups. One group was praised for "being really smart"; the other was praised for "having worked really hard."

Subsequently, the students were requested to take another test with the choice of an easy one on which they were likely to do well, or a more difficult one on which they were likely to make mistakes. 90 percent of the students who were complimented for working hard selected the more difficult test whereas a majority of the students who were complimented for being smart selected the easy test.

Dweck (2010) pointed out the difference between "fixed mind-sets" and "growth mind-sets." In the former, students either believed they were good at something or they were not. With this belief, mistakes underscored failure.

Students with "growth mind-sets" believed that some students are better or worse in some subjects but anyone can improve. Given this mind-set, students could accept failure better because it was considered part of learning (growth). Moreover, when students were taught about "growth mind-sets," *motivation improved.*

Covington (1992) discovered that students, especially those who operate on avoiding failure and competition, are highly motivated by being informed of their knowledge gain. This positive report on their progress, even if small, leads students to want to learn further. It is also now recognized that one of the most potent student motivators is *choice* (Erwin 2004). Teachers who place a high priority on allowing students to choose their methods of instruction and even assessments, and who communicate a trust in the students to make the best choices for themselves produce learners who become intrinsically motivated to succeed.

Csikszentmihalyi (1990) reported that when students are passionate about something, they will overcome obstacles to achieve. There is for a vast majority of students at least one subject, topic, or activity that excites and, therefore, motivates them. Identifying this passion and capitalizing on it during learning will lead to a student's progress. For example, a teacher who knows his/her student loves baseball can use it to teach how to compute averages.

Long-term memory is best developed when the learning has meaning for the student. The brain is a meaning maker and welcomes anything that helps it understand. Meaning is enhanced when content is organized, especially by using advance organizers, concept maps, graphic organizers, and other visual tools (Hyerle 1996; Ewy 2003; Tate 2003), and when fewer subjects are processed, in depth rather than in breadth. Gallagher (2010) reported that students scored higher on state exams when their teachers covered subjects in breadth; however, students who were taught in depth earned higher grades once in college.

Another effective way to increase learning is by using *narratives* instead of explanations. When appropriate content is related through drama or a story instead of just telling or reading, there is a significant increase in remembering the content over a longer period of time (Nuthall 1999; Marzano 2002). Telling about a battle through a play or a narrative is more effective than just telling about the battle or reading about it in prose form.

Moreover, Nuthall (1999) reported that students cannot learn content just once. They need *a minimum of four exposures* in order for the content to be assimilated for the long term. He found that these four exposures should be *different,* reviewed and, therefore, reinforced in several diverse ways, with no more than two days occurring in between. The focus of these exposures should be on deepening understanding of the content.

Traditional learning theory informed us that feedback was important for learning. We now know that feedback and goal setting used together are powerful in improving student performance, even more powerful than either of them used separately. Also, the frequency of feedback obtained through assessments is positively related to student achievement (Marzano 2007).

While it was considered that learning should be generally from whole to part, it is now evident that some students are field-dependent and others are field-independent. This means that the teacher has to present certain content in both ways.

We know that the use of mnemonics helps memory. However, mnemonics use realizes its full potential only after the students have a sound understanding of the content (Marzano, Paynter, and Doty 2003).

Regarding the emotional environment of the classroom, it has been recently demonstrated that there are several characteristics that are conducive to promoting a positive classroom environment. These are having a caring attitude, setting high standards, and having all classroom members including the teacher show mutual respect for each other (Oakes and Lipton 2003).

Weiss (2007) reported research indicating that carefully choreographed teacher gestures emulated by the students during relevant instruction seemed to increase memory of the content. He provides as one example the sweeping of the teacher's left hand on the left side of an equation and the sweeping of the teacher's right hand on the right side of the equation to show that the value on the left side of the equation should equal the value on the right. Having the students repeat this hand gesture helps them understand and apply the concept.

As you read this chapter, you probably noted that the research on teaching and learning has caused a shift that has influenced teaching practice, particularly with teacher and student roles in several areas. These are summarized in Table 1.3 below. It is important for you to concentrate on these changes because they will guide you in the remaining chapters.

Chapter Summary: As teacher effectiveness research began to emerge in the 1970s, the implications of this research were largely implemented in the classroom under the direction of the teacher. More recent research has added to our depth of knowledge about how students learn. This includes having students more personally involved in their own learning, having some control over what and how they learn, learning in more social settings, and owning some responsibility for the learning of other class members.

Constructivists have emphasized the social and personal uniqueness of each learner's experiences, the need for a holistic approach to learning, and the introduction of broad ideas into the curriculum.

Brain research has demonstrated the importance of the emotions in learning, of introducing the appropriate amount of stress, focusing on student-centered

Table 1.3. Practices of Traditional and Contemporary Teachers

Traditional Teacher (Learning Is Teacher-Directed)	Contemporary Teacher (Learning Is Student-Centered)
Determines goals	Allows students to include their own goals
Delivers knowledge	Has students discover information and construct their own knowledge
Provides same learning method and activities for all students	Offers a variety of choices
Provides same assignments for all students	Offers choices according to student needs
Delivers instruction to the whole class	Provides additional opportunities for small group and individual work
Provides same assessments for all students	Offers assessment choices
Learning is passive	Learning is active
Provides knowledge in the content areas	Provides content area knowledge in addition to student self-knowledge
Focuses on teaching	Focuses on assessment as a guide to teaching
Looks at the achievement of the class as a whole	Stretches each student to the next level
Provides extrinsic motivation	Stimulates student self-motivation

learning, hands-on learning, and ensuring that the learning has meaning and is challenging.

Student learning styles and types of intelligences should be considered when planning instruction. To accommodate the diversity of styles, the teacher should deliver a variety of activities and offer students choices.

Chapter 2

Implementing Curriculum and Instructional Planning Skills

In Chapter 1 you reviewed learning principles you may have already studied and have also gleaned new information. Learning theory should be embedded in all your planning. As you proceed through the next chapters, you will read about skills that are imperative for planning. However, it is one thing to know about effective planning skills and another actually to be able to implement them.

> Whoever acquires knowledge but does not practice it is as one
> who ploughs but does not sow.
> Saadi

Knowledge of any teaching skill reaches its full potential when you can translate that knowledge into performance.

A FRAMEWORK FOR ACQUIRING TEACHING SKILLS

Learning even the most basic skills takes time, and developing teaching skills is a lifelong endeavor. A framework for acquiring teaching skills was offered by Joyce and Showers (1995, 2002). This framework includes the following: theory exploration, demonstration, practice with accompanying feedback, and adaptation and generalization.

1. Theory exploration. As a professional, the teacher must first understand the guiding principles of the research and oversee their use. You have already accomplished this knowledge by studying the first chapter and will accomplish more when you complete the text. You can further

explore planning skills through additional readings and discussions with colleagues.

2. Demonstration. In this phase the skill to be improved or the new skill is modeled for the teacher. Examples of the skill in action may be conducted through written samples; a live demonstration by a peer; an outside expert; through videotapes; or computer simulations. Teachers have often complained that in their teacher education programs, professors never modeled or provided adequate examples of the practices that were promoted (Reiman and Thies-Sprinthall 1998).

3. Practice with accompanying feedback. It has often been said that the three most important things in real estate are location, location, and location. It can also be said that the three most important activities in developing teaching skills are practice, practice, and practice.

The role of practicing cannot be overemphasized. Practice is required to develop any skill whether it is in the arts, sports, or teaching. You can do some of the practice on your own (unit planning, constructing teacher tests, rubric construction). But when your practice session involves interaction with students, it should be recorded through audio or videotaping so that performance is documented.

Though you can practice and evaluate your own performance, practice is more effective when it occurs with colleagues. Teaching used to be a very lonely profession. When a teacher closed his/her door, s/he had to fend for him/herself with no input from colleagues, only an occasional observation and checklist evaluation from a supervisor or principal.

On the occasion of his retirement, John (Jack) Welch (2000), former CEO of General Electric, communicated to his employees that whatever they can do well on their own, they can do much smarter with others. Teachers are now working much smarter by diagnosing students together; planning together; co-designing and selecting assessment tools and curriculum materials; observing each other; and giving one another feedback regarding performance. Peer interaction has been demonstrated as being necessary for teacher growth (Danielson 2006).

As soon as possible after the practice session, you should receive feedback regarding your performance from your colleagues. Immediate feedback allows you to become aware of parts of your performance that were successful and those that needed adjustment. Receiving this feedback prevents poor performance from becoming routine.

When your performance is interactive in nature, *microteaching*—teaching a short lesson to a small group of your students, concentrating on only a few skills, usually not more than three—should be used. It is essential that the microteaching session be audio- or videotaped.

Since a microteaching lesson is short and focuses on just a few skills, the teacher can specifically concentrate on developing just those particular skills and evaluating them readily. It is simple to count how many times they have appeared in the microteaching session so that subsequent microteaching sessions can document the increase of effective behaviors. Practice under microteaching conditions can then continue until the desired level of achievement has been realized.

4. Adaptation and generalization. There is no point in developing planning skills or any other classroom skills if they are not actually implemented in the classroom. Once the skills have been practiced in a clinical setting with a small group of your peers or students, the skills can then be implemented with the whole class. Video- or audiotaping interactive skills remains a critical necessity so that you can receive feedback for yourself and from your mentors/colleagues. In all cases it is essential that you self-evaluate and self-reflect.

THE POWER OF COACHING RUBRICS

To assist you in self-reflection as you endeavor to improve your teaching skills and acquire new ones, you will be provided throughout this book with a collection of personal guided observation instruments—*coaching rubrics.* A coaching rubric is a set of criteria for developing performance. The criteria in each rubric were designed collaboratively after teachers researched the rubric topic.

Coaching rubrics do exactly what their name implies. They coach and guide your performance. They will also document your growth. Documentation is of particular consequence because it has been reported historically that there is a gap in perception between what teachers think they do in the classroom and what they actually do (Good and Brophy 1974; Hook and Rosenshine 1979; Sadker and Sadker 1994; Delpit 1995).

Besides serving to summarize important content throughout this book, coaching rubrics serve many other functions. Coaching rubrics

expose teachers to best practices (mastery performance);
offer a medium with which to internalize best practices;
constantly remind teachers of best practices;
analyze present teaching performance;
compare present performance to best practices by identifying skills yet to be mastered;
refine present skills;

serve as tools for acquiring a new repertoire of skills;
foster communication and dialog among colleagues to continually identify
excellent teaching criteria;
provide a forum for discussing with colleagues better examples of criteria;
provide a structure for adjusting criteria and for creating new rubrics when
an innovation and/or new research emerges; and
evaluate teaching skills after practice.

The coaching rubrics offered will empower you to take control over your
own development immediately.

The Difference between Coaching and Scoring Rubrics

Coaching rubrics are different from scoring rubrics with which you are likely
to be already familiar. Scoring rubrics are a set of criteria for judging performance. In a scoring rubric the criteria (descriptors) are arranged in a hierarchy
that ranges from the poorest to the best performance.

A scoring rubric is holistic in that performance is either scored numerically
(1–6) or verbally (such as "emerging" to "outstanding") according to a set of
criteria (descriptors). Holistic rubrics assess overall quality of student work
such as organization of a report, creativity in writing, or critical thinking. For
a score to be assigned, all criteria (descriptors) have to be taken into account
simultaneously (Brookhart 2004).

Example: In a scoring rubric for map legends, the following scores (1, 2,
or 3) represent the corresponding performance levels.

You will observe in the Map Legend Scoring Rubric, Figure 2.1, that
performance levels are ranked and all levels of performance have to be
considered before judging which score (1, 2, or 3) to assign.

In contrast, the criteria in coaching rubrics are not necessarily arranged in
a hierarchy. Coaching rubrics are analytic in that each criterion (descriptor)
assesses specific aspects of performance and is evaluated separately, not by
rating the criterion but by identifying specific examples of the criterion.

Level 3 (Higher Order): creates an original legend to communicate spatial
arrangements and directions
Level 2 (Complex): interprets map subtleties that go beyond just reading the
legend
Level 1 (Basic): states literal meanings of legend items

                                          (Adapted from Lazear (1998, 56))

Figure 2.1. Map Legend Scoring Rubric

Table 2.1. Scoring and Coaching Rubrics

Scoring	Coaching
Judge performance	Develop performance
Criteria arranged in a hierarchy (performance levels)	Criteria not necessarily arranged in a hierarchy
All criteria evaluated together to assign a score (holistic)	Each criterion evaluated separately (analytic)
Score (usually numerical) assigned	Specific and accurate examples of criteria must be indicated

The criteria must also be specific and observable enough so that more than one person observing the performance will be able to agree if each criterion has been demonstrated. Specificity and observability give the rubric reliability. (Wiggins 2005).

How to Use Coaching Rubrics

Coaching rubrics are easy to complete. After experience with the first coaching rubric, teachers have often expressed how simple these rubrics are to work with and how effective they actually are in improving professional practice.

As an illustration, consider Table 2.2, the Coaching Rubric for Professional Development. The criteria in this rubric were developed by teachers after studying effective practices in professional development. The rubric is filled in partially to explain how to use the remaining rubrics in this book. Before you continue reading, examine this sample rubric carefully. Viewing the rubric will provide you with a frame of reference and a context for the explanation that follows.

You will notice that the coaching rubric above is divided into two columns—Criteria (Descriptors), and Performance Indicators (Examples), and that some of the Performance Indicators are completed and others are blank. The column on the left lists specific research-based skills (criteria) associated with a particular rubric.

Coaching rubrics represent mastery performance. When working with coaching rubrics, you should understand from the beginning that it is not expected, necessary, nor in most cases possible that anyone can perform all the criteria all the time (Wiggins 1998). However, since the criteria are determined because they positively correlate with student achievement, implementing most of the criteria will increase the chances for reaching all learners successfully.

As already indicated, the criteria in a coaching rubric are not necessarily listed in order. For instance, you can join a professional organization before identifying reading for personal broadening. You can identify peers with whom to work before doing either of the above.

Table 2.2.   Coaching Rubric for Professional Development (T)

Criteria (Descriptors)	Performance Indicators (Examples)
The teacher identified reading for personal and professional broadening	identified Classroom Instruction That Works by Robert Marzano et al.
read the materials and was able to describe what was learned	read text, learned that the nine major instructional strategies which affect student achievement are: identifying similarities and differences; summarizing; reinforcing effort; homework and practice; using non-linguistic representations, cooperative learning; setting objectives; generating and testing hypotheses; using questions, cues, and advance organizers.
used the new learning acquired from the materials in the classroom	used similarities and differences when teaching verbs by comparing them with other verbs and contrasting them with other parts of speech
evaluated the effect of the new learning on instruction	evaluated students on subsequent test on which they performed significantly better than they had before I made the comparisons/contrasts and just gave them definitions and examples
identified a relevant professional association (or associations)	identified the ASCD
joined the professional association(s)	joined the ASCD in June
participated in the association's activities and can describe what was learned	
transferred the new learning acquired from the professional association to the classroom and evaluated the effect of the new learning	
identified a mentor to assist in professional development	identified veteran master teacher Marian Floyd
identified others with whom to network	identified and contacted June Larson and Roy Pinzer from neighboring districts
identified ways to act as an agent to arrange for complementing my teaching	
collaborated with colleagues to obtain feedback for self-reflection	collaborated with fellow 4th grade teachers Lisa, Tom, and Frank
used guided observation for self-reflection	used the Coaching Rubric for Lesson Planning and Implementation with my colleagues to evaluate my videotape

(Continued)

Table 2.2. *(Continued)*

Criteria (Descriptors)	Performance Indicators (Examples)
sought input from learners	sought input from class every Friday in both writing and in classroom discussion regarding how well the week went and what could be done to improve instruction on the part of both the students and myself
used a self-reflective journal	used a self-reflective journal to jot down what happened each day. Arranged with Marian Floyd to discuss my journal once a week.
developed a portfolio for self-reflection	
As a result of the above, identified own professional development needs	
devised a plan to meet the needs	
If learning/perfecting a particular skill/model was identified as a need for development,	
explained the theory supporting the skill/model	
If necessary,	
arranged to have the skill/model demonstrated by an expert or video simulation	
practiced the skill/model with feedback (under microteaching conditions where applicable) until a desired level of achievement was attained	
implemented that skill/model in the classroom with the whole class	
evaluated the implementation of that skill/model in the classroom with the whole class	

The column on the right presents the Performance Indicators. The teacher (colleagues/evaluators) must put in writing in this column exactly how each criterion was demonstrated, providing specific, detailed, and appropriate examples. This process provides objective and more reliable performance data, making it easier for several observers (peers/colleagues) to agree that the performance has actually occurred.

Documentation of the examples is more focused and precise because the same verb and tense stated in the criterion is also used in the indicator. Verbs used in the Criteria (Descriptors) are expressed in the past tense describing what the teacher actually did, not what s/he plans to do. For instance, the third criterion in the Coaching Rubric for Professional Development is, "Enlisted peers with whom to collaborate."

Inappropriate ways to state the Performance Indicator would be stating what will be done in that category; putting a check, writing "Satisfied," "Completed," "Yes," or an equivalent term next to the corresponding criterion; numerically scoring the criterion; or offering an irrelevant example. Appropriate ways of stating the Performance Indicator for the above would be writing the names of the persons who agreed to be collaborators next to the corresponding criterion such as, "Enlisted (same verb and tense as the one in criterion) Paul and Sally from my teaching team." Otherwise, the Performance Indicator for this criterion would remain blank.

Because the documentation is so specific, coaching rubrics are more informative than the traditional type of rubric that judges performance through rating scales where raters place a check mark for each criterion in the corresponding box. Traditional rubrics, with scale variations (1–4, 1–5, 1–7), are commonly used to evaluate teachers.

However, these rubrics ". . . don't give specific enough information . . . to use for further learning" (Brookhart 2004, 77). Receiving a reported rating (score), such as three for "Average" on any scale used, while it does give some feedback, does not inform the teacher during the self-reflective process what "Average" performance actually is nor guide him/her how to improve in that category.

You have already observed that there are blank spaces under Performance Indicators in the Coaching Rubric for Professional Development presented in Table 2.2. Spaces that are not filled provide specific feedback identifying where performance could be improved.

Table 2.3. Completing Performance Indicators for Corresponding Coaching Rubric Criteria

Correct Completion	Incorrect Completion
Use the same verb	Use a different verb
Use the same tense	Write what will be done
Provide a specific example	Provide a general or vague example
Provide a relevant example	Provide an irrelevant example
	Use terms such as "Yes," "Completed," or "Satisfied," place a check mark, or score numerically.

The first session using any rubric provides baseline data regarding performance on that rubric. From the baseline data it can then be determined which additional criteria (descriptors) should be demonstrated or increased, and which ineffective criteria demonstrated, if any are identified as such on the rubric, should be avoided in future performance. After obtaining the baseline data, the teacher can then practice, addressing only a few criteria at one time.

In their attempt to offer a teacher evaluation system that goes beyond using observation forms and changing them periodically, Danielson and McGreal (2000) have offered a blueprint with three essential attributes: the "what," the "how," and "trained evaluators."

The "what" includes clear criteria for exemplary practice based on current research; the "how" involves the ability of school districts to guarantee that teachers can demonstrate the criteria; and "trained evaluators" can assure that regardless of who is conducting the evaluation, the judgment is consistent, and, therefore, reliable.

Coaching rubrics fulfill all three criteria suggested by Danielson and McGreal (2000). These rubrics express criteria for mastery performance (exemplary practice), help teachers demonstrate criteria by indicating which have and which have not been evidenced by appropriate examples, thereby identifying areas needed for practice, and provide a forum for "reliable evaluations" where the teacher him/herself must indicate and peer evaluators must agree which specific and accurate examples of criteria were implemented during actual performance.

Moreover, in the discussions of the examples among all participants, suggestions can be offered for better examples that could have been implemented. This interaction is professionalism at its best because it is highly effective in improving instruction and growth for all participants (Danielson 2007).

At a time when teaching degrees, training, and certification are being questioned as definitions of a "highly qualified" teacher, a new approach has been advocated in a longitudinal study of daylong classroom observations (Pianta 2007). "Watching teachers in action, using systematic, validated observational approaches, allows trained observers to see very clearly what good teachers do to foster learning" (p. 11). Coaching rubrics assist teachers and their colleague observers to ensure that agreed-upon researched criteria correlated with student achievement are understood and actually implemented in the classroom.

Using the coaching rubrics, you are now prepared to apply the framework for acquiring teaching skills (Joyce and Showers 1995, 2002) introduced earlier in this chapter: theory exploration, demonstration, practice with feedback, and adaptation and generalization. You should understand why the criteria in the coaching rubric are essential (theory exploration).

Familiarity with the research and discussion with peers are crucial processes in assisting participants in both identifying and then internalizing the criteria. If there is a question about any criterion that is not clear, an example of the criterion should be provided (demonstration). Practicing using the coaching rubric can then follow in a controlled environment. You may recall the old adage that practice makes perfect. Wolfe (2001) reminded teachers that practice also makes permanent.

And Vince Lombardi taught his football players that perfect practice makes permanent. These are the reasons that you must practice correctly with complete understanding of the rubric criteria and why they are important. Frequent practice is important because not all classroom events will necessarily provide you with the occasion to demonstrate each criterion and do so consistently. When the performance is interactive in nature within a limited time frame, microteaching should be used (practice with accompanying feedback).

As previously stated, microteaching can be conducted with a small group of your students. If you and your colleagues are satisfied with your performance, you can then implement the new skills with your entire class (adaptation and generalization).

Some coaching rubrics, such as one that may be developed for lesson planning, have criteria that can be demonstrated within a class period. Other coaching rubrics take a longer time to implement, such as the Professional Development rubric offered above and the implementation of the Coaching Rubric for Unit Planning. Coaching rubrics that take a longer time to implement are coded (T).

---

1. Identify collaborators (colleagues) and ensure that you and your colleagues fully understand and agree with the rubric criteria (descriptors).
2. Rubrics that take time (T) should be checked periodically to determine progress. When performance involves interacting with students within a class period (such as Lesson Planning and Implementation), audiotape or videotape the delivery.
3. As soon as possible after the performance, document it with colleagues by writing next to each criterion under the Performance Indicators column a specific and relevant example where you demonstrated any of the criteria. Write the indicator using the same verb and same tense stated in the criterion.
4. Identify no more than three additional criteria. Concentrate on only those criteria in subsequent performance using microteaching with audiotaping or videotaping whenever student interaction is involved.
5. Continue identifying additional criteria to be demonstrated and documenting that performance until a mutually agreed-upon level of achievement is reached.

Figure 2.2. Directions for Using Coaching Rubrics

Above all, it must be clear that coaching rubrics are dynamic. These living documents are works in progress, guidelines whose criteria should be modified when new research develops. As more studies reveal different criteria for performance excellence and as new and validated strategies and criteria are proposed, collaborators should revise rubrics and/or develop new ones.

Also, it is essential to understand that a teacher can demonstrate all the criteria in the rubric and yet be ineffective. The reason is that teaching is more than the sum of its parts. There are always intangibles involved that can contribute to effective or ineffective performance.

Chapter Summary: Knowledge of teaching skills is useless unless this knowledge can be translated into performance. Teaching skills can be acquired by understanding the theory behind them, having the skills demonstrated, practicing the skills with feedback, and transferring them to the classroom. As with all other skills, teaching skills take time and practice to develop.

Coaching rubrics are guided observation instruments that assist teachers in acquiring, developing, and evaluating teaching skills.

Chapter 3

Assessment/Evaluation of Learning

In most books on teaching skills, the topic of assessment/evaluation is placed *after* instructional planning. But assessment is such an integral part of instruction that here it is being reviewed *before*. The current trend is to determine first how you will assess and evaluate what the students will learn before planning the actual instruction (Wilcox 2006). Planning *high-level* assessments in advance will assure that you deliver instruction that will meet the assessments, thus giving you a mind-set to keep you focused on the key to successful instruction—student achievement.

THE DIFFERENCE BETWEEN ASSESSMENT AND EVALUATION

Assessment is the process of gathering information on student performance in order to make informed instructional decisions. This information may be collected through a variety of formal and informal means.

Formal assessments usually include the use of standardized tests, pre-tests, classroom tests, portfolios, and performance tasks—projects and presentations. Informal assessments include observing performance on homework and classroom assignments, student participation in classroom discussions, samples of student work, student feedback, student-to-student and student-to-teacher interaction, or performance on quizzes.

Assessment is used to promote learning by providing teachers with constant feedback on the effectiveness of their instruction. Assessment serves as a rudder for instruction because if the instruction is not working, the teacher must adjust the instruction (change course) to ensure student achievement by doing something *different.*

Table 3.1.   Formal and Informal Assessments

Formal	*Informal*
Standardized tests	Observation
Pre-tests	Interviews
Classroom tests	Quizzes
Portfolios	Homework
Performance tasks	Class assignments
Projects	Casual student comments
Student self-assessments	Samples of student work
Presentations	Class discussions
Interviews	Student self-assessment
Questionnaires	
Checklists	
Placement tests	

Assessment is just as essential for students. It makes learning more efficient by concentrating their attention on what is important and encourages student self-monitoring and self-evaluation using clear and objective criteria. Assessment also promotes motivation by informing students of their achievement. Studies have shown that when assessment is a regular and frequent part of classroom procedures and the students are aware of their progress along the way, student achievement is higher (Bangert-Drowns, Kulik, and Kulik 1991; Kika, McLaughlin, and Dixon 1992; Stiggens 2002, 2005).

When examining Table 3.1, you should observe that in several cases, formal and informal assessments are *not mutually exclusive* but can be used interchangeably.

Evaluation is the process of making a judgment on or assigning a value to student performance, such as assigning a grade once the information has been gathered through assessments. There are in general three types of evaluation: diagnostic, formative, and summative.

Diagnostic evaluation occurs before or at the beginning of instruction to determine what knowledge, skills, and experiences the students already have. This is valuable planning information that makes it possible for the teacher to know which students are ready for new learning and which students may need instruction before being exposed to the new material.

Also, the teacher will be able to determine students' interests and which students may need instructional accommodations or need to work individually

Social/Personal
How does the student get along with others?
What self-concept does the student demonstrate?
How do other students treat him/her?
What is the general appearance of the student?
How has the student shared knowledge/skills/materials with others?
What attitudes does the student convey?
How many other students selected him/her in a sociogram?

Academic
In what subject(s) is the student strong/weak?
Which subjects does the student seem to enjoy?
Where are there consistent errors?
What types of activities seem to engage the student?
What work habits does the student demonstrate?
What does the student do to demonstrate that s/he can self-assess?
What organizational skills does the student demonstrate?
What prerequisite skills necessary for present learning does the student demonstrate?

Behavior
How does the student demonstrate cooperative or uncooperative behavior?
Give an example of how the student follows (or does not follow) rules.
What acting out behaviors, if any, does the student demonstrate? What was happening in the classroom at the time?

Figure 3.1. Questions for Student Observation

or in groups. Diagnostic evaluation can be performed by observing and interviewing students, examining the results of standardized tests, checking anecdotal records, or administering pre-tests or placement tests.

Figure 3.1 lists general categories for observation (social/personal, academic, and behavior) followed by specific observable behaviors.

Note that in all the questions in Figure 3.1, none can be answered just *yes* or *no*. Specific examples must be given to each question. What other questions would you add under each category?

Even the most experienced observers can sometimes miss noticing relevant behavior or can misinterpret behavior. Be sure that the behaviors you observe are consistent and that they occur under different learning conditions.

A way to determine student interests as well as receive additional pertinent diagnostic information is through a personal interview. The interview should be a pleasant, relaxed experience where the student feels comfortable, because students do not reveal their feelings in a tense environment.

Structured questions are helpful, but the teacher must be ready to explore further information (that can come from students) before continuing with the

What are your favorite subjects?
What hobbies do you have?
Who are your best friends?
Which sports do you like?
What do you enjoy doing?
What do you not enjoy doing?
Which are your favorite TV programs?
What kind of music do you like?
From which activities do you best learn? (Videos, lectures, projects, reading, learning activity centers, worksheets, manipulatives, other)
What do you do in your leisure time?
Do you like material presented in logical order or without structure?
Do you prefer to listen, read, watch a video, or work with your hands?
Do you like to be told a rule or generalization followed by examples, or discover the generalization after being given examples?
Do you prefer working alone, in small groups, or in large groups?
What is the name of the most recent book you read?
What is the name of the most recent magazine you read?
What questions would you like to ask me?

Figure 3.2. Questions for Student Interview

more formal format. For example, if a student says that s/he hates math, the teacher may want to probe him/her by asking, "What might make math more enjoyable?" even though that question had not been planned.

As you go through the list of interview questions, reflect on which would be appropriate at various age levels and how the knowledge of each answer might influence instruction.

Now that you have read the list, what questions would you add?

You cannot assume that students will have answers to all questions. The areas in which they have no answers may provide you with teaching opportunities. For instance, you may want to provide hobby options as a choice of activities for a student who has no hobbies.

Though information about family is always helpful, probing too deeply in this area can be problematic unless a student voluntarily offers information. With increasing numbers of students coming from single parent and extended families, you cannot take for granted that students can answer traditional questions regarding mothers, fathers, or siblings.

Always remember that effective teachers are good listeners. Listening is critical not only while conducting interviews but during all interactions with students. The old maxim states, "You learn more by listening than by talking."

Information gleaned from Figure 3.3 Student Diagnosis Form should help teachers perform an appropriate diagnostic evaluation of students.

Name_____ Age/Grade_____

Standardized test results:

Achievement

Diagnostic

Aptitude

IQ

Other

Classroom test results:

Relevant family information:

General health:

Information from:

Parent/guardian meeting(s)

Prior teachers

Intelligence strength(s):

Verbal/linguistic

Logical/mathematical

Visual/spatial

Musical

Bodily/kinesthetic

Interpersonal

Intrapersonal

Naturalist

Learning preferences:

Cultural (Be careful to avoid stereotypes.)

Style

Field-dependent

Field-independent

Modality

Figure 3.3. Student Diagnosis Form as a Guide to Instructional Planning *(Continued)*

Auditory

Visual

Tactile/kinesthetic

Exceptionalities noted (if any):

Relevant information from:

Observation

Interview

Samples of student work

General strengths:

Weaknesses in need of remediation:

General prescription for student:

Figure 3.3.   *(Continued)*

Formative Evaluation

Formative evaluation (also referred to in the educational literature as *formative assessment*) is an instructional tool that determines the progress of students at all points during the instruction process. Formative evaluation is educative, with the main purpose of providing feedback while the instructional program is still malleable by both teachers and students through continuous collection of information (assessment) regarding how they are meeting the goals and objectives of instruction, so that adjustments can be made by both to ensure success before it is too late.

The purpose of formative evaluation is not the comparison of students or the assignment of grades but to improve instruction on the part of both teachers and students, and students should be made aware of this distinction (Popham 2008). Awareness of their performance makes students responsible for modifying their own learning tactics for the purpose of achieving an instructional goal. To reiterate, formative evaluation is a process whose overriding purpose is generating evidence so that, if necessary, teachers and students can adjust what they are doing to improve learning.

The formative evaluation process must be planned in advance. Before a teacher can decide whether to make an instructional adjustment, s/he must first determine at what point in the subskill or building block knowledge acquisition toward achievement of a final instructional goal or objective this decision will be made. Before assessment feedback is received, the teacher must decide what will initiate an instructional adjustment. This decision is based on a pre-determined minimum required level of both individual performance as well as a pre-determined level of class performance.

For example, a teacher may decide that each student should receive a minimum 80 percent achievement on a long division quiz and that 90 percent of the class should receive this score. On the basis of these results, a teacher may include additional instruction or exclude planned subsequent instruction.

In gathering information for the adjustment, the teacher may use observations; classroom questions; discussions; quizzes; performance on assignments; and student self-assessments (Popham 2008, 2011). Once the teacher decides to adjust instruction, this adjustment can take the form of different input experiences, reinforcement experiences, student grouping, or any other adjustment method that makes sense.

Summative Evaluation

Summative evaluation occurs at the end of instruction, whether that is a lesson, a unit, or a course, to determine how well the students have achieved the goals and objectives. At that point the teacher makes a final determination of what was learned. For both teachers and students it would obviously be better to know constantly how students are doing so that by the time they get to be evaluated, they could improve their performance. Information for summative evaluation may be obtained through classroom tests, portfolios, projects, performance tasks, and standardized tests.

Before continuing with a discussion of assessment/evaluation, it should be pointed out that the appropriate type of assessment must correspond with an instructional goal. If the goal is *declarative knowledge* —what students should know and understand (vocabulary acquisition or knowledge of cultural lifestyles), then objective tests would be in order. If the goal is *procedural knowledge* (Chapter 1) —what the students can actually do as a result of knowledge (solve a problem or develop writing skills), then a performance assessment would be appropriate.

Table 3.2. Evaluation

Diagnostic	Formative	Summative
Conducted at or before the beginning of instruction	Conducted during instruction	Conducted at the end of instruction
Provides input for initial planning	Provides continuous feedback so that instructional adjustments can be made	Determines how well instructional goals have been met

Finally, if the goal is *disposition development* (interests, attitudes, and mind habits such as reflecting on experiences, knowing how to find additional information, coming up with original questions, or searching different viewpoints), then evidence such as student self-reflective journals, portfolios, or teacher observations would need to be collected over a period of time. It would make no sense to "measure" a student's persistence in pursuing work by a matching or multiple choice test question (Tomlinson and McTighe 2006).

ASSESSING/EVALUATING THROUGH TEACHER-CONSTRUCTED TESTS

Classroom Quizzes and Tests

As stated above, tests are valuable in measuring declarative knowledge. Quizzes and tests differ in that quizzes are usually shorter in administration time and less comprehensive in content coverage. Quizzes occur daily, or after several days of instruction, and tests are usually given at the end of a unit. Before reviewing how to construct tests, the general attributes of tests as well as the specific attributes of various types of classroom tests should be mastered.

Attributes of Tests

Validity. A test's *validity* is the extent to which the test measures what it says it is measuring. Does the test do the job it was intended to do? Does it measure what students have been charged with learning?

Of particular concern to teachers is *content validity*, also known as *curricular validity*. The curricular (content) validity is the degree to which the test questions represent an adequate sampling of what the objectives of the chapter, course, or instructional program were intended to cover. If the teacher spent more time on three out of 10 of the objectives, a comparable percentage of test questions (30 percent) should reflect those same objectives. Students often express frustration when a teacher tests them more on content that was not covered in class as opposed to content that was covered.

Reliability. The extent to which a test is consistent in measuring what it measures is its *reliability*. Is the test dependable, stable, and trustworthy? Does the test have scoring consistency from one measurement to the next? If the same test is given to the same student within a short time frame or to similar students, would the results be the same or very close?

To ensure reliability, a variety of measures should be collected on each student. These multiple measures would include not only tests that determine declarative knowledge but also a combination of performance tasks and products that measure procedural knowledge.

Types of Tests

Norm-referenced test. This is a test in which the student's score is compared to the average score (norm) achieved by a citywide, statewide, or nationwide sample of students. The norm is based on the actual performance of pupils of different grades or ages in a standardized group and provides a frame of reference for comparing a student's score with those of other students of the same grade or age.

Since the norm is a midpoint on a norm-referenced test, half the students in the sample group score above the midpoint (norm) and half the students score below. Though norm-referenced tests have some value for broad comparison purposes, they do not provide information about a specific student skill.

Criterion-referenced test. A test designed to provide information on the achievement of specific knowledge or skills set up in advance is a criterion-referenced test. This type of test usually covers small units of content.

Example:

Given a list of spelling words, the student will be able to spell correctly eight out of 10 words.

Note that in this type of test, the skill is specific. The student must meet the criterion indicated (spell correctly eight out of 10 words) rather than be compared with other students, and it is also possible for all students to meet the criterion.

Constructing Classroom (Paper and Pencil) Tests

In this era of educational accountability, tests are being used for both assessment and evaluation. As soon as the teacher puts on his/her assessor's hat, s/he becomes a test preparer. And if the teacher is going to have to prepare tests, s/he should do the job properly and professionally.

Basically, there are two types of classroom tests: essay and objective.

Essay Tests

As with all types of test questions, essay questions have advantages and disadvantages. The advantages are that essay questions

1. can test the types of objectives that call for the student to develop without suggestions or alternatives a response in his/her own words regarding higher level abilities such as analyzing and solving problems, evaluating situations, or presenting evidence,
2. provide less opportunity for the student to guess the correct answer or take advantage of context cues, and
3. take less time to construct.

The disadvantages are that essay questions

A. take a long time to score,
B. have scoring that tends to be subjective and unreliable, and
C. represent a relatively small sample of the student's achievement.

Suggestions for Writing Effective Essay Questions

1. Use the simplest wording to ensure maximum clarity.
2. Always word the questions to convey the exact task required.

Examine the following two essay questions to see if you can identify the difference between the tasks required.

A. "Discuss the causes of the Civil War."
B. "Explain how slavery was one cause that contributed to the Civil War."

The first question (A), using the word "Discuss," *does not specify* the information sought. Other *non-specifically* framed questions begin with words such as "What do you know about . . . ?" or What do you think of . . . ?."

The second question (B) is more structured, and therefore, more *specific*.

The student knows what to do (explain) to answer the question. Other specific questions begin with words such as "Compare," "Describe," "Summarize," or "Contrast."

3. Do not offer a choice of questions unless they are equal in instructional importance and difficulty.
4. Include just enough essay questions to provide ample time for the student to examine each question before answering, to review each answer, and to revise when necessary.

To improve objectivity in scoring essay questions:

1. Indicate for each question which factors will be considered in evaluating the answer. Scoring rubrics, already described in Chapter 2 and detailed

Table 3.3.   Coaching Rubric for Constructing Essay Questions

Criteria (Descriptors)	Performance Indicators (Examples)
framed clearly around a *specific problem* *limited in scope*	
employed directions for responding by using terms such as *explain, describe, contrast, compare* instead of less structured terms such as *discuss,* or *what is your opinion of*	
communicated *extent* and *depth* of the response desired	
corresponded to instructional objectives of the content covered	
limited to measuring instructional objectives not readily measured by objective-type questions	
consisted of a larger number of short essays instead of one or two long essays	
offered no choice of response	
worded for simplicity and clarity	

further later in this chapter, will facilitate objectivity and reliability in evaluating essay questions.

2. Rate all the responses to the same question before rating the next.
3. Try to score all answers to a question without interruption.
4. Have the students identify themselves by social security numbers or by any other way to assure anonymity.

When using the coaching rubrics that follow to evaluate different types of tests, begin by evaluating the tests you and/or others have already constructed or taken in each category. On the basis of the coaching rubric evaluated, make recommendations for improving the formerly constructed tests so that they will conform to the criteria (descriptors) for best practices. Be sure to first review the Directions for Using Coaching Rubrics described in Chapter 2.

Objective Tests

Objective tests offer the student the opportunity to give a brief answer in which s/he either selects or supplies the response. Advantages of objective tests are that they measure instructional objectives where writing skills per se are not important or measure instructional objectives best assessed by short answers. Distinct disadvantages are that they are difficult to write well and

Table 3.4. Advantages and Disadvantages of Essay and Objective Tests

Essay Tests		Objective Tests	
Advantages	*Disadvantages*	*Advantages*	*Disadvantages*
Test higher level thinking	Take a long time to score	Can cover a wide range of objectives	Difficult to write well
Offer less opportunity for guessing	Scoring tends to be subjective and unreliable	Offer more objective scoring	Test in general lower level thinking
Take less time to construct	Represent a small sample of student achievement	Offer questions that require brief answers	Take a long time to construct

take a long time to construct. Table 3.4 summarizes the advantages and disadvantages of essay and objective tests.

Objective tests include several categories: true-false (T-F); short answer (completion); matching; and multiple choice.

General Suggestions for Writing Objective Tests

To ensure that your questions are most effective:

1. Avoid copying statements verbatim from references or texts.
2. If the answer to a question is dependent on an authority or knowledge of expert opinion, provide the name of the authority or expert.
3. Construct questions using simple, direct language.
   What is your reaction to the following true-false (T-F) question?
   "T F Non-organic nutritious substances absorbed through ingestion are fundamental for the growth and maintenance of blood and bones."
   You probably reacted to the wordiness of the question.

   The question would be better worded in the following way:

   "T F Minerals in our food help the growth of blood and bones."
4. Avoid interdependence among items.
   What would be the effect of having the next two questions appearing on the same test?
   A. "What is the mean of the following set of scores? 85 87 93 98 68 75 82"
   B. "How many points from the mean would Patricia's score be?"

You undoubtedly realized that if the student makes a computational error in (A), his/her answer to (B) would automatically be incorrect and s/he would be unfairly penalized.

5. Construct "clueless" questions so that no one question provides a clue for another.
   Examine the following two True-False questions:

   "T F A histogram is a graphical representation of a frequency distribution."
   "T F In graphing a histogram to represent a frequency distribution, cumulative relative frequencies may be used."
   An aware test-taker would recognize that the second question provided a clue to the first.
6. Avoid patterning of answers. To make the test easier to score, some teachers may use a repeated pattern of responses such as DCBA in a multiple choice question or TFFT in a true-false question. Frequently, the student can identify and even looks for the pattern. Did you ever do this?

Specific Suggestions for Writing Objective Tests

True-False (T-F) Questions

True-False questions test factual information, not understanding or application. When developing T-F questions, do the following:

1. Use a statement that is entirely true or entirely false.
2. Phrase the question for clarity, avoiding long, involved statements and qualifying clauses. When preparing a T-F question, if you write both a statement that is true and a corresponding statement that is false, you will have less of a chance of writing an ambiguous question.
3. Avoid questions using the words *never, no, only, always, all,* or their equivalents. A sophisticated reader will know that T-F questions containing these words are usually false. Avoid also using terms such as *may, can, sometimes, usually, generally,* or their equivalents. A clever test-taker will know that statements using these words are usually true.
4. Avoid using negative statements, especially the double negative. If a negative statement must be used, underline the negative term.
5. Avoid using trick statements that have an insignificant error in the statement.
   "The Battle of Hastings occurred in 1066 B.C."
   The student may know the year, but not notice the B.C.
6. Keep the length of true and false statements the same. Because true statements contain more qualifiers and limitations, true statements tend to be longer.
7. If you choose to use the modified True-False question, the kind that requires a student to change an answer if it is false to make it true, this question decreases the even chance of guessing and is more challenging.

Table 3.5. Coaching Rubric for Constructing True-False Questions

Criteria (Descriptors)	Performance Indicators (Examples)
expressed statements clearly and briefly	
wrote statements free from intricate language and qualifying clauses	
focused core of question at beginning of sentence	
worded statements as completely true or completely false	
contained no trick items	
stated in positive terms	
wrote statements without the double negative	
used statements that avoided clues such as generally, may, might, could, never, perhaps	
constructed both true and false statements to be approximately the same length	
highlighted part of statement, if student was asked to correct a false statement	

> However, be sure to mark clearly by means of underlining, italics, or bold type the word or phrase that is to be changed.
> "T F The President of the Confederacy during the Civil War was *Abraham Lincoln*."

In the above example, not only would the student have to know that Abraham Lincoln was *not* the President of the Confederacy, but that Jefferson Davis *was*.

Matching Questions

Matching questions are easy to score, need little reading time, and can cover a large number of questions in a short time. As in the case of true-false questions, matching questions are limited to factual information.

The matching question provides a list of premises (Column A) and responses (Column B) where the student fills in the response in the space in front of the premise.

Examine the following matching question:

"In the space provided before each opera in Column A, write the numeral preceding the name of the corresponding composer listed in Column B.

Column A (premises)	Column B (responses)
_____a. Carmen	1. Donizetti
_____b. La Traviata	2. Verdi
_____c. The Magic Flute	3. Mozart
_____d. The Flying Dutchman	4. Gounod
_____e. Lucia di Lammermoor	5. Giordano
	6. Bizet
	7. Wagner"

Note that in the above question the following criteria were employed:

1. The premises and responses were short.
2. The premises and responses were arranged for maximum clarity and convenience for the student.
3. The basis upon which responses were to be matched to premises was clear. The wording could have been to write the number of the matching item in Column B to Column A, but the wording in the example question above focused instead on writing the numeral preceding the name of the corresponding composer.
4. There was an unequal number of premises and responses, thus making it more difficult for students to guess the correct answer by process of elimination.
5. The premises and responses were homogeneous. All referred to operas and their Composers, with no out-of-context clues for correctly matching a response with a premise. If a contemporary composer of popular music such as Barry Manilow or Elton John, or an artist such as Rembrandt were one of the responses, they could easily have been eliminated.

Short Answer (Completion) Questions

Short-answer questions test specific facts. These questions may be framed as a question or as an incomplete statement.

"Who was the President of the United States during the Korean War? _____."

"The President of the United States during the Korean War was _____."

To construct a professional short answer (completion) question, attend to the following:

Table 3.6. Coaching Rubric for Constructing Matching Questions

Criteria (Descriptors)	Performance Indicators (Examples)
constructed homogeneous premises and responses (all related to the same category)	
introduced directions which expressed clearly the basis on which matching was to be made	
Premises and responses presented in relatively short language	
arranged for clarity	
used longer statements as premises, shorter statements as responses	
contained no extraneous clues	
included at least two more responses than premises	
indicated permission in the directions, if same response was allowed more than once	

1. Make sure that there is only one line segment per single response.
   For example, what happens when a student attempts to answer the following two questions?
   "The gas we exhale is _____ _____."
   "The city in the United States with the largest population is_____
   _____."

   The fact that two spaces were provided in each statement is a clue that the answer in both cases above has two words.

2. Compose a statement for which there is only one correct answer.
   What problems would students confront in the following two questions?
   "The population of Florida is_____."
   "Ernest Hemingway wrote _____."

   In both of the above questions, more than one answer can be correct. In the first question, a student can give a numeral, indicate that the population is increasing, wealthy, or growing older, or provide a myriad of different correct answers. In the second question, any novel or writings of Hemingway would be acceptable. It would be better to write, "Who wrote *A Farewell to Arms*?"

How could you reword the first question (on Florida) so that there would be only one correct answer?

3. Avoid questions with context clues.
   Example:
   "An _____ is the part of speech that describes a noun." Using "An" instead of "A(n)" allows the student to guess that the response begins with a vowel or silent "h" if s/he was not sure. Of all the parts of speech, only two begin with a vowel: adjective and adverb.
4. Give the students a focus by placing the blank at the end of the sentence. The previous example could be improved to read, "The part of speech that describes a noun is a(n)_____." Using this phrasing, the student can begin to formulate an answer before reaching the space.
5. Phrase questions for clarity.
   "The ____ is computed by _____ the scores in a test and _____ by the number of scores." This question is chopped-up and confusing. It would be better worded as, "How could the mean be computed from a set of scores?"
6. Make all line segments of equal length with no more than two blank spaces. Look again at the prior example. The size of the line segments gives a clue regarding the size of the words to be inserted.
7. In computational problems, state the units you want and the degree of precision. "If the length of a rectangle is 38 1/3 inches, and its width is 2 1/6 feet, its perimeter is_____." The student should know if you want the answer in inches or feet, and the degree of precision (nearest inch, nearest foot).

Table 3.7. Coaching Rubric for Constructing Short Answer (Completion) Questions

Criteria (Descriptors)	Performance Indicators (Examples)
focused question at beginning	
constructed all spaces of equal length	
placed blank space(s) at end	
expressed clearly enough to produce only one correct answer	
contained no grammatical clues	
if computational, indicated degree of precision expected	
indicated units to be expressed	

Multiple Choice Questions

These questions are the most flexible of all the objective-type test questions because they can measure both factual as well as higher-level understanding. Multiple choice questions are also the most difficult to construct.

A multiple choice question contains an item stem and a set of responses. The item stem can be expressed either as a direct question or an incomplete statement. The responses, usually four or five in number, contain one correct answer and the remaining choices as distracters.

The item stem should do the following:

1. State a problem or ask a question clearly and briefly, including only essential information for solving the problem.
2. Provide enough information to give the student a focus.

   "Carbon dioxide
   A. is 20 percent of the air we breathe.
   B. is heavier than air.
   C. is present on the moon's atmosphere.
   D. is available only as a gas."

This question can be improved by rephrasing it as follows:
"Which of the following statements gives an accurate characteristic of carbon dioxide? It is
   A. 20 percent of the air we breathe.
   B. heavier than air.
   C. present on the moon's atmosphere.
   D. available only as a gas."

Note that in the above, phrasing the item stem as a question provides better clarity for the reader.

3. Be phrased in such a way that the same words do not have to be repeated in the response. In the first of the two examples provided in number 2 above, "is" was repeated in each response. In the second example the word(s), "It is," were included in the item stem so that in the response clumsy repetition was not necessary.
4. Include enough information so that the question may be answered first without checking the responses.
5. Be free, as in writing completion questions, of the grammatical clue "a" or "an" when using the item stem as an incomplete statement.

6. Avoid, as in writing True-False questions, an item stated in negative terms, or else underline the negative term.

The responses should do the following:

1. Be such that knowledgeable people in the field would agree on the best answer.
2. Be plausible enough so that a student cannot eliminate answers due to lack of knowledge.

   "The Italian who composed *The Masked Ball* was
   A. Puccini
   B. Bellini
   C. Tchaikovsky
   D. Verdi"

In this question, response *C* is not plausible because Tchaikovsky was not an Italian. Therefore, this response may be eliminated due to context, not knowledge.

3. Be similar enough so that a student cannot eliminate answers due to lack of information. In general, the more the responses are similar, the more difficult the question. Contrast the following two sets of responses to the same question.

   "In what year did Columbus discover America?
   A. 1100   A. 1412
   B. 1492   B. 1442
   C. 1630   C. 1468
   D. 1776   D. 1492
   E. 1812   E. 1498"

You will note that in the first set, responses are so different that a student would have to know only that Columbus came to the New World around the 1400s.

In the second set, the student's knowledge of the year would have to be more precise.

4. Have only one possible correct answer.

   "Hemingway achieved his greatest fame as a (an)
   A. painter
   B. architect
   C. writer

    D. film-maker
    E. novelist"

You should have been able to see that both *C* and *E* would be correct answers.

5. Do NOT include words or phrases used in the item stem. This use may provide a clue to a student who lacks the appropriate information. Note that in the following question you will be able to select the correct answer even if you have no idea what the answer could be.

"In the process of thermionic emission
    a. the positive plate attracts electrons
    b. a metal is magnetized
    c. kinetic energy is changed to potential energy
    d. electrons are emitted when a material is heated"

The fact that "emission" was used in the item stem, and "emitted" was used as one of the item responses made it easy to select *D* as the correct answer.

6. Provide an appropriate number of choices for the grade level (in general, two to three choices for second graders, three to four choices for third and fourth graders, and four or more for older students).

7. Avoid overlapping.
    "How many U.S. presidents were lawyers?
    A. Fewer than 5
    B. Fewer than 8
    C. More than 8
    D. More than 10"
    More than one response would be correct.

8. Avoid "none of these" as an alternative unless the response can be expressed in exact terms.
    "Barbara has 10 nickels, 3 quarters, 5 dimes, and 8 pennies. How much money does she have?
    A. $1.53
    B. $1.62
    C. $1.87
    D. None of these"

Also, if a student knows that only one of the answers is correct in any question, s/he could eliminate "none of these" as a response.

9. Avoid "all of the above." The student can eliminate "all of the above" by knowing that only one of the other answers was incorrect.

To format clear and consistent multiple choice questions:

1. Use small or capital letters instead of numerals for responses. Since the questions themselves are generally listed as numerals, employing letters as responses is less confusing.
2. Place the letters corresponding to the responses directly beneath the beginning of the item stem.
3. If the item stem is a direct question, capitalize the first word of each response. If the item stem is an incomplete sentence, do not capitalize the first word of each response, and place a period at the end of each response.
4. If the responses are numerals,
   A. arrange the responses from smallest to largest.
   B. when working with decimals, place decimal points one underneath the other, and use the same number of decimal places.
   C. when using dollar signs, place the dollars signs one underneath the other.
5. Use a random process for locating responses.

New Short-Answer Test Items

You have already read that one criticism of short-answer questions is that they tend to measure lower-level knowledge. To ensure that students have mastered a deeper understanding of content, new short-answer test items are now being used. These tests integrate several skills: analyzing, interpreting, drawing inferences, and logical writing.

Note the difference between the conventional (traditional) short-answer questions and the new questions in the two following illustrations.

First illustration:

Traditional test item: "When experimenting to determine how much water different soils can hold, all of the following equipment would be needed EXCEPT a

   a. funnel.
   b. vegetable dye.
   c. filter.
   d. catch container."

(Note that in this traditional test question, the use of a (an) would not be necessary because all choices begin with a consor.ant, not any choice with a vowel or silent h.)

Table 3.8.   Coaching Rubric for Constructing Multiple Choice Questions

Criteria (Descriptors)	Performance Indicators (Examples)
Item Stems	
framed as a question or incomplete statement	
expressed with only one central problem	
expressed clearly	
contained no extraneous clues	
contained no negative statements or highlighted negative statement	
expressed so that no words in the premise were repeated in the response	
offered only one correct response	
provided enough information so that students could formulate an answer before examining choices	
Responses	
offered mutually exclusive choices	
offered all plausible and attractive choices	
written grammatically consistent with item stem	
expressed with parallel construction	
arranged in logical order, when appropriate	
located at the ends of questions or incomplete statements	
employed "none of these" only when the answer could be expressed in exact terms	
excluded "all of these" as a choice	
tested items so that experts in the field could agree on the correct answer	

Now look at the new test item with similar content in Figure 3.4 Soil Water Absorption.

A group of students tested different soils to compare how much water they each can hold water. They used the following setup:

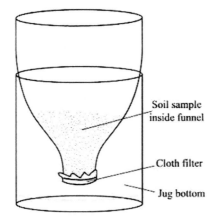

Soil sample inside funnel

Cloth filter

Jug bottom

They used the following procedure:

1. Put some sand, clay or garden soil into a funnel.
2. Pour water into the funnel and measure how much drips through.
3. Repeat for all 3 soil types.

Describe two improvements that could be made to their procedure. Explain how each improvement would make their data and conclusion more reliable.

_____

_____

_____

_____

_____

_____

Figure 3.4. (*Source:* Reprinted with permission of the Connecticut State Department of Education. http://www.ct.gov/sde)

The second example of a comparison between a conventional (traditional test item) and more thought-provoking short-answer question is illustrated in Figure 3.5 The Woggle.

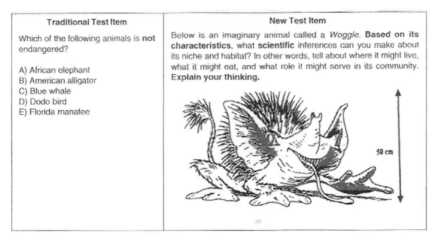

Traditional Test Item	New Test Item
Which of the following animals is **not** endangered? A) African elephant B) American alligator C) Blue whale D) Dodo bird E) Florida manatee	Below is an imaginary animal called a *Woggle*. **Based on its characteristics**, what **scientific** inferences can you make about its niche and habitat? In other words, tell about where it might live, what it might eat, and what role it might serve in its community. **Explain your thinking.**

Figure 3.5.   (*Source:* Reprinted with permission of the Connecticut State Department of Education. http://www.ct.gov/sde)

You can see in both of the examples that the new test items incorporate analysis, interpretation, the drawing of inferences, and clear writing skills. Therefore, these new types of short-answer questions can no longer be criticized for measuring only lower-level skills.

Involving Students in Constructing Tests

Students are currently being assisted in becoming lifelong learners who assume more responsibility for their own learning. As part of this responsibility, students are coming up with rules for the classroom; participating in constructing their own questions about content they are studying; designing their own learning; and assessing and evaluating that learning. As part of the assessment and evaluation process, it is also important for students to participate in constructing tests and in eventually developing rubrics.

Think of what it takes to develop a test. First the material must be mastered in depth. Then the content must be manipulated in different ways to construct test questions. Students can develop questions as a culminating activity, can administer the test to other students, and can check each other's work. The situation can also be *reversed,* so that students can be provided with answers to tests and then design questions that will elicit those answers.

Test construction is an excellent way for students to review a chapter or a unit. You can teach them, depending on their age and grade level, what you learned in this chapter about designing tests. You can also have students analyze test questions to see how they meet the criteria described in this chapter.

If you model professional test construction, your students will have a better opportunity to design professional test questions themselves.

Test Variations

Quick feedback such as that sought through short-answer questions can also be obtained from letter-card responses, whiteboard responses, and the traffic-signal method described by Popham (2008). Each of these three methods involves all the students in the responses.

Using the letter-card response, every student is given a set of eight white index cards, with each card boldly marked A, B, C, D, E, T, F, and ?. The teacher reads or places on an overhead a multiple choice item, and when given the appropriate predetermined signal, students respond by holding up one of the response choices from A through E.

A quick look at the responses informs the teacher of the students' knowledge status. If as much as a third of the students selects the B card when the correct response is E, this informs the teacher that content related to both responses needs instructional adjustment. The T and F can be used for True-False questions and a student can use the card, ?, when not sure of the answer to either the multiple choice or True-False question.

Because the letter-card response limits the students in their response options, erasable whiteboards can be used instead. The teacher presents the students with a question that requires a short response. The students write that response on the whiteboard. When prompted by the teacher, the students hold up their response, giving the teacher the opportunity to check on the class achievement level. Students then erase their responses at the teacher's signal and get ready for the next question.

The traffic-signal technique is a little different from the preceding two methods because it employs the student's judgment regarding how much the content level is understood. This technique is an adaptation of the use of the three colors in traffic lights—green signifying go, yellow meaning slow down, and red indicating stop.

Each student receives a red, yellow, and green cup. The student superimposes the yellow cup over the red and the green over the yellow. If during instruction the student keeps the green cup on top, this conveys to the teacher that the student understands the content to the point that s/he can teach it to another student. If the student places the yellow cup on top, this signals a level of uncertainty regarding the content. A red up on top would indicate to the teacher that the student does not understand the material. A yellow or red cup informs the teacher that instruction adjustment is necessary.

ADDITIONAL ASSESSMENT/EVALUATION OPTIONS

In addition to classroom tests and other quick feedback techniques, a wide range of assessment/evaluation options is available to teachers. These options include informal methods, academic prompts, and alternative assessments (Wiggins 1998, 2005).

Informal methods. It has already been stated that many of the diagnostic methods suggested in this chapter, such as observations and interviews, are also used in assessment/evaluation. Additionally, teachers can analyze samples of student work, administer quizzes, and check homework to obtain feedback regarding how well students are accomplishing the objectives. Even though diagnosis usually occurs before instruction, it is also continuous.

Academic prompts. Academic prompts are open-ended questions that go beyond recall (Wiggins and McTighe 1998, 2005). Academic prompts require critical thinking demonstrated by preparing a response, product, or performance under school or examination conditions. Typical academic prompts do not have a best strategy or single answer for problem solving; they do require the development of a strategy, since the prompts provide no structure; they may or may not be known in advance of instruction; they require higher levels of thinking and analysis; require a defense of answers or methods; and require judgment-based scoring based on criteria and performance standards.

Example:

> After studying a science unit, the student, with materials provided by the teacher, designs and constructs for other students an original science kit that includes directions for use.

Alternative assessment. According to Ryan (1994), it has been alleged that the following quote was displayed on Albert Einstein's office wall: "Not everything that counts can be counted, and not everything that can be counted counts."

It was always clear to teachers that though paper and pencil and standardized tests are important, they do not tell the whole story about students. An overemphasis on testing tells students what the school values, and it is the role of the schools to promote loftier goals than those evaluated largely with paper and pencil and standardized tests.

Moreover, tests do not identify for both the student and the teacher exactly where the student is having a problem nor do tests adequately describe student performance. Tests themselves do not connect school with the outside world.

Performance Tasks and Products

Performance tasks and products provide alternative assessment techniques often referred to in the educational literature as *performance assessment* or *authentic assessment.* As opposed to completing tests, students must show what they can *do* as a result of knowledge gained when they are involved in authentic assessments. In performance assessment students must *generate* rather than select a response. "Products guide students in moving from consumers of knowledge to producers with knowledge" (Tomlinson and Eidson 2003, 11).

Students are actually performing a designated activity to demonstrate competence (Mitchell 1992). These performance projects provide high-level challenges representing problems that must be faced in the "real world" (authentic) outside of school and make school more relevant by engaging students in meaningful applications. The level of complexity of the task depends on the student's stage of development.

Meyer (1992) pointed out that the terms *performance tasks* and *authentic tasks* are often used interchangeably. Though both require that students come up with their own responses and apply knowledge, performance tasks tend to be more contrived. For a task or product to be authentic, all the following attributes must be present:

1. The student must perform the subject, as opposed to just talking or reporting about it.
2. The task or product must be one representing a real-life situation, whether it is solving a problem confronted in personal life, as a citizen, or in the work environment.
3. The student must apply knowledge and skills by solving a previously unsolved problem.
4. The student must integrate a repertoire of knowledge and skills in the application.
5. Guidelines, standards, resources, and adequate feedback must be provided so that the student may self-adjust.
6. The task should be about something important.
7. The task must be challenging for the present level of student performance.

Though tasks and products are used synonymously, there are subtle differences between the two, with the product being more advanced.
Examples:

Task	Product
Analyzing a budget using specific criteria	Creating an original budget using the same criteria

Comparing and contrasting two battles	Designing a strategy to make the losing side in a battle become the winning one

Tasks and products are not the same as instructional activities. An instructional activity is designed to *facilitate learning of* one or more objectives. Tasks and products are designed to *assess* the extent and level to which the objectives (achievement targets) have been mastered. Threading a sewing machine is an activity that teaches a student how to thread; redesigning the machine to make the threading more efficient is a task; building the redesigned machine and then organizing a marketing strategy to promote it would be a product.

For a task or product to be valid, it must be one that demonstrates achievement of the goals of instruction. There are many tasks that may meet the criterion of authenticity, but if they do not assess how the students have met the objectives of a chapter or unit, the tasks do not meet the criterion of validity.

Student Portfolios

A student portfolio is a collection over time of student work that documents progress. A portfolio is not just any collection of work placed into a folder. In order to have maximum worth as an assessment tool, the purpose of the portfolio must be perfectly clear to both teacher and student. The purpose determines what is to be collected, which criteria will be used to review the collection, and how the portfolio will be scored.

Teacher and student are active in the process of portfolio evaluation in which they decide together what work may be used, removed, or added, as the process of portfolio development continues, so that it may produce valid, reliable evidence of achievement. Danielson and Abrutyn (1997) suggested that students spend time sharing portfolios.

The portfolio may serve as a

- capstone project, the crowning achievement produced by a student;
- display or showcase project used for a professional to make a judgment, such as a collection of the best art projects for submission to an art school for program admission;
- sample of the student's best work;
- example of student growth;
- indicator of the student's ability to self-assess and improve performance.

Constructing Rubrics for Performance Tasks, Products, and Portfolios

Performance tasks, products, and portfolios achieve full potential when they are accompanied by scoring rubrics. In Chapter 2 you were already introduced to a coaching rubric, a set of criteria that develops performance, and reviewed a scoring rubric, a set of criteria for judging performance.

You will recall that in a scoring rubric, the criteria (descriptors) are arranged in a hierarchy that ranges from the poorest to the best performance. Scoring rubrics allow teachers and students to judge or rate objectively student performance. If scoring rubrics are constructed well, they also have the critical function of allowing students to self-assess their work and, as a result, self-adjust and improve.

Teachers and students sometimes get so involved with the assessment component in a rubric that they forget that the rubric is an important *teaching tool*. It offers criteria that allow students to move to higher levels of achievement.

Scoring rubrics contain " . . . an identified behavior within an assessment task; quality or performance standard; description of the desired standard; and a scale to be used in rating student performance" (Taggert et al. 1998, 58–59). Before a scoring rubric (or a coaching rubric) can be constructed, the person who prepares it must determine what constitutes quality performance in a representative work.

Wiggins and McTighe (1998, 2005), two leaders in the field of assessment, suggested that samples of students' and professionals' work should be analyzed first to determine what range of excellence they demonstrate. It is essential that rubrics be constructed on the basis of the absolute best possible performance, because if they are constructed the way students are currently performing, the students will remain at that performance level.

Once the best performance is determined, then minimal performance should be identified. After both the poorest and best performances are described, intermediate levels between the two are determined, and a scoring rubric can then be presented quantitatively as a scale. The scale can range from 1–4 or 1–10 with the most common scoring rubric presenting a scale from 1–6, with 1 as the lowest level of performance and 6 the highest.

Scoring rubrics may also be expressed qualitatively as poor through outstanding, novice through professional, emergent through fluent, or any other equivalent system depending on the type of performance being assessed. It is recommended that the number of categories in the quantitative or qualitative scale be *even* because judgment tends toward the center. If a scale of 1–5 is used, many evaluators, even with specific criteria, will tend to select the midpoint, 3.

Look once again at Figure 2.1, the Map Legend for Scoring Rubrics, presented in the previous chapter. Decide whether this tendency might lead to selecting Level 2 (Complex) because it is in the middle (between 1 and 3).

Corresponding to each point or level on a scale is a set of performance descriptors that indicates clearly what criteria must be demonstrated to qualify for that score. Criteria should always be described in *positive* terms, what the performance was, not what the performance was not. It would be a better-stated descriptor as, "made basic computational errors," as opposed to, "did not have the ability to compute basic problems."

The criteria should not be evaluative (fair, good, excellent) and should discriminate sufficiently from each other so that each level of achievement can be distinguished with no overlapping. Clear, discriminating criteria give validity to the rubric. You have already read in Chapter 2 that specificity and observability give reliability to the rubric.

As mentioned earlier in this chapter, using a well-prepared scoring rubric to grade essay questions would give the scoring validity and higher reliability (Wiggins 2005). Wiggins and McTighe (2005) asserted that the rubric should be written *before* deciding what task or product to assign. The criteria identified in the rubric would be able to guide the selection of the task that would best provide the opportunity for meeting the criteria.

Many educators believe that when the students are developmentally ready, they should *participate in creating* the rubric so that the criteria can be internalized. Regardless of whether or not students participate in rubric construction, it is essential that they be presented with the rubric *before* they begin working on a task, product, or portfolio, and are clear regarding the meaning of each criterion.

Recently, *document-based questions* (DBQs), those based on original documents such as charts, maps, cartoons, songs, graphs, letters, posters, photographs, pictures, or short quotes, have been introduced in many classrooms for both instruction and assessment. These documents provide primary sources for learning, and are, therefore, more brain-compatible.

Many states are using DBQs to teach and assess learning standards. The student is provided with a set of these original documents, two to eight in number depending on the grade level, all related to a theme. The student examines these documents and answers one or more questions pertinent to the documents. These questions are known as "scaffolding" questions because their responses lay the foundation (scaffold) for an essay question that follows in which the student integrates the knowledge gained from the document questions. The essay is then evaluated with a scoring rubric.

Figure 3.6 is an example of a DBQ with five documents for Grade 5 Government followed by a scoring rubric for that DBQ, Figure 3.7.

Government
Grade 5

The following question is based on the accompanying documents (1 - 5). It is designed to test your ability to examine and interpret the meaning of the documents. Then you will write a final essay which uses important information from the documents you have analyzed.

Directions:
- Write an introductory paragraph.
- Use specific details from at least three documents in Part A.
- You may include any other outside information that you have learned.
- Finish with a concluding paragraph.

Historic Background: The United States of America was build based on the ideas of freedom and opportunities for citizens to have a voice in their government. A democratic government works well when its citizens take an interest in what is happening and understanding how their government works.

Many historical events have influenced and shaped our roles and responsibilities as citizens and our participation in a democratic country.

Task:

For Part A, read **each** document carefully and answer the question or questions after each document. Then read the directions for Part B and write your essay.

For Part B, use your answers from Part A, information from the documents, and your knowledge of social studies to write a well organized essay. In the essay you should:

> Explain how the rights and responsibilities of American citizenship have developed throughout history.

Figure 3.6. *(Continued)*

Document 1:

1. What do the part of the snake represent?

_____

_____

_____

_____

2. Explain what "Join, or Die" means.

_____

_____

_____

_____

_____

_____

_____

Figure 3.6. *(Continued)*

Document 2

The Stamp Act required tax stamps (right) to be placed on newspapers and pamphlets

1. What items were taxed under the Stamp Act?

_____

_____

_____

_____

_____

2. What action did the colonist take in response to the Stamp Act?

_____

_____

_____

_____

Figure 3.6. *(Continued)*

Document 3:

Excerpt from the
Declaration of Independence, approved
by the Continental Congress in 1776.

We hold these truths to be
self-evident: That all men are
created equal; that they are
endowed by their Creator with
certain **unalienable** rights; that
among these are life, liberty, and
the pursuit of happiness; that, to
secure these rights, governments
are **instituted** among men,
deriving their just powers from
the **consent** of the governed.

endowed: given
unalienable: basic
instituted: founded
deriving: getting
consent: agreement

1. Identify two rights that the colonists had as a result of the Declaration of Independence.

1)_____

_____

2)_____

_____

Why was the Declaration of Independence an important statement for our country?

_____

_____

_____

_____

_____

Figure 3.6. *(Continued)*

Document 4

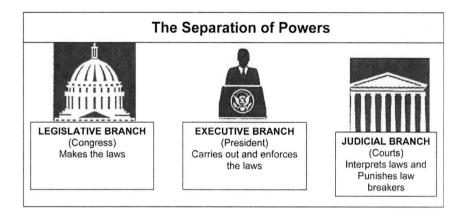

The Separation of Powers
LEGISLATIVE BRANCH (Congress) Makes the laws	**EXECUTIVE BRANCH** (President) Carries out and enforces the laws	**JUDICIAL BRANCH** (Courts) Interprets laws and Punishes law breakers

1. Identify the three branches of government.

1_____

2_____

3_____

2. Why was separation of powers important to American democracy?

_____

_____

_____

_____

_____

_____

Figure 3.6. *(Continued)*

Document 5:

1. What is one important responsibility of an American citizen?

_____

_____

_____

_____

_____

_____

_____

_____

Figure 3.6. *(Continued)*

Part B:

Directions: Using the documents, the answers to the questions in Part A, and your knowledge of social studies, write a well-organized essay about American citizenships.

In your essay, remember to:
- ♦ Tell how the rights and responsibilities of American citizenship have developed throughout history.
- ♦ Include an introduction, body and a conclusion
- ♦ Include details, examples, or reasons to develop your ideas
- ♦ Use the information from the documents in your answer.

_____

_____

_____

_____

_____

_____

_____

_____

_____

_____

_____

_____

_____

_____

_____

_____

_____

_____

_____

_____

_____

_____

_____

Figure 3.6. *(Continued)*

Figure 3.6. (*Source:* From "Teaching with Documents" www.edteck.com/dbq by Peter Pappas, Reprinted with permission, http://peterpappas.blogs.com.)

Note that the criteria in this rubric are based on the directions and the task identified at the beginning of the DBQ and are repeated below.

Directions: Write an introductory paragraph.
Use specific details from at least three documents in Part A.
You may include any other outside information that you have learned.
Finish with a concluding paragraph.

Task: Explain how the rights and responsibilities of American citizenship have developed throughout history.

Score of 6: Developed the task (theme) completely and clearly
Used a substantial number of documents
Supported the task with additional and substantial relevant information
Organized the essay well with a beginning, middle, and conclusion beyond the restatement of the theme

Score of 5: Developed the task (theme) consistently
Used several documents effectively
Supported the task with additional relevant information
Included a beginning, middle, and conclusion

Score of 4: Developed the task (theme) partially
Incorporated some information from documents
Incorporated some relevant outside information
Organized the essay in a satisfactory manner

Score of 3: Developed the task (theme) in a confused and poor manner
Used documents ineffectively or not at all
Wrote an essay that covered only one section
Contained major errors

Score of 2: Showed little understanding of the question
Provided poor or no use of documents
Provided irrelevant or no outside information
Showed lack of organization

Score of 1: Made little or no effort to write the essay

Figure 3.7.   Grade 5 Government DBQ Essay Scoring Rubric

Table 3.9 presents the Coaching Rubric for Constructing Scoring Rubrics. After viewing this rubric, examine the Grade 5 Government DBQ Essay Scoring Rubric you just read to see if/how it conforms to criteria 3, 4, 5, and 6. (You would have no way of knowing in this rubric if the other criteria were implemented.)

Table 3.9. Coaching Rubric for Constructing Scoring Rubrics

Criteria (Descriptors)	Performance Indicators (Examples)
analyzed a wide range of work samples before determining criteria for assessing the task	
described the performance extremes before determining criteria	
expressed performance criteria in clear, descriptive language free of evaluative terms	
differentiated clearly among performance levels so that students can self-assess and self-correct	
stated criteria in positive terms at all levels	
presented an *even* number of quantitative or qualitative levels	
designed criteria with student input, when appropriate	
presented rubric and discussed criteria with students *before* they began to work on task or product	

Assessment FOR Learning

Stiggins (2002, 2005) has promoted the idea that assessment must be not only *of* learning but also *for* learning. While assessment of learning is performed to demonstrate evidence of student accomplishment, assessment for learning is performed to increase student accomplishment.

Stiggins (2007) points out that, historically, assessment was used to differentiate and rank students, thus producing winners and losers. With the current focus on assisting all students, assessment has now shifted from demonstrating learning to assisting learning so that everyone experiences success. Given the proper assessments, students are becoming increasingly responsible for their own learning by keeping track of their achievement and making instructional suggestions regarding how to improve.

In this new environment the teacher first ensures that s/he creates assessments that accurately reflect student achievement. S/he makes students aware of learning goals, presents these goals clearly, and provides outstanding examples of student work. Students self-assess frequently using small amounts of descriptive (rather than judgmental) feedback so that they are not overwhelmed. With practice, students can then create their own descriptive feedback and establish goals for the next learning venture.

Students are involved in comparing and contrasting different qualities of student work to come up with their own version of scoring rubrics; creating their own short-answer questions before a test is finally administered to pinpoint weaknesses to be remediated and areas of strength attained; identifying pre-determined areas of growth to demonstrate in portfolios; and communicating their accomplishments and improvement with classmates and families.

Stiggins (2007) emphasizes that students' emotional reaction to results decides what they will do with the results. In the final analysis, a score must go beyond validity and reliability and concentrate on the student, especially if it leads him/her to give up. Assessment FOR learning yields productive student responses to assessment so that everyone is a winner.

The importance of assessment for learning cannot be overemphasized. Effective assessment builds student confidence, keeps students motivated, and provides the foundation for unparalleled achievement gains.

Assessments for the Innovation Age

We have moved from an industrial to an information-based economy, and are now shifting to an innovation-based economy. This type of economy requires that students can create new knowledge, analyze and solve problems, and imagine new ways to promote work.

Change and the acceleration of change are salient features of today's world. When accommodating to meet these changes, students must acquire a skill set that will assist them to adapt to new situations and create new solutions. These skills are analogous to those proposed in Sternberg's triarchic view of intelligence—analytic, practical, and creative (Chapter 1). This skill set acquisition will keep students competitive with those of Europe and Asia.

Education has to go beyond teaching facts and skills; it must prepare students to integrate and apply knowledge. Correspondingly, educators must embrace a more comprehensive view of measuring this learning. Assessments must offer a wide range of strategies to determine how students can apply and integrate knowledge. Measures should include complex and challenging real world and virtual performance tasks.

Assessments will have to

e. be predominantly performance-based;
f. analyze what types of conceptual strategies students use to solve problems;

g.   produce data that will inform teachers how to provide more informative instruction for students;

h.   provide opportunities for both teachers and students to obtain feedback so that both can grow;

i.   offer a continuous process that is well-aligned to the concepts and major ideas being taught.

These criteria will be delivered through cutting-edge technologies. Some technologies are already taking the form of having students demonstrate their information; communication; technological; research; management; and presentation skills within a virtual city.

Computer-administered assessments will organize and deliver complex tasks that chart student cognitive processes and provide fast feedback. Assessments will be run on hand-held computers to give teachers insights into student thinking by generating a performance profile. The diagnostic data produced will provide the information that teachers can use to adjust instructional delivery (Fadel , Honey, and Pasnik 2007).

Instructional delivery is beginning to come under more scrutiny in this age of innovation as educational policymakers realize that today's accountability tests do not present a valid picture of how well students are being taught (Popham 2007). Instead, they currently actually measure socioeconomic status. He states that tests that cannot distinguish between effective and ineffective instruction are just as "dumb" as weighing yourself on a scale that was not influenced by the weight of the person using it or taking your temperature with a thermometer not affected by heat.

Popham believes that just being aware of the need for tests that accurately reflect instructional sensitivity—the extent to which students' test performance reflects accurately the instructional quality specifically delivered for students' mastery on these assessments—will be the impetus to design these tests. As an example, he cites the construction of tests that eliminated test bias once this problem was identified.

Student Sensitivity in Designing Assessments

Before concluding this section, it should be stressed that student differences must be taken into account when designing assessments and evaluations. Students must have the writing skills necessary to answer essay questions. There are students who may have the information but cannot communicate that information in writing. These students should be accommodated by being given the opportunity to answer orally or by any other relevant means.

Students must have the reading comprehension necessary for answering objective questions. These learners should not be penalized for their lack of reading ability, and may need accommodation in assessing their knowledge.

Although assessment tasks and products represent deeply involved activities, that still does not make them immune from the need to be culture free. Tasks should be selected in a way that is free from cultural bias. Students should be given choices in selecting tasks.

Necessary accommodations should be made in assessing/evaluating any student with special needs. When testing, assessing, and evaluating, it is best to use a variety of approaches (Guskey 1996).

Assigning Grades (Marks)

Assigning grades is not one of the most pleasant or easy chores that teachers perform, but it serves several important functions.

Grades

- help both students and parents keep informed on achievement, thus giving students the feedback and, therefore, the motivation and opportunity to improve performance;
- assist teachers in instructional planning; and
- provide identification for administrators to select those eligible for honors, graduation, and special programs; and for counselors to determine a student's interests, strengths, weaknesses, and vocational or career potential (Airasian 1994).

School districts usually decide the process for assigning grades, and, perhaps, may have a report card already designed. Usually the report cards differ according to grade level, with elementary reports more descriptive, and secondary reports containing letter or numerical grades.

The school district relies on a philosophy about a frame of reference when recommending how grades should be assigned. Should the students be compared against themselves; to other students in the class; to how they achieved specified standards; to how they achieved according to ability or effort, or to how much improvement occurred from one report card to the next?

As with every system in life, no grading system is perfect. There are positives and negatives in each decision regarding which grading method to use. But the central question in the decision should be, "Does this grade really represent achievement?" To ensure that it does, lowering grades for misbehavior, giving pop quizzes, counting effort and attendance, and allowing extra credit assignments should be avoided. They all distort the actual achievement of students.

There is a certain amount of subjectivity in assigning grades (Guskey 1996). To represent achievement as objectively and validly as possible, it is important that the final grade in any marking period be drawn from a variety of sources. These would include scores on quizzes, tests, oral/written reports, homework, or other non-authentic assessment sources, as well as ratings from authentic sources such as tasks, products, and portfolios. Whatever process is used in determining grades, it should be communicated clearly to students and parents at the beginning of the school year in writing in the course outline and in a note or e-mail sent home to parents.

There is a difference between scores and grades. Scores are accumulated along the way and are formative, providing assessment feedback to students and teachers. Grades are assigned at the end of a pre-determined time frame, are summative, and provide a final evaluation of the student's work.

There are several types of grading systems to report student achievement. Though there are no right and wrong ways to assign grades, Marzano (2000, 2006) recommended that teachers should take the following two assumptions into account: the most important reason for grades is to provide feedback regarding performance to both parents and students, and a criterion referenced approach provides the best way to grade content-specific learning goals. With Marzano's recommendation in mind, decide for yourself which of the following would meet his assumptions.

- Letter Grades. Letter grades are used most frequently. They may range from *A* through *F*, from Unsatisfactory (U) through Superior (S), or may just be stated as Pass (P)-Fail (F). A percentage standard should be selected for each letter (e.g., 95 for *A*, 85 for *B*, 75 and 65 respectively for *C* and *D*).

A point system is helpful in deciding a final letter grade. Student work is assigned points, the sum of which is used to determine a grade. If 300 points is the most a student can accrue and, as indicated above, 95 percent is the cutoff for an *A*, a student who achieves 0.95×300 (or 285 points) would receive an A, 0.85×300 (or 255) a *B*. Using the same cutoffs, what number of points would receive a *C* or a *D*? By using a point system, both the student and teacher know at any stage in the marking period the student's grade achievement in any subject.

- Numerical Grades. Numerical grades represent the percentage of content from 0–100 the student has achieved on several different assignments or tests. These percentages are then averaged. There are validity issued involved with averaging in this system because it assumes equal weight to content that may be different in importance and emphasis.

Table 3.10.   Report Card with No Course Grades

NAME: Jennifer Achiever

GRADE LEVEL: 11

Standards	Standards Rating on Rubric			
*CIVICS	1	2	3	4

Understands how politics enables a group
of people to reach collective decisions -------------------------------- 2.75

Knows formal institutions that have the
authority to make and implement binding
decisions---3.5

Understands the nature of political authority--3.75

Understands the sources of political authority -------------------------------------- 3.75

Understands why politics is found wherever
people gather as a group -- 3.5

Understands major arguments for the necessity
of politics and government--- 4.0

Understands some of the major competing ideas
about the purposes of politics and government ---------------------------3.0

Understands how the purposes served by a government affect relationships between
the individual and government and between government and society as a whole
---3.0

Communication standard Written work -- 3.5

Communication standard Oral--2.0
Non-achievement factor(s) Effort --- 3.5
                           Attendance --- 4.0
                           Behavior--- 4.0

(*Source*: Marzano (2000, 107). Adapted by permission of McREL. *Civics standards from Kendall (2011).
   Reprinted by permission of McREL.)

Table 3.11. Sample Report Card

Name of Student: Susan Superior

Quarters	First	Second	Third	Fourth
Reading/Literature Standards				
Uses a variety of reading strategies				
Comprehends grade level material				
Reads grade level material accurately				
Reads a variety of materials				
Responds to literature (oral, written, artistic)				

Key: 1. Does not meet expectations 2. Progressing toward meeting expectations 3. Meets expectations 4. Consistently exceeds expectations

(Source. From "Succeeding with Standards. Linking Curriculum, Assessment, and Action Planning" (112), by Judy F. Carr and Douglas E. Harris. Alexandria, VA: ASCD. © 2001 by ASCD. Reprinted with permission. Learn more about ASCD at www.ascd.org.)

- Descriptive Evaluations. Descriptive evaluations are written statements that describe the quality of student work. Though written commentary can pinpoint more explicitly students' accomplishments and needs, these descriptions are time-consuming for both writer and reader, and tend to have less objectivity and validity than other grading systems.
- Grades for Rubrics. Taggart et al. (1998) described some ways to grade rubrics. Each category may be assigned points so that the total number of points equals 100. A percentage is then computed based on the student's performance. A letter may be assigned to each level within the rubric. If the highest level is a *4*, the *4* can be converted to an *A*, a *3* to a *B*, a *2* to a *C*, etc. Taggart et al. (1998) cautioned, however, that when using this procedure, the rubric be constructed to represent adequate performance.
- A pass/fail system may also be used. A specified level is determined for passing, and a student may have several opportunities to achieve the passing criteria.

Teachers are often pressured by parents and/or students to change grades. These pressures come from the fact that students may be removed from band, sports, or other activities unless a certain level of achievement is attained and maintained. Grades are also important in computing class rank, a determinant in college and university admissions. If you have clearly thought through your grading procedure, you should remain steadfast in keeping the grade you assigned, for it should represent what you awarded on the basis of what the student *earned.*

New Trends in Grading

Marzano (2000, 2006) offered a future look at grading. Since he believes that numerical grades represented as a percentage and grades represented as a letter are uninformative in offering details needed to give evidence of student achievement, he has suggested a new type of report card with no grades.

This report card would have the student's name and grade level at the top and include all the subjects taken during a marking period, usually about six weeks. A column on the left would list the standards to be achieved in each subject and rows would provide on a scale of 1–4 the student's rubric ratings on those standards, with *1* being the lowest, and *4* the highest. This type of report card could even accommodate non-academic factors such as behavior, attendance, and effort.

A sample of what this kind of report card adapted from Marzano (2000) for one course might look like is offered in Table 3.10. The standards of other subjects taken by the student along with communication standards and non-achievement factors would be listed under the Civics standards to complete the whole report card.

Carr and Harris (2001) suggested a similar type of report card distributed on a quarterly basis. The student's name would be on top, the standards would be specified on the left, and a rubric score (1–4) would be on the right. A key is presented on the bottom with indicators for the assigned score. A sample for one standard category (Reading/Literature) is shown in Table 3.11.

Before concluding this chapter, it must be pointed out that in this age of technology there are more efficient ways for teachers to keep track of grades rather than with paper and pencil. Some companies are designing programs to make record-keeping easier.

Many states are now scoring assessments electronically. The scores are correlated with the state standards and reported in a way that informs the teacher which standard each student has or may not have achieved. This input assists the teacher regarding which students may need remedial instruction so that the standard(s) will be achieved.

An integral part of the assessment process is *teacher self-assessment.* Frequently, this assessment is implemented by watching videos of the class and teacher in action. After that time the teacher self-reflects and often gets both student and colleague input regarding the video and how both teacher and student performance can be improved (Ferlazzo 2011).

Chapter Summary: While assessment is the process of collecting a variety of information on student performance, evaluation is making a judgment on the performance based on the information collected.

Assessment provides data about student achievement as well as data to improve learning. This informed feedback assists in instructional planning for both teachers and students.

One way to assess/evaluate students is through teacher-constructed tests, whether they are quizzes, which are shorter in content and time needed, or tests, which are longer and more comprehensive. Tests measure knowledge and understanding goals. In order for tests to be of value, they should be valid—measure what is intended to be measured, and reliable—consistent in their results.

There are two general types of tests: norm-referenced and criterion-referenced. Norm-referenced tests compare students to average scores achieved by students in a sample group. Criterion-referenced tests evaluate pre-determined specific skills.

Two types of classroom tests are essay and short answer. Both have advantages and disadvantages and should adhere to specific guidelines for proper construction. New short-answer questions are now being used to measure higher-level learning.

In addition to tests, academic prompts, performance tasks and products, and portfolios can be used to evaluate instructional goals. Authentic performance assesses what the students can do with knowledge and understanding.

Scoring rubrics provide objective means for teachers and students to both assess and improve performance. Scoring rubrics have a scale from the lowest to the best performance, with a set of corresponding performance descriptors. It is preferable that the scale offer an even number of descriptor choices and that the descriptors be stated in positive terms. When possible, students should participate in rubric construction. Rubrics should be available to students before beginning tasks.

To enhance student motivation and achievement, assessment should be conducted *for* learning as well as *of* learning.

Computer-assisted technologies will assist teachers in obtaining information to assess students' thinking processes and skill applications for staying competitive in a global innovation economy.

Assigning grades (a final evaluation) is a fact of life for teachers. There are several systems that can be used for assigning student grades. These systems reflect the school evaluations and scores for rubrics constructed for performance tasks and products.

Currently, there is a trend toward having report cards with no grades. These report cards use a rubric scale to indicate student achievement of standards.

Electronic scoring assessments of state learning standards are increasingly being used to indicate which specific standard(s) a student may have yet to attain. This information helps teachers know which students will need remedial instruction to achieve the standard(s).

Teacher self-assessment is integral to any assessment/evaluation system that is implemented in the classroom.

Chapter 4

Reviewing Unit and Lesson Planning Basics

Before considering how to plan effective instruction, always be cognizant of the fact that you are preparing students for society in the twenty-first century. In this society, people will be changing jobs approximately every five years. The demands of these new jobs will require skills associated with team membership; listening; self-management; time management; assuming responsibility; and following schedules (Secretary's Commission on Achieving Necessary Skills 1991). High job performance will result when there are high expectations of employees who are allowed to set their own goals for achieving these expectations, when the employees receive prompt feedback, and exhibit good listening skills (Cummings 2000).

States throughout the nation are currently revamping education to meet the demands of the twenty-first century by including life skills, a wide range of intellectual skills, and social skills. There is agreement between leaders in both industry and academia that students have to learn to become innovative, solve problems, and interact successfully with people from many different cultures (Gewertz 2008).

To bolster your students' twenty-first-century needs within classrooms that are increasing in social, emotional, cultural, and academic diversity, it is imperative that planning and instruction be conducted in a *supportive learning environment.* In this environment, the teacher is a facilitator who fosters not only students' academic growth but also their personal and social growth.

The classroom is a learning community in which there is *shared responsibility* for the success of all community members. The teacher's role is one of a guide and coach as opposed to a person who pours information into students' heads or determines classroom rules and procedures without student input. There is a warm friendly atmosphere and a spirit of cooperation in which each has a stake in the success of all other members. This atmosphere produces a comfort level in which students are more willing to take risks and participate to enhance accomplishment.

Recently, several characteristics have been demonstrated to be conducive to promoting a positive emotional classroom environment. As already indicated in Chapter 1, these include having a caring attitude, setting high standards, and having *all* classroom members including the teacher show mutual respect and support for each other (Oakes and Lipton 2003). In short, there is a sense of community where all classroom members are connected with one another.

Supportive research has indicated that rapport with the teacher and fellow classmates made students feel linked and willing to participate, thus enhancing cognitive and affective learning (Frisby and Martin 2010). Data from research conducted by the Redwood City School District (CA) and Stanford University's John W. Gardner Center partnership and reported by Lavin (2011) confirmed " . . . that a safe and caring setting is the ideal climate for learning. Caring classrooms have students who treat one another with respect and teachers who foster this behavior by letting students know they are not allowed to make fun of others for a wrong answer or mistake" (p. 3). Moreover, in these positive classrooms, motivation was increased along with its attendant result, achievement.

This supportive learning environment welcomes student questions; is non-judgmental; fosters the attitude that it is all right to make mistakes because we all do and learn from them; and does not allow students to be subjected to ridicule from anyone in the learning community. Students are given the time to think and are challenged at their appropriate levels. When necessary, students help each other in achieving goals and completing assignments.

The seating arrangement in the classroom is critically important in implementing an effective curriculum. Whenever possible, students should work in small groups (Chapter 7). When working in large groups, students should sit in a circle where they all face each other and can address each other in a more personal way. In this setting, all students are easily visible to the teacher and to each other, with little opportunity for students to conduct non-related activities. The teacher is free to move around more easily, thus giving him/her contact with everyone in the class.

In a supportive learning environment, the teacher is enthusiastic and plans units and lessons carefully with input from the students, when appropriate. S/he expects all to participate in activities and assists with the rest of the class in helping any student who has difficulty.

Once you have established this supportive learning environment with your students, you will be well on your way to planning and implementing twenty-first-century curriculum and instruction more effectively.

THE IMPORTANCE OF PLANNING FOR INSTRUCTION

When the Teacher of the Year in Los Angeles was interviewed for the cable TV program, "Breaking Point: The Education Crisis in America," on the Fox News Channel (November 23, 2003), the gentleman was asked what the secret to his teaching success was. His response was that his success was due to only four words, "There are no shortcuts." This was his way of saying that he did not take the path of least resistance, but planned and implemented everything that was necessary to ensure student success.

Planning is one of the most important responsibilities of teachers and it must be taken very seriously. Excellent planning is time consuming, but *carefully thought-out plans* give students the greatest chance for achievement.

If there is anything you can expect as a teacher, it is the unexpected. Plans are effective if they are applied flexibly. Some teachers put so much into planning, have so much invested, that they want to carry out every item, even if they seem to be losing the students.

The best plans can go awry, so it is productive to develop alternative plans if, during instruction, what you are doing is not successful. Also, an unexpected situation can occur that you can take advantage of, resulting in more learning than from actually following what you had originally planned. You must be adaptable enough to change course, if necessary, so that the new direction will result in higher achievement.

Sources for Units

A unit plan is a written guideline for instruction centering around a topic, connected topics, problem, or theme, usually lasting from one to several weeks or for a marking period. The unit is a *framework* from which daily lessons are planned.

Before you actually begin to plan a unit, you should receive input from several sources: colleagues, learners, and parents. All three have tended to be neglected participants in the past.

Colleagues. Whatever type of planning you do, you should avoid teaching as a lonely profession by teaming with other professionals in the planning process. In Chapter 2 you read that collaboration is much more effective in developing teaching skills than working on your own. When you plan collaboratively, you plan smarter, have more support, and are better able to coordinate the use of materials and resources all collaborators will need.

Many school systems have begun to adopt the procedure of curriculum mapping (Jacobs 1997, 2009) districtwide. This process provides the opportunity for each teacher in the school district to indicate in broad terms what is actually being taught in his/her classes month by month throughout the school calendar year. For instance, an eighth-grade social studies teacher could write:

Month	Topic
September	Civil War
October	Reconstruction
November	Rise of industry
December	
January	
February	
March	
April	
May	
June	

continuing to identify general topics for the remaining months, December through June.

Since what is taught throughout K–12 by every teacher is expressed on the map so broadly, curriculum mapping is an effective tool for producing a big picture and context for making collaborative curriculum and instructional decisions. Being aware of what is being taught at all levels on a month-by-month basis allows curriculum decisions that avoid gaps and redundancy and provide for greater integration of subject matter. Equally important, curriculum mapping presents a focus for *deciding what assessments* will be used for the curriculum.

Learners. Your students should also have input into what is taught and how it is taught. Learners' personal interests should be taken into account as well as their ideas regarding how they best learn. You cannot rely solely on learners' interest, however, because that would limit the scope of what you teach, and your role is to broaden learners' exposure to new content and experiences. Yet, you should still include students' suggestions in your planning.

Parents. Parental involvement in planning is a trend that is being adopted in many school districts. Buchen (2004) has argued that there is a trend toward " . . . the emergence of parents as the newest and perhaps the most major pivotal players of education in the future" (p. 31). Marzano (2003) reported that of the eleven factors he identified that influence a school's success, parental involvement is in the top five. Parents are often invited to participate on curriculum committees and even on search committees for new faculty and administrators.

Many positive results are achieved when parents are involved in schools (Reynolds and Teddlie 2000). Parents who participate are more likely to support the school politically. They bring their own talents as resources, provide an extension of the curriculum after school, and can offer tutoring as needed not only for their own children but for others as well. There are also fewer discipline problems in classrooms where parents are involved.

Research regarding parental involvement documented improvement in student achievement regardless of education and socioeconomic level of parents or the age of the student (U.S. Department of Education 1994). And in a study conducted by Columbia University and reported by Zuckerbrod (2007), low-income students whose parents participated in school life performed equally well whether these students attended public or private schools.

There are, in general, long-term and short-term plans. Long-term plans can cover a year, a semester, a marking period, or a week, and are determined by how the academic year is organized by a school district and school. Long-term plans help sequence the content that is taught, allow realistic time frames for that content, form the basis for more thorough unit plans, and identify which subjects are related and whether or not they will be integrated. Short-term plans involve daily lessons that focus on one or a limited number of objectives, making it easier to allow for ongoing adjustments in instruction.

Planning can also be affected by scheduling. Many school districts have introduced block scheduling on the secondary level, where a longer time is set aside on a regular basis so that teachers can plan ahead for content and activities that may be pursued in depth, instead of having these activities interrupted by a traditional time frame. The teacher could also allow for breaks within the time block (Jensen 2005).

Content (Curriculum) Sources for Units

Traditionally, curriculum sources came from societal needs and values, textbooks, the interests of learners, and from state and local curriculum guides. In many respects all of these are still used. However, the sole reliance on these sources began to change in the 1980s as citizens, constantly complaining about the "mediocrity" of education in the United States, began to demand more accountability.

The impetus for the possibility of more comprehensive change came in 1989, when the National Council of Teachers of Mathematics, NCTM, became the first professional organization to propose standards for its discipline. In 1994 the Educate America Act provided funding for the development of national standards. This legislation was amended in 1996 for the purpose of assisting states in producing their own standards. However, with global economic competition a major concern for the country, a movement occurred to produce national standards to replace state standards (Allen 2009).

As of this writing, 48 states are involved with common core state standards. These standards were developed because it was recognized that existing standards across the states were uneven. It was necessary to adopt more rigorous common state standards that would identify for all school districts throughout the nation what students should know and be able to do at each level from K–12.

The mission statement for these standards is as follows:

> The Common Core State Standards provide a consistent, clear understanding of what students are expected to learn, so teachers and parents know what they need to do to help them. The standards are designed to be robust and relevant to the real world, reflecting the knowledge and skills that our young people need for success in college and careers. With American students fully prepared for the future, our communities will be best positioned to compete successfully in the global economy (http://www corestandards.org).

According to the Common Core State Standards Initiative's website (2010), the common core standards

- are aligned with college and work expectations;
- are clear, understandable, and consistent;
- include rigorous content and application of knowledge through high-order skills;
- build upon strengths and lessons of current state standards;
- are informed by other top-performing countries so that all students are prepared to succeed in our global economy and society; and
- are evidence-based.

So far, common core state standards have been developed for English and mathematics. They can be downloaded from the Common Core State Standards Initiative website (http://www.corestandards.org). These standards are being implemented slowly and should be fully implemented by 2014. Common core standards for other curriculum areas are also being developed along with standardized assessments that will be aligned with the common core standards (Ciurczak 2011).

Since standards express what students should know and be able to do, there are, clearly, both content and performance implications in this definition.

Standards are broad statements that express what students are expected to learn by the time they finish high school. The critical question regarding the content that is taught, whether predetermined standards or not, is whether " . . . what is taught is worth knowing in the first place, and that it is treated in sufficient depth to engage students' interest and offer them a challenge" (Cotton 2000, 4).

To clarify and refine standards, which are stated in very broad terms, it is necessary to identify what related knowledge or skills are needed at various grades, developmental, or grade-level intervals. These subcomponents of standards are known as *benchmarks.* To make the process of identifying benchmarks more manageable, they are generally stated at a few key levels, for example, grades 2, 5, 8, and 12, though many school districts have identified them for all levels.

The work of Kendall and Marzano (1997) provides an illustration of a standard in science along with its possible benchmarks for grades 12 and 8.

Standard: Understands basic concepts about the structure and properties of matter.

Benchmark that could flow from this standard on a 12th grade level:

Knows that the physical properties of a compound are determined by its molecular structure (e.g., constituent atoms, distances and angles between them) and the interactions among these molecules.

Benchmark that could flow from this same standard on an 8th grade level:

Knows that atoms often combine to form a molecule (or crystal), the smallest particle of a substance that retains its properties (Kendall and Marzano 1997, 25).

The above examples should make it clear to you that standards eventually become benchmarks which are more focused and narrow for different developmental (or grade) levels. These benchmarks are further broken down into goals that are more manageable for developing within a limited time period (1–6 weeks).

The standards movement has both advocates (Tucker and Codding 1998; Glatthorn 1999) and critics (Caine and Caine 1994; Kohn 2000; Sylwester 2000). Yet, standards are a fact of life.

Despite the complaints about standards, Carr and Harris (2001) asserted that the best way to succeed with them is by having the teacher

inform students of the skills involved in the standard;
match the content to the students' developmental levels;
provide access to non-text resources;
ensure that instructional time is used flexibly;
provide a safe environment both physically and emotionally;
offer engaging activities that build on prior knowledge;
perform a variety of teaching roles;
assign students to perform a variety of learning roles;
integrate and apply learning in meaningful contexts;
involve students in assessment;
establish performance criteria that are clear; and
use assessment techniques that allow for the adjustment of instruction.

What Carr and Harris (2001) are saying is that there is no excuse to avoid using effective teaching when implementing standards. And with bipartisan politicians along with business, labor, and educational leaders supporting a common nationwide curriculum (Dillon 2011), you must deal with standards whether you like them or not.

In addition to traditional and current curriculum sources, a new curriculum trend is now international (Cavanagh 2006). Through the Internet and other technologies, students from different nations can now communicate with peers in other countries to design projects, work collaboratively on them, and learn about each other's cultures. Currently, approximately one million students from the ages of 5–19 participate in this global network exchange daily. These students represent 115 countries and 20,000 schools including 600 in the United States.

This international trend is a positive step, because a discussion on curriculum and standards cannot be concluded unless attention is given to requirements offered by Jacobs (2010). She points out that any new standards,

Table 4.1.   Content (Curriculum) Sources for Units

Curriculum	*Sources*
General Goals	Common Core State Learning Standards
Goals for Specific Subject Areas	State and District Curriculum Guides, Subject-Specific Professional Organizations
Sets of Related Goals (Benchmarks) and Specific Corresponding Objectives	Classroom Unit Plans
Specific Objectives from Unit Plan	Classroom Lesson Plans

regardless of how rigorous they may be, will remain an anachronism unless they promote the use of twenty-first-century digital and networking tools, address global perspectives, and identify interdisciplinary linkages for real-world applications. Implementation of these networking tools will force school districts to rethink their scheduling.

Organizing Units

Units may be organized in several ways. This organization may be as topic units, integrated units, or thematic units. Some texts have different labels for these different units, but the label is less important than the intent and approach.

Topic Units. Topic units center around narrow content such as "Fractions," "Poetry," "Mammals," or focus on one standard such as "Understands developments in foreign policy and domestic politics between the Nixon and Clinton presidencies" (Kendall and Marzano 1997, 189). A standard itself can be translated into a unit topic. In the previous example, the topic title could be "Developments in Foreign Policy and Domestic Politics between the Nixon and Clinton Presidencies." The standard can also be turned into a question, "How Did Foreign Policy and Domestic Politics Develop between the Nixon and Clinton Presidencies?"

A topic unit tends to be the least brain-compatible, since the context and content are limited. Secondary school teachers may have to rely more on the topic approach because they frequently have up to five different preparations, with less time for collaboration with teachers from different subject areas. Teachers using the topic approach should attempt to correlate as many other subjects as feasible to tie in with the content presented.

Integrated Units. Integrated units usually link two or more subjects together. Using the above examples of topic units, ("Fractions," "Poetry," and "Mammals"), fractions could be studied with music, poetry could be coordinated with the history and music at the time the poetry was written, and mammals could be studied with climate, geography, and economics.

Two standards from different but related areas of the same subject can also be studied in an integrated unit. In social studies the standard from history referred to above, "Understands developments in foreign policy and domestic politics between the Nixon and Clinton presidencies," could be connected and studied with a standard from economics, "Understands how Gross Domestic Product and inflation and deflation provide indications of the state of the economy" (Kendall and Marzano 1997, 489).

The integrated unit is more brain-compatible than the topic unit because integration connects different subjects together—history and economics in the prior example—instead of presenting subjects in isolation. Elementary and middle school teachers usually have more liberty to collaborate in planning for integrating their subjects and teaching them simultaneously.

Thematic Units. The thematic approach to developing units organizes content around a specific theme or idea. "Terrorism," "The Aging Population," "Technology," and "Preparing for Hurricanes" are examples of themes. They deal with big questions, big ideas, and broader issues. Problems and questions stemming from themes are examined and solved using the content from several subjects. The answers and solutions often lead to further questions and problems.

For example, science, history, economics, and politics are just a few disciplines that could contribute to solving problems caused by "The Aging Population," a theme already cited above. The fact that science is helping people live longer has implications for the quality of life, social security, prescription drugs, nursing homes, health care in general, and a myriad of other issues. Think of the political, social, economic, historical, and geographic implications of preparing for Hurricane Katrina and its aftermath.

The thematic approach is the most brain-compatible since it leads to deeper understanding by drawing on several subjects to explore content. Elementary teachers who teach all subjects within self-contained classrooms have better opportunities than middle and high school teachers who are in subject-specific classrooms to plan thematic units with other teachers at the same grade level. However, teaching in a thematic way is recognized by educators as so important that school districts are trying to find ways for secondary teachers from the same disciplines to plan with each other as well as with teachers from other disciplines.

Whether planning topic, integrated, or thematic units, collaboration and correlation of content will be easier if the district has adopted curriculum mapping (Jacobs and Johnson 2009).

Goals and Objectives

Before you actually plan a unit, you must review and understand the difference between goals and objectives and how to write them properly. Goals and objectives are important because they will help both you and your students determine how successful your teaching and their learning has been.

Goals. In general, goals are outcomes (results) of instruction expressed as long-term statements regarding what the students will accomplish. Standards and benchmarks are examples of goals. For the purpose of your unit, however, goals state what the students should accomplish with respect to the content by the end of the unit. Obviously, goals are not accomplished in a day. They clearly offer direction and overall thrust to the unit within its time frame.

Table 4.2. Goals and Objectives

Goals	Objectives
Results (outcomes) of instruction	Results (outcomes) of instruction
Achieved over the long term (at end of unit)	Achieved over the short term (at end of lesson)
Stated in broad terms	Stated in specific terms
Sources of instruction in themselves	Derived from goals

Though you may have your own goals in planning and teaching a unit, goals should emphasize not what you want to achieve, but results you want the students to achieve. When age appropriate, students should also determine in addition to your goals their own goals to accomplish by the end of the unit.

Objectives. Objectives are frequently referred to interchangeably in curriculum literature as behavioral objectives, instructional, or performance objectives. (Those that are referred to as educational objectives are often actually goals because, even though they include the word objective, educational objectives are achievable over a longer period of time.)

Objectives derive their content from goals, and as opposed to goals, are achievable in the short term. Objectives are written to communicate clearly to students what they are expected to achieve. This communication is particularly important, because as indicated in principles of learning verified by brain research (Chapter 1), students who are aware of objectives are more likely to attain them.

Before reviewing what objectives are, first be clear regarding what they are *not*. They are not teacher-oriented, stating what the teacher is going to do. They are student-oriented, expressing the results or outcomes of instruction. They are not activities the students will do, but are results of having participated in those activities. To summarize, objectives are student-oriented and describe what the student will be able to do at the end of and as a result of instruction.

When a teacher states that s/he will discuss an overhead of a cell, this is not an objective. It is what the teacher will do. To discuss and view an overhead is an activity that can lead to what the students can do as a result, namely, identify the parts of a cell and describe their function.

How to Write Instructional (Behavioral, Performance) Objectives

Mager's Version According to Mager (1984, 1997), objectives have three attributes: an observable performance, a condition, and a level of achievement (criterion).

1. The observable performance represents a desired performance also known as a target behavior. The performance should be overt (visible) and describe explicitly what the student will be able to do as a result of instruction. The performance should be expressed as an observable verb that is clear enough so that several people viewing the student would be able to agree that the performance is actually taking place.

   What is the difference in your ability to observe behavior by using the verbs *learn* and *define* in the following objectives?

   The student will be able to learn vocabulary words.

   The student will be able to define vocabulary words.

   Do not resume reading until you have answered the question.

If you wanted the students to learn vocabulary words, how would you know whether or not the students had learned them? Is the learning observable? Could several people agree that learning had taken place unless the students did something specific to demonstrate that learning? The student would have to do something such as define the word or use it correctly in a sentence. Demonstrating after instruction what the students were not able to do before instruction provides evidence that learning has taken place. Of course, if the student can perform the objective before instruction, there is no need for instruction.

   In the following list of verbs, which are overt (visible and observable), and which are not?

   see
   state
   list
   view
   recite
   differentiate
   compare
   know

See, view, and *know* are ambiguous and, therefore, considered "*no-nos*" because they are not overt. Other ambiguous "no-nos" are "grasp the meaning of," "believe," "appreciate," "realize," or comparable terms. While non-observable verbs can be used as general statements in goals, these verbs should not be used in objectives.

Some observable verbs can be used improperly. "Demonstrate the understanding of," "Demonstrate the knowledge of," or "Demonstrate an awareness of" mean essentially *to understand* or *to know*. Therefore, *demonstrate* is *not* appropriately used in these examples.

However, "To demonstrate the way the blood flows through the heart" is observable, so in this example *demonstrate* can be used. The intent in "Develop a critical understanding" also means *to understand*, which is *not* observable. But if an objective states, "Develop a plan for evacuating victims from a particular building," then *develop* in this case *is* observable and used appropriately (Mager 1997).

It is also important to distinguish between verbs used as activities and verbs used as objectives (results). *Cut* different shapes and superimpose them on a template (an instructional activity) can lead to *identify* shapes (a result). *Pour* water from a quart pitcher into as many cups as possible should lead to *state* how many cups equal one quart. *Study* is an activity that could lead to an objective. However, after a lesson on how to study, study itself may be the result.

2. A condition. When writing objectives, it is essential to consider what might influence the shape of the performance by considering under what condition(s) or circumstances the student will be able to demonstrate performance. Stating the condition eliminates miscommunication by clarifying any situation that would have a significant impact on performance.

For instance, what would have happened to allow the student to perform the objective, or what materials will be allowed or prevented from being used during the performance? What are the real-world circumstances under which the performance will be expected to take place?

Consider the following objective: the student will be able to deliver the soliloquy from Hamlet.

Will the student be allowed a text or not? If the intent is to have the student show that s/he has memorized the content, then the delivery would occur without referring to the text. If the intent is to have the student demonstrate oral interpretation, then the text could be used. If the objective is the former, then it should be restated as, "Without referring to the text, the student will deliver the soliloquy from Hamlet."

The purpose of the objective should determine the degree of specificity. If you can picture the student performing the objective, it will help you decide whether or not a condition is implied or should be stated.

"Given a protractor, the student will be able to measure all the angles in the trapezoid."

"Given a list of 20 words, the student will be able to put them in alphabetical order."

"The student will be able to break up a list of 20 words into syllables without using a dictionary."

"While blindfolded, the student will be able to identify five different fruits."

It is not necessary to state, "At the end of the lesson, the student will be able to . . ." because it is assumed that the student will need instruction in the lesson. If the student can already perform the objective, then no instruction regarding that objective is required. It is also redundant to keep stating, "The student will be able to . . ." for each objective in a list.

The question arises whether or not every objective should state conditions. Mager (1997) suggested, "Add enough description to an objective to make it clear to everyone concerned just what you expect from the learner. If what you expect is made clear just by stating the desired performance and the degree of excellence you desire . . . then don't add conditions arbitrarily" (p. 106).

3. Level of achievement or criterion. To write a clear objective, it is *sometimes* necessary to refine it by stating the minimal level of acceptable performance the students must demonstrate. The levels are usually stated numerically (N), within time frames (T), or as a combination of the two (NT).

> The student will be able to do the following:
> state at least three examples of verbs (N)
> write a paragraph with no punctuation errors (N)
> calculate five addition-of-unlike-fractions problems within five minutes (NT)
> spell all of the words from the spelling list correctly (N)
> spell nine out of 10 words from the spelling list correctly (N)
> spell 80 percent of the words from the spelling list correctly (N)
> calculate to the nearest inch the length of a table (N)
> compute within ten minutes all division problems (NT)
> identify three causes of the Civil War (N)

Table 4.3. Anatomy of a Mager Objective

Condition	Observable Performance	Level of Achievement (Criterion)
Without the use of a dictionary	the student will spell from the assigned list	18 out of 20 words correctly
Given a protractor	the student will measure on the worksheet	all angles correctly
After watching the video	the student will list	three personality traits of the hero

run a mile in fifteen minutes (T)

Note that in the objective, "The student will be able to define a verb," the student can either define a verb or not. The level of achievement (viz., accurately) is implied, so it would make no sense to state that the student would be able to define a verb with 80 percent accuracy. Yet, teachers frequently write this level of achievement in objectives. Be sure to use thought and common sense when writing objectives.

Gronlund's Version Some teachers have found listing all the criteria in Mager's objectives burdensome. Gronlund (2004) has offered a more flexible way to write objectives for unit and lesson planning. Some teachers find his approach easier to work with. He begins with a general objective (educational objective or goal) applicable to any grade level or course, and then proceeds to the specific related outcomes (instructional [behavioral, performance] objectives) that would be appropriate to that grade.

Example: Comprehends basic principles (general objective also known as an educational objective or goal)

1.1 States (instructional, behavioral, performance objective) the principles in his or her own words.
1.2 Identifies (instructional, behavioral, performance objective) an example of the principle.
1.3 Distinguishes between (instructional, behavioral, performance objective) correct and incorrect applications of the principle.
1.4 Predicts (instructional, behavioral, performance objective) an outcome based on the principle (Gronlund 2004, 19).

As previously stated in this chapter, the general objective in the above example is a long-term statement that is actually a goal. The four objectives are specific and state what the student must do to demonstrate achievement of the goal. These are the instructional (behavioral, performance) objectives.

What should be evident is the importance of both goals and objectives. Their purpose is clarity, so that both you and the students will know what they are to achieve, and both you and the students will be able to determine whether or not they have done so.

Not using appropriate objectives is like getting into a car and driving without a roadmap, GPS, or knowing where you want to go. Time, energy, and money are wasted and the driver may get to a place not intended or drive around in circles getting to no place at all. Knowing the destination (objective) makes it locatable on the map and provides guidance for the most efficient and direct way to arrive. Also, standards and benchmarks are eventually broken down into objectives.

Standards➤➤➤Benchmarks (Larger goals)➤➤➤Goals (Smaller)➤➤➤Objectives

Classifying Objectives

Objectives can be categorized according to their learning outcomes (results). The objectives are generally grouped under three main categories known as *domains*. These domains are the cognitive, the affective, and the psychomotor.

The Cognitive Domain Cognitive objectives have as their thrust the information or content knowledge taught in schools. Bloom et al. (1956) developed a taxonomy of objectives in the cognitive domain. They are arranged in a hierarchy from simple memory to the most complex levels of thinking. Each level of the hierarchy uses information from lower levels. The lower levels are concerned with factual information; the higher levels are concerned with manipulating that information.

Some factual information must be learned before higher levels of thinking can proceed. For example, a student cannot design a space suit for getting to the moon unless he has factual information about the moon. A persistent problem that often occurs in schools, however, is that too much learning remains on the lower levels.

Bloom et al. (1956) proposed six levels in the cognitive domain. The levels are these: knowledge, comprehension, application, analysis, synthesis, and evaluation.

Knowledge. On the knowledge level, students recall basic information or specific facts. This knowledge would include remembering terms, principles, theories, procedures, people, events, dates, or places. Some verbs commonly used at the knowledge level follow:

state
define
identify
recognize
list
recite
outline
name
select

Example: The student will be able to name the nine planets.

Comprehension. Students can take the basic information gained on the knowledge level and translate, compare, interpret, or describe it in their own words on the comprehension level. Verbs generally associated with the comprehension level include these:

compare
summarize
describe
generalize
restate
rewrite
give an example of
demonstrate
estimate

Following through with the above knowledge level example, the student will be able to name the nine planets, this same objective on the comprehension level could read,

"Given models of the nine planets, the student will be able to distinguish among them."

Application. This level involves having the student, once s/he understands the information, able to use it or transfer the information to a new situation. Appropriate verbs may include the following:

manipulate
modify
use
relate
demonstrate
predict
apply
perform
solve
construct

Example: The student will be able to construct a timeline to demonstrate the distance of planets from the sun.

Analysis. At the analysis level the student breaks information into its component parts. Understanding at this level involves the structural form and content of the material. Verbs frequently associated with this level are analytic verbs such as these:

arrange
distinguish between or among
discriminate
differentiate
classify
separate

Example: The student will be able to differentiate the orbits of the planets according to gravity and centrifugal force.

Synthesis. On the synthesis level the student puts information together in new ways. The student may solve a problem or come up with a plan that does not exist. Verbs used on this level may include the following:

put together
devise
construct
assemble
generate
predict
rearrange

Example: Given assigned new masses of the planets, the student will be able to redesign the solar system.

Evaluation. Evaluation is the highest level of the cognitive domain. This level includes making informed opinions, judgments, and decisions based on clear criteria.

Verbs that may be employed follow:

interpret
rate
evaluate
support
appraise
defend

Example: The student will be able to justify his/her design of the new solar system.

The content selected, which immediately follows the verb in an objective, is just as and perhaps more important than the verb. "The student will distinguish nouns from verbs" is very different from the objective, "the student will distinguish among several different plans for constructing a method for leaving a building in the event of a fire." The verb "distinguish" is the same in both objectives, but in the first objective, the content is on the comprehension level, and in the second, the content is on the analysis level.

Table 4.4 summarizes the cognitive domain. Marzano (2001) has offered a new taxonomy of educational objectives in the cognitive domain based on Bloom's work. While acknowledging Bloom's "incredible contribution to educational theory and practice" (p. ix), Marzano claimed that in the half century that has passed since the original work in 1956, " . . . no successful attempt has been mounted to update or replace the taxonomy. Yet in that same half century, understanding of how the mind works, the nature of knowledge, and the interaction of the two have advanced dramatically" (p. viii).

Retaining the first four levels of Bloom's taxonomy, Marzano (2001) and Marzano and Kendall (2007) added *metacognition* and *self-system thinking*, a total of six levels. This taxonomy also describes three knowledge domains, those of information, mental, and psychomotor procedures, all of which are operant at all six levels.

Table 4.4. The Cognitive Domain

Levels	Task	Corresponding Verbs
Knowledge	Recall basic information or specific facts; remember terms, principles, theories	State, define, identify, list, recognize, recite, outline, name, select
Comprehension	Take basic information and translate, interpret, or describe it in student's own words	Compare, summarize, describe, generalize, restate, rewrite, give an example, demonstrate, estimate
Application	Transfer new information to a new situation	Manipulate, modify, use, relate, demonstrate, predict, apply, perform, solve
Analysis	Break information into its component parts	Arrange, distinguish between, discriminate, differentiate, classify, separate
Synthesis	Put information together in new ways	Devise, construct, assemble, generate, predict, rearrange
Evaluation	Make informed opinions, judgments, and decisions based on clear criteria	Interpret, rate, evaluate, support, appraise, defend

Table 4.5. Cognitive Domain Comparisons

Bloom	Marzano	Anderson Et Al.
Knowledge	Knowledge Domains -Information -Mental -Psychomotor	Knowledge (4 Dimensions) -Factual -Procedural -Conceptual -Metacognitive
Comprehension	Comprehension	Remembering
Application	Application	Understanding
Analysis	Analysis	Applying
Synthesis	Metacognition	Analyzing
Evaluation	Self-System Thinking	Evaluating Creating

Anderson et al. (2001) have also added their voices to the need for updating Bloom's taxonomy. They offered four dimensions of knowledge: factual, conceptual, procedural, and metacognitive. For each of these categories Anderson et al. (2001) have adapted Bloom's six levels to provide a list of their own cognitive processes: remembering, understanding, applying, analyzing, evaluating, and creating.

When you feel that you are well-grounded in Bloom's taxonomy, you may want to progress to studying and implementing those suggested by Marzano (2001), Marzano and Kendall (2007), and/or Anderson et al. (2001).

The Affective Domain While the cognitive domain develops knowledge or information, the affective domain is concerned with a student's attitudes, values, and interests, thus presenting another dimension in considering the education of the whole student. Krathwohl, Bloom, and Masia (1964) developed a taxonomy of objectives in the affective domain. It contains five levels: receiving, responding, valuing, organization and characterization.

Receiving. The first level reflects the willingness of a student to pay attention to a particular stimulus or phenomenon without coercion. Corresponding verbs are these:

follows
demonstrates
listens
selects
chooses
gives

Example: The student listens to a classical music selection.

Responding. In the responding level the student demonstrates behavior that responds voluntarily to the original stimulus. Verbs at this level include these:

assists
discusses
reads
performs
selects
chooses

Example: Given a range of tapes from classical to contemporary, the student chooses to listen to the tape of a classical music selection.

Valuing. At this stage of affective development, the student accepts beliefs and values. Verbs included at this stage are as follows:

argues
justifies
invites
joins
protests
supports

Example: The student argues that classical music is superior to rock.

Organization. At the organization level the student builds a personal value system, assigning worth and relative importance to each value. Verbs associated with this level include these:

defends
integrates
adheres
prepares
relates
explains

Example: The student organizes a classical music club.

Characterization. At this highest level of the affective domain the student behaves consistently with his/her beliefs and values. Action verbs may include the following:

revises
performs
influences
verifies
displays

Example: The student convinces peers to purchase a subscription to orchestral performances.

As in the case of cognitive objectives, verbs used in affective objectives can be used on several levels, but it is what follows in terms of demonstrating the behavior that actually determines the level.

Table 4.6 summarizes the affective domain.

The Psychomotor Domain The psychomotor domain completes the development of the whole child, but not without disagreement regarding what should be included. Originally conceived as developing proficiency in skills, especially control of gross and fine motor skills, the psychomotor domain now contains more creative and inventive skills.

Table 4.6. The Affective Domain

Levels	Task	Corresponding Verbs
Receiving	Willingness of a student to attend to a particular event, stimulus, or phenomenon suggested by another without coercion	Demonstrates, listens, selects, chooses, gives
Responding	Demonstrates behavior that responds voluntarily to the original event, stimulus, or phenomenon	Assists, discusses, reads, performs, selects, chooses
Valuing	Accepts beliefs and values Argues, justifies, invites, joins, protests, supports	Argues, justifies, invites, joins, protests, supports
Organization	Builds a personal value system	Defends, integrates, adheres, prepares, relates, explains
Characterization	Behaves consistently with his/her beliefs and values	Revises, performs, influences, verifies, displays

Harrow (1977) developed a taxonomy of objectives that deals with physical as well as more creative aspects. Her taxonomy ranges from the lowest level, such as using a mouse, to the highest level, designing new hardware (or software). Four levels are represented in Harrow's taxonomy: movement, manipulation, communication, and creation.

Movement. At this level, students are involved with gross motor coordination. Verbs commonly associated with this level are these:

walk
run
jump
carry
lift
grasp

Example: The student will remove the parts of a car model from its container.

Manipulation. Once gross motor skills are demonstrated on the movement level, the manipulation level is concerned with fine motor skills. Tune, turn, adjust, assemble, thread, paste, and build are some choices of verbs that involve fine motor skills.

Example: The student will construct the model of the car.

Communication. At this level feelings and ideas of students are communicated. Verbs common to this level are as follows:

draw
explain
write
describe

Example: After completing the model of the car, the student will describe his feelings about the project.

Creation. Not only is creating the highest level of the psychomotor domain, but many believe that it is the highest level of all domains. In creation, the student must integrate achievement in all domains. Appropriate verbs at this level include the following:

Table 4.7. The Psychomotor Domain

Levels	Task	Corresponding Verbs
Movement	Display of gross motor coordination	Walk, run, jump, carry, lift, grasp
Manipulation	Display of fine motor coordination	Tune, turn, adjust, assemble, thread, paste, build
Communication	Express feelings and ideas	Draw, explain, write, describe
Creation	Integrate achievement in all domains	Perform, design, create, invent, choreograph

perform
design
create
invent
choreograph

Example: The student will redesign the shape of the model car body to lower wind resistance.

Table 4.7 summarizes the psychomotor domain.

Table 4.8 presents a summary of all domains.

Even though the three domains were reviewed as separate entities, they are actually interconnected. In planning, there is a need to integrate them rather than consider them as separate. For example, acting out the rotation of the earth involves movement, which emanates from the psychomotor domain. This movement can be used in order to learn about a cognitive objective—the earth rotates on its axis. And as has already been stated, creation integrates achievement in all domains (Anderson et al 2001).

It is not necessary or even possible to write objectives at all levels in all domains. Mager (1984) himself considered any attempt at doing this inefficient. What is important is that when you plan, you attempt to cover

Table 4.8. Summary of Domains and their Levels

Cognitive	Affective	Psychomotor
Knowledge	Receiving	Movement
Comprehension	Responding	Manipulation
Application	Valuing	Communication
Analysis	Organization	Creation
Synthesis	Characterization	
Evaluation		

several different levels, tugging and pulling students to higher levels of achievement. You should expect higher levels of achievement, even from lower-ability students. If you do not expect performance at higher levels, you are not likely to get it.

Chapter Summary: Planning is one of the most important teacher responsibilities. When teachers plan instruction, they should remain cognizant of the fact that they are preparing students to develop skills needed to succeed in the twenty-first century.

Unit planning provides a flexible roadmap for organizing content around a specific topic, problem, or theme for a period of one to several weeks. Units offer a structure for planning daily lessons. Even the most dynamic plans will not be successful unless they are implemented in a supportive learning environment.

Sources for units include colleagues, learners, parents, state and district learning standards, curriculum guides, and textbooks. Learning standards are further divided into benchmarks which identify how the standards should be addressed at different grade levels. Just because teachers are working with standards does not mean that they cannot use effective teaching methods.

Curriculum mapping allows teachers throughout the school district to identify what is being taught in every subject at each grade level, in order to allow collaborative planning and to avoid gaps in or duplication of content.

Units can be organized by specific topics, by integrating two or more topics, or by using themes that draw from several subject areas.

Goals express the outcomes (results) of instruction over the long term, such as a year, semester, or at the end of a unit. Objectives (behavioral, performance, instructional) express the outcomes of instruction over the short term, such as after a lesson. Objectives include an observable verb, a condition, and a level of achievement. Many times the condition and level of achievement are implied.

What is most important about goals and objectives is that they are stated clearly and are communicated to the students. Goals and objectives also assist students in monitoring their own learning.

Objectives can be classified according to three domains—the cognitive, affective, and psychomotor. Cognitive objectives are concerned with content knowledge and information. Affective objectives deal with attitudes, values, feelings, preferences, and interests. Psychomotor objectives cover motor skills as well as creative and inventive skills.

Teachers should provide curriculum and instruction that reflects all domains.

Chapter 5

Maximizing Unit Planning for Student Achievement

Madeline Hunter, who contributed so much to applying research to lesson planning, later reflected that if she had to do it over again, she would have concentrated on unit planning rather than on lesson planning. She is quoted as saying that she saw lessons as fluctuating too much each day, with units giving an important overall guide and focus to instruction (Marzano, 2002). This chapter reviews unit planning first because it provides a context and framework from which to plan individual lessons.

When planning units, it is important to distinguish the difference between curriculum and instruction. There are several different ways to define curriculum, but for the purposes of this presentation, curriculum is concerned with *what* specifically will be taught within a subject or content area. Instruction focuses on *how* that content is taught, or what methods (input) will be used to best convey the content. Both curriculum and instruction decisions must be made in planning.

There is not one way to plan a unit. *There is not one way to plan a unit.* THERE IS NOT ONE WAY TO PLAN A UNIT. This is not an editorial error. The sentence was stated three times to make a point. Also, a unit plan is a *flexible* guide which should be adjusted as you proceed to meet the needs of your students.

It should also be noted that before you plan a unit, you should have a good handle on what the students already know so that you can connect prior knowledge to the new knowledge to be obtained in the unit. If you have performed a diagnostic evaluation using formal and informal assessments such as pre-tests, observations, and interviews, this evaluation process will assist you in determining students' prior knowledge. The Student Diagnosis Form as a Guide to Instructional Planning, presented in chapter 3, Figure 3.3, is a tool you can use to perform a comprehensive diagnosis of each student.

Though there are varieties of ways to plan topic, integrated, and thematic units, almost all plans have certain elements in common. Before you continue reading about unit planning, take some time to stop and write what general components you may be presently using in developing a unit, and in which order they should occur. Then look at the overview presented below to compare your components with those in the outline. With the overview as a guide, take a few moments to write what you might be currently implementing before reading further.

The unit planning presented in this text is a combination of learning principles, constructivism, and the "backward design" as presented by Wiggins and McTighe (1998), McTighe & Wiggins (2004), and Tomlinson & McTighe, 2006.

UNIT COMPONENTS

Examine the unit plan outline in Figure 5.1

What to Include in Each Unit Component before the Assessment/Formative Evaluation Component

Grade _____	Subject(s) _____
Learning Standard(s)	
Topic/Theme _____	Time Frame_____
Introduction	
Organizing ideas	Essential questions
Content Outline	
Goals (results/outcomes)	
Objectives	
Assessment/Formative Evaluation	
Instructional Procedures	
Instructional Materials and Resources	
Correlations with Other Curriculum Areas (if a topic approach is used)	
Assessment/Summative Evaluation	

Figure 5.1.   Unit Plan Outline

Planning Guidelines

In order to plan (and deliver) a unit most effectively, Brooks & Brooks (1999) have proposed some general guiding principles upon which you should concentrate based on current teaching practices: ascertain what knowledge the student already has mastered; present an overview of the unit content introducing large concepts before smaller ones; encourage student participation in planning the unit by seeking and incorporating their questions and goals; whenever possible, use primary sources and hands-on learning experiences as opposed to worksheets and textbooks; assess continuously; have students experience learning largely in groups instead of having the teacher present information; provide experiences that allow for students to discover knowledge and construct their own theories; interact with students as a facilitator of knowledge instead of as a conveyor of information.

With the outline of the unit plan and the above guiding principles in mind, you are now ready to begin reviewing each component before reviewing the assessment/formative evaluation component.

1. Learning Standard(s). Identify which learning standard or standard combinations your unit will address.
2. Topic/theme. This part includes the unit title. It should be narrow enough to give the unit a focus. "Weapons" and "Medical Discoveries" are unit titles that are too broad. Also, if the title is presented as a question, this format will tend to capture the interest of the students. For example, the broad unit titles above can be narrowed down and changed to questions such as, "How has weaponry changed throughout the ages?" and "How have recent medical discoveries influenced the average lifespan?"
3. Introduction. In this section make sure it is clear in your own mind, and then put in writing the overall nature and scope of the topic or theme to be taught, considering the grade and learners. Lee Iacocca, former Chairman of the Chrysler Corporation, is quoted in ben Shea (2002) as having said, "The discipline of writing something down is the first step toward making it happen" (p. 80). As your planning becomes more proficient, you will probably get to the point where you write less. But you will still have to go through the same thought process.

    Identify the organizing (big) ideas and essential questions that the unit will address. Jacobs (1997) has presented a set of criteria for generating the essential questions. These criteria are:

. . .Each child should be able to understand the question.
. . .The language . . . should be written in broad, organizational terms.
. . . Each question should be distinct and substantial.
. . .The questions should be realistic given the amount of time allocated for the unit.
. . .There should be a logical sequence to a set of essential questions.
. . .The questions should be posted in the classroom (Jacobs, 1997, pp. 30–32).

Essential questions serve as an umbrella for the unit. Therefore, activities, assignments, and assessments should be designed to assist students in answering the essential questions. The questions should be arguable, relevant to students' lives, and student-friendly. Essential questions should focus on deeper meaning, not the type that are answerable in a word or sentence (Udelhofen, 2006).

Some examples of essential questions are: How does what we eat affect our health? How did the cultures of the North and South contribute to the causes of the Civil War? Non-examples of essential questions are: Which foods contain calcium? What battles did the Union win?

Tomlinson & McTighe (2006) suggest that teachers should use standards to begin considering essential questions.

A more specific strategy involves "unpacking" the nouns and verbs in the standards. The nouns point to "big ideas" and companion questions, whereas the verbs are suggestive of the assessments. Because one needs a solid base of content knowledge to identify the enduring ideas and essential questions, we recommend planning with a partner or team whenever possible. In this case, two (or three) heads are almost always better. (p.32)

Allot just enough time to cover the applicable content. In order to make your instruction appropriate to the developmental level of the student, remember the general rule that very young children's units should be relatively short, approximately one week, with increasing numbers of weeks as students proceed through upper elementary and middle school grades to approximately six weeks for high school students.

With the reality of time constrictions in mind, identify the major skills, concepts, problems, and issues that will be covered. Explain the importance of the unit, why it should be studied, what relevance it has to the students, and how you will communicate that relevance. Plan one or two initial activities to stimulate interest and questions.

For example, if you are planning a unit on a topic such as the Civil War for high school students, you may want to show a film or parts of a film about the war such as *Gone with the Wind* or *Glory*. For an elementary school unit on Reptiles, a trip to the zoo would be a suitable activity for stimulating interest and questions.

If developmentally appropriate for your students, at this point it would be beneficial for you to apply the first two parts of the popular four-part KWLH strategy used to guide student inquiry.

> K stands for, "What do I already *k*now about this subject?"
> W asks, "What do I *w*ant to know?"
> L represents, "What did I *l*earn?" and
> H stands for, "*H*ow I can learn more?"

Have the students involved personally by writing answers to the questions, What do I already *k*now? and What do I *w*ant to know? This information can be part of your diagnostic evaluation because the information is valuable in assisting you in deciding if parts of the content you originally planned to cover should be modified. The last two parts of KWLH, What have I *l*earned? and *H*ow can I learn more? can be determined after instruction.

4. Content outline. The first step, and perhaps the most difficult at this point, is determining essential from supplemental content (Marzano, 2003). You cannot teach it all. After you have decided on the essential content and essential questions, the content outline serves as a general guideline regarding the sequence of instruction. Narrow the thoughts you wrote in the introduction by writing in outline form what the students will learn in terms of topics, subtopics, concepts, issues, problems, and skills. Given the general time frame you have indicated, assign an approximate time you will allot for each topic, question, and concept identified.

   Whenever possible, *obtain student input regarding content.* For example, if you are preparing a unit on the culture of a particular group, ask the students if there is anything in particular that they would like to learn about that group. Student input will be easier if you have used initiating activities introducing the unit to stimulate questions.

   Have a list of key terms the students should know, preferably in order of introduction. These terms should be displayed. But unless you are teaching vocabulary per se as part of your unit, your focus should be on activities, not on vocabulary development.

   Always take advantage of current events that can be used to make more relevant connections to your content and instruction. For instance, if there is to be an important election, tie this in to a unit on elections. If there has been a recent earthquake, tsunami, hurricane, tornado, or

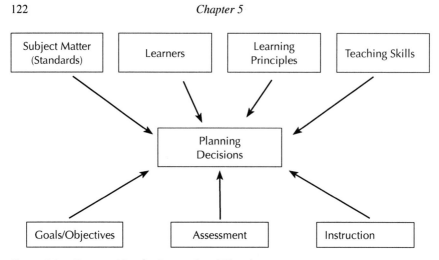

Figure 5.2. Concept Map for Instructional Planning

volcanic eruption, incorporate the economic impact of these events into a unit on economics or have the students study the causes of earthquakes, tsunamis, hurricanes, tornadoes, or volcanoes in a science unit.

A valuable part of planning the content outline is determining a content organizer for the students. This organizer may be an advance organizer where the content is presented in a written hierarchy of concepts, or a graphic organizer such as a concept map where the content is represented visually (Hyerle, 1996, 2004; Ewy, 2003). An example of a concept map that should help you understand the planning process for teaching is presented in Figure 5.2.

5. Goals derived from benchmarks. In the previous chapter you were reminded that goals are achieved over the long term and, when written for units, are the results the students should accomplish by the time the unit is completed. Goals can be the actual benchmarks determined from the standards you have identified for your unit or can be refined further if you find that the benchmarks are too broad for your particular purposes. The latter is usually the case.

When considering goals for your unit, be aware that Wiggins & McTighe (2011) have identified four characteristics necessary for unit goals. They should be *t*ransferable to other contexts (T); lead to deeper *m*eaning and big ideas (M); reflect *k*nowledge of the content (K); and (4) develop *s*kills (S).

In addition, goals should lead not to just knowledge but deeper understanding. Wiggins and McTighe (2011) have indicated that this type of understanding is demonstrated by the students' ability ". . . to *explain*, *interpret, apply, shift perspective, empathize,* and *self-assess . . .*" (p. 4, italics in the original). When goals reflect these attributes, a high level of corresponding authentic performance (Chapter 3) can then be designed to indicate student achievement at these levels.

Goals clearly offer direction and overall thrust to the unit. Once developed, the goals should be communicated explicitly to the students along with the reasons the goals are important, how they can be applied in the real world, and how they will affect the students personally.

Unless goals (and subsequently, the objectives) are conveyed to the students, they may not achieve the knowledge the teacher intended, even if the activities that develop the goals are stimulating (Nuthall, 1999). The previous sentence is so critical that you should stop and re-read it. Not only is in necessary to inform students of goals but also to convey high expectations that the goals will be achieved.

Some teachers advocate presenting goals and their importance to the students in writing. Students should be asked to prepare a journal (log) where they will record your goals for them and put in writing their own personal goals relative to the unit. "I want to understand the root causes of terrorism," "I want to learn about the Israeli-Palestinian conflict," or "I want to understand my own feelings of revenge against terrorists" are examples of personal goals.

> Encourage students to set their own goals, share them with others, and talk about why they chose them. Ask students to put some stakes in the goals: "What will happen when you reach your goal, and what will you experience?" When students realize they may experience, for example, increased satisfaction, this discovery creates emotional hooks to the goals. If the hooks are strong, attentional resources get a boost. (Jensen, 2005, p. 37)

Students can then monitor their own work by periodically referring to your goals and theirs to assess progress and to decide if a change in behavior (yours and/or theirs) will better achieve the goals. Whatever the goals you decide to pursue, whether they be the benchmarks themselves or goals you derive from the benchmarks, it is important that they be challenging for all students (Marzano, 2003).

Be aware of the fact that in today's diverse classrooms, one student's challenge is another's boredom. If you have performed the prerequisite assessments (observations, interviews, pre-tests) to make a diagnostic evaluation, you will be in a better position to know what the students already know and, therefore, which goals will be challenging.

Goals are extremely important in any organization (Covey, 2004). Though he promoted his ideas for the success of the industrial community, he deemed them applicable also in education. Covey proposed several situations relevant to schools regarding goals. They should be clear to all, measurable, planned together and have corresponding assessments. All students and the teacher should hold each class member accountable for achieving goals. And most important, there must be a positive safe and supportive classroom environment in which students feel valued thereby willing to work on achieving goals (Adapted from Covey, 2004, pp. 370–71).

When all class members function in cooperation with each other and support each other, there is a high probability that all will achieve the goals. The teachers should foster this type of cooperation.

To increase the chances that students will achieve the goals, scoring rubrics (Chapter 3) should be designed (with students, when appropriate) for each teacher and student goal as soon as the goals are established (Marzano, 2007). Scoring rubrics known to students in advance of instruction not only remind students of what they should achieve but allow students to self-assess along the way.

Many teachers find it useful to turn goals, just as unit titles, into questions that are subsequently exhibited in the classroom. The goal, "Understanding the root causes of terrorism" can be changed to, "What are the root causes of terrorism?" Questions are more engaging for students and provide guidance in assisting them in determining how well they are achieving the goals.

Some additional examples of goals in both stated and question form are: "The students will collect and use information and data in research," or in question form, "How can information and data be collected and used in research?"

"The students will understand the course of World War II at home and abroad," or in question form, "How was World War II conducted at home and abroad?"

6. Objectives: Unpacking Standards. The goals you identified must be further broken down into objectives.

Standards

Benchmarks (Larger Goals)

Smaller Goals

Objectives

An assessment framework from Colorado's Grade 8 mathematics standards is presented in Table 5.1 followed by a specific example.

Additional benchmarks and objectives then follow for this Colorado standard, but you should be able to note the sequence in the specific

Table 5.1. Colorado's Standards CSAP Mathematics Assessment Framework (Grade 8)

Assessment Framework—defines what will be assessed on the State paper and pencil, standardized, timed assessment (CSAP). This document is organized as follows:

Standard	Indicates the broad knowledge and skills that all students should be acquiring in Colorado schools at grade level. Each standard is assessed every year.
Benchmark	Tactical description of the knowledge and skills students should acquire within each grade level range (i.e., K–4, 5–8, or 9–12).
Assessment Objectives	Specific knowledge and skills measured by CSAP for each grade level assessed. Assessment Objectives are assessed on a cyclical basis.

Specific Example:

Standard 1	Students develop number sense and use numbers and number relationships in problem-solving situations and communicate the reasoning used in solving these problems
Benchmark 1	Demonstrate meanings for integers, rational numbers, percents, exponents, square roots and pi (π) using physical materials and technology in problem-solving situations
Assessment Objectives	Use equivalent representations of positive rational numbers and common irrational numbers (for example, locate rational numbers on a number line and demonstrate the meaning of square roots and perfect squares)

(*Source*: Reprinted by permission of the Colorado Department of Education. cde.state.co.us.)

example above how the standard leads to a benchmark (goal) which is further narrowed into objectives. It is up to the individual teacher to decide if the benchmarks should be broken down into smaller goals before being divided further into objectives.

The state of Rhode Island has offered a website of archived lesson plans, samples of student work, and videos showing how they are all aligned with standards. Rhode Island offers this website as a way of thinking about the teaching and learning process as opposed to imposing a way of teaching. The website is offered to all and can be accessed at www.ride.ri.gov/instruction/curriculum.

Another illustration of breaking down standards has been selected from the work of (Kendall & Marzano, (1997). Examine the process offered for grades 3–5 in science:

Standard: "Understands essential ideas about the composition and structure of the universe and Earth's place in it."

They propose the following benchmarks (component parts) for that standard:

- Knows that the Earth is one of several planets that orbit the sun, and that the moon orbits around the earth
- Knows that the patterns of stars in the sky stay the same, although they appear to slowly move from east to west across the sky nightly, and different stars can be seen in different seasons
- Knows that planets look like stars, but over time they appear to wander among the constellations
- Knows that telescopes magnify distant objects in the sky (e.g., the Moon, planets) and dramatically increase the number of stars we can see
- Knows that astronomical objects in space are massive in size and are separated from one another by vast distances (e.g., many stars are more massive than our Sun but so distant they look like points of light). [pp. 75–76]

Note again that the benchmarks clarify the standard. Since benchmarks are goals, they are still stated in broad terms. Therefore, the use of the terms "understand" and "know" are acceptable. Depending on the grade you are teaching, and prior knowledge of your students, you can select the benchmarks that are appropriate for the time frame allotted and break them down into smaller goals, if necessary, and then narrow these goals down further into objectives.

Examine the first benchmark (goal) offered by Kendall and Marzano (1997) already presented above—Knows that the Earth is one of several planets that orbits the Sun, and the Moon orbits around the Earth

There are several instructional concepts embedded in this benchmark (goal). Can you identify them before continuing?

They include: star, Earth, planet, orbit, rotation, revolution, Sun, and Moon.

A possible set of objectives that could flow from the above benchmark (goal) is:

- Define a star
- Define a planet
- Distinguish between a planet and a star (sun)
- State that there are nine planets
- Name the nine planets in order of distance from the sun
- State at least three important features of each planet
- Define an orbit
- Define revolution

- Act out a planet revolving around the sun
- Define a moon
- Distinguish between a planet and a moon
- Distinguish between a moon and a star
- Describe our moon's features
- Distinguish between living on the moon and living on the earth
- Define rotation
- Act out simultaneously the earth's rotating on its axis while revolving around the sun
- Demonstrate the moon orbiting the earth
- Explain why the same side of the moon always faces the earth
- Define a year according to each planet
- Identify planets that have moons
- Draw a timeline of the earth and moon in relation to the sun
- Construct a "living" solar system with students playing roles of planets, our moon, the sun, with planets and moons rotating and orbiting in their respective ways
- Construct a model of the solar system
- Construct models of planets demonstrating size order
- Plan a moon trip
- Design a space suit for getting to the moon and surviving on it
- Design a solar system game
- Organize an astronomy club
- Join an astronomy club

You will observe that the above objectives cover several levels of the cognitive, affective, and psychomotor domains (Chapter 4). In order to determine the diversity of your unit plan objectives, it would be helpful to examine a behavior-content matrix (Bloom et al., 1971). A simplified version of this matrix can be used by referring to the checklist in Table 5.2 and placing a slash next to the level that corresponds to each of your unit objectives. It is not necessary to memorize this list but to use it as a reference.

The purpose of knowing about and using the three domains is *not* to have every level of each domain represented but to ensure challenge and variety for all the students in your class.

When writing objectives, examine them to be sure that they flow from the goal, whether this be one you created from the benchmark or the benchmark itself, include several levels of the different domains, and incorporate suggestions from students. Then be sure to communicate the objectives, as eventually delivered in each lesson, to the students.

Table 5.2.   Domain Level Checklist

COGNITIVE DOMAIN

Knowledge

Comprehension

Application

Synthesis

Evaluation

AFFECTIVE DOMAIN

Receiving

Responding

Valuing

Organization

Characterization

PSYCHOMOTOR DOMAIN

Moving

Manipulating

Communicating

Creating

Planning the Assessment/Formative Evaluation after Planning the Objectives

7. Assessment/Formative Evaluation. You have already assessed and made a diagnostic evaluation on the basis of that assessment before or at the beginning of the unit. As you proceed through the unit, it is critical for you to measure your progress and that of the students to decide if any re-teaching is necessary. To make this decision there must be an alignment among classroom assessments of student performance, the curriculum, and actual instruction (Cotton, 2000).

A detailed presentation of assessment, evaluation, and scoring rubrics was offered in chapter 3. The topic is reviewed briefly here to ensure continuity of the thought process involved in unit planning, and especially to stress the importance of determining the assessments (Step 2) immediately after planning objectives (Step1) and before instructional decisions are made (Step 3). McTighe & Wiggins (2004) have emphasized the value of this "backward design" in unit construction. Since their approach is being used increasingly in school districts, you should be thoroughly familiar with it.

We have chosen the unit as a focus for design because the key elements . . . big ideas, enduring understandings, essential questions, and
performances of understanding—are too complex and multifaceted to
be satisfactorily addressed within a single lesson. . . . Nonetheless,
we have found that the larger unit goals provide the context in which
individual lessons are planned. Teachers often report that careful attention to Stages 1 and 2 sharpens their lesson planning, resulting in
more purposeful teaching and improved learning . . . [This attention]
should include core assessment tasks that all students would perform to
demonstrate their understanding of key ideas and processes (Of course,
these tasks would be accompanied by agreed-upon scoring rubrics.)
[pp. 26–27].

The backward approach is different from that which has been traditionally employed because once objectives have been written, teachers
wanted to instantly proceed to planning instructional activities to assist
the students in achieving the objectives. After all, isn't achieving objectives what teachers want to accomplish?

However, Wiggins (1998) suggested that teachers would be better off
if they learned to think first as assessors instead of teachers. He recommended that immediately after writing an objective, the teacher should
put on his/her assessor's hat and ask the question, "What counts as
evidence of student learning?" In other words, what would the teacher
be looking for to make him/her decide whether or not the students are
meeting the objectives?

During this stage, assessment is a continuous collection of feedback
received to make a formative evaluation to see how the students are
performing so that, if necessary, instruction can be adjusted. If the
objective is stated clearly, it will give direction to the assessment and
then to instruction. For instance, if the objective is that the student will
be able to compute the length of a hypotenuse, the teacher must first
determine what counts as evidence that the student can do this. Will it
be by observing him/her perform calculations, by administering a quiz,
by having the student create and solve his/her own triangle problems, or
any other appropriate activity?

The teacher has to know whether or not to move on or to re-teach
the computation in a different way. If the objective has to be re-
taught, what alternatives would be provided? Once the objective and
assessment are in place, the teacher is in a better position to decide
what instruction will be needed to most likely have the student demonstrate achievement. This task is more clearly accomplished if the
objective includes an assessment statement (a condition) as illustrated in Table 5.3.

Table 5.3.   Objectives and Corresponding Assessment Statement

Content Component of Objective	Condition (Assessment Statement)
Label the parts of a flower	on a drawing of the structure of a flower
Identify an adjective	by distinguishing adjectives from a list of all the parts of speech
Explain the causes of the Civil War	in a set of coherent paragraphs

In summary, Wiggins and McTighe (1998) stated:

> . . . the teacher will address the specifics of instructional planning—choices about teaching methods, sequence of lessons, and resource materials—after identifying the desired results and assessments. Teaching is a means to an end. Having a clear goal helps us as educators to focus our planning and guide purposeful action toward the intended results (p. 13).

The current trend is for teachers to, "Approach instruction as assessment" (Fogarty, 1999, p.6). The book you are currently reading also recommends that assessment should be at the core of instruction.

You will recall that assessment can be formal or informal and that data may be determined through procedures such as asking questions, observing students, interviewing them, or by quizzes or tests. During the assessment process, students should be responsible for monitoring their own progress in achieving their own personal goals as well as the teacher's unit goals.

As already mentioned earlier in this chapter, an effective way they can do this is by having the students keep a journal (log) noting their achievement, a journal both they and you can check periodically. Students who are not progressing well should assume responsibility for their own performance by suggesting ways of changing their methodology in order to meet goals (Popham, 2008, 2011).

One valuable way to assess student performance is by analyzing samples of student work (Wiggins, 1996). The teacher may do this independently, with other teachers, and/or set up student teams to examine each other's work. They could ask the questions such as,

"What evidence is there that knowledge has been attained?"
"Where are there persistent errors?"
"Where are there misconceptions?"
"What prerequisite knowledge had not been mastered that allowed misconceptions to occur?"

On the basis of the analysis, all or some of the students can move on, or the content can be re-taught in a different way for those in need. One of the pervasive criticisms of remedial instruction is that during remediation, students are exposed to the same methodology that was ineffective for them in the first place.

Cotton (2000) has researched validated approaches to re-teaching. One of these approaches is, "Using different materials and strategies for re-teaching than those used for initial instruction, rather than merely providing a 'rehash' of previously taught lessons" (p. 26).

Examining samples of student work in *all* subjects is a productive way to perform diagnostic teaching by analyzing errors and determining understanding as well as misunderstanding. As already recommended, this examination is most effective when it is performed collaboratively with other teachers.

Figure 5.3 is an example of a work sample, Astronaut Disaster, written by an advanced ESL student. This sample is followed by Figure 5.4, a commentary by the readers after analyzing the student's work.

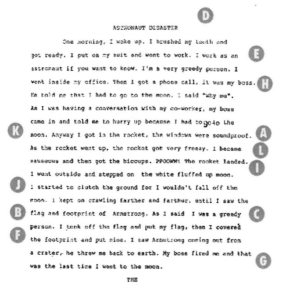

Figure 5.3.

English as a Second Language
Work Sample & Commentary: *Astronaut Disaster*

The task
Advanced level ESL students were asked to respond to a reading unit on space and time by writing and illustrating a short story. The work shown here was part of a 32-week reading and writing program in which students were asked to respond to the literature read during the unit. Their edited stories were compiled into a book.

Circumstances of performance
This sample of student work was produced under the following conditions:

alone	in a group
in class	**as homework**
with teacher feedback	with peer feedback
timed	**opportunity for revision**

This work sample illustrates an advanced level ESL performance for the following parts of the standards:

E1c Reading: Read and comprehend informational materials.

E2c Writing: Produce a narrative account.

What the work shows
E1c Reading: The student reads and comprehends informational materials to develop understanding and expertise and produces written or oral work that:
• restates or summarizes information;
• relates new information to prior knowledge and experience;
• extends ideas;
• makes connections to related topics or information.

Click to Enlarge

A The student used information from nonfiction books about space travel to produce a believable description of a journey to the moon in a rocket: "…the windows were soundproof. As the rocket went up, the rocket got very frenzy….PPOOWW! The rocket landed."

B The ideas gathered through reading and research are recast within a story that incorporates the ideas in a new context. The historical fact that Neil Armstrong placed a flag and left his footprint on the moon contributes to the plot of the story.

C The story makes a connection between the student's knowledge about the history of space travel and the actions of the character: "As I said, I was a greedy person. I took off the flag and put my flag, then I covered the footprint and put mine."

E2c Writing: The student produces a narrative account (fictional or autobiographical) that:
• engages the reader by establishing a context, creating a point of view, and otherwise developing reader interest;
• establishes a situation, plot, point of view,

The student used an imaginative and creative approach to producing a fictional response to literature. The work incorporates many of the elements of narrative accounts, such as situation, plot, point of view, setting, character, and conflict. The student created the fictional persona of an astronaut who is

Figure 5.4. *(Continued)*

setting, and conflict (and for autobiography, the significance of events);
- creates an organizing structure;
- includes sensory details and concrete language to develop plot and character;
- excludes extraneous details and inconsistencies;
- develops complex characters;
- uses a range of appropriate strategies, such as dialogue and tension or suspense;
- provides a sense of closure to the writing.

sent to the moon on a rocket, meets Neil Armstrong, and must face the consequences of his actions.

D The title, "Astronaut Disaster," establishes the (space travel) context. In addition, the title develops reader interest with the word "disaster" by encouraging the reader to anticipate a dangerous space adventure.

E The student created the persona of a self-centered, cavalier character, e.g., "I work as an astronaut if you want to know."

F The student incorporated conversational introductory phrases which hold reader interest and are appropriate for the purpose and tone of the narrative.

G The student maintained the cavalier persona of the character throughout the narrative.

H The work has a sequential organizing structure, telling the story in a chronological fashion from character introduction to conflict resolution, e.g., "…I woke up. I brushed my teeth…I put on my suit and went to work…then I got a phone call…my boss fired me and that was the last time I went to the moon."

G The student made effective use of relevant detail and concrete language that contribute to the realism of this fantasy tale. The student also used details to create suspense and maintain reader interest, e.g., "I took off the flag and put my flag, then I covered the footprint and put mine."

I The student used a range of strategies in the work such as tension/suspense, humor, dialogue ("why me"), descriptive language ("…I started to clutch the ground…."), and onomatopoeia ("PPOOWW!").

This work contains certain language constructions that indicate the student is at an advanced stage of second language acquisition. Second language learners create rules from the grammatical information they encounter and gradually revise these rules in the direction of the target language. Errors are not a sign of failure, but provide insight into how learners process and apply the features of language.

J In the sentence, "I started to clutch the ground for I wouldn't fall off the moon," the student used "for" instead of the purpose clause "so that." This is an indication of transference of a native language structure.

K The work shows three instances of run-on sentences which could be remedied by providing the student with continued appropriate instructional opportunities including extensive reading and writing.

C ESL students may have difficulty in using phrasal verbs, e.g., "I took off the flag and put my flag." The teacher can ask the student to rethink this sentence during editing or provide options such as "I took down the flag and put up my flag," or "I took the flag down and put mine up."

L The ESL student may use some vocabulary inappropriately, e.g., "greedy," "frenzy," and "clutch." These attempts to use these words in the work show a desire to be expressive.

Figure 5.4. (*Source:* Reprinted by permission of the Board of Education of the City School District of the City of New York.)

Figure 5.5 is a sample of student work—the unassisted, un-timed writing sample of a 10-year-old special education 4th grade boy. The writing was performed after reading a story in which Native Americans attacked Pilgrims in their homes and set these homes on fire. The Pilgrims retaliated by shooting at the Native Americans.

Examine the work, preferably with colleagues, by answering the following questions, as recommended earlier by Wiggins (1996):

"What knowledge seems to be firmly acquired?"
"Where are there persistent errors/misconceptions?"
"What prerequisite knowledge had not been mastered that allowed errors/misconceptions to occur?"
"How can these errors/misconceptions be remediated?"

> I think the book was grate my favorite part was when he fired the gun I also like the Illustrashuns. They look so real. My favorite picture is when he fired the gun. That is why when he fired the gun is my favorite part. Because of the illastrashons.

Figure 5.5. Student Work Sample

It is clear from the writing sample that the student needs remediation in sentence structure; homophones; spelling; capitalization; grammar; and idea expansion. This remediation is no small challenge.

Steiny (2010) has described the way she has students learn from their errors. She distributes a standard form with three squares across a large grid. In the first box the students rewrite the problem (or question that had the error). In the second box they determine what they did wrong by describing the misunderstanding. And finally, in the third box, they redo the problem (correct the error).

What to Include in the Unit Components Following the Assessment/Formative Evaluation Component

8. Instructional procedures. After making explicit both objectives and methods of assessment, the next decision is selecting the best possible way to teach the objectives so that the student will be able to demonstrate performance on the assessments. McTighe & Wiggins (2004) described this process as first identifying the desired results (goals and objectives),

then determining what would be acceptable evidence that the goals and objectives have been met, and finally planning the corresponding learning experiences. McTighe & Wiggins (2004) have stated that using this backward design ". . . helps to avoid the twin sins of activity-oriented and coverage-oriented curriculum planning" (p. 25).

There should be a choice of instructional activities provided for students, especially when it comes to independent work.

> A menu of activities provides a great opportunity to break the old paradigm of giving all students the same task at the same time and giving all students the same amount of time to finish. . . . It starts with the main dish—that is, the activities that are required for all students (yet students can do them in any sequence, providing an element of choice). The side dishes include tasks that offer extensions to the unit and reflect the multiple intelligences. Students might be required to complete three of six side dishes, and they get to choose which three. The dessert portion of a menu usually includes related activities for which no product is required; they are enriching and optional. Both side dishes and optional dessert portions may be set up as learning centers around the classroom. (Cummings, 2000, pp. 43–44)

A guide teachers have for many years found useful in making decisions for general instructional activities is the Cone of Experience, Figure 5.6, adapted from the work of Dale (1969), also known as the learning experiences ladder (Kellough & Carjuzaa, 2006). Specific learning activities are usually reserved for lessons (chapter 7).

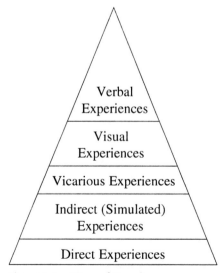

Figure 5.6.   Cone of Experience

Examine each category on the cone from the bottom up.

Direct experiences. The best way to learn how to dissect a frog is to dissect a frog. The best way to learn how to cut glass is by actually cutting it. In these direct experiences the student is dealing with the real object and is learning by actually doing with hands-on experiences. Most of the five senses are involved.

Indirect experiences. Frequently it is not possible to have the real experience. One cannot travel through the solar system, nor create a real nuclear chain reaction. The next possible experience to preserve active involvement and the use of senses is exposure to a model or mockup (a working model) of the solar system or of a chain reaction. Role playing the movement of different parts of the solar system or acting out a chain reaction will also involve students with many of their senses. Dramatizing an experience such as the trial of Galileo, while not the actual trial itself, would still give the participants the feeling of actually being there.

Vicarious experiences. These experiences still engage the learner but with fewer senses. Computer and video programs fall into this category. Virtual reality games can make the student feel s/he is in that situation. A video of the blood flowing through the body is a vivid example of that process. Field trips to museums, exhibits, or to a meeting of the United Nations are vicarious experiences in that the student is primarily relegated to the role of an observer.

Visual experiences. Charts, maps, timelines, pictures, diagrams, slides, cartoons, comics, and overheads are some examples of visual experiences. A diagram of the circulatory system or a chart showing the structure of government would be specific examples. Students are limited to only the sense of sight in learning through visual experiences. Yet these experiences can clarify meaning and enhance concept development.

Verbal experiences. During verbal experiences students are engaged in listening or reading and are using only one sense. These experiences include listening to other students, the teacher, a guest speaker or another resource person, or reading the textbook. Learning at this level is largely symbolic with students less actively involved.

Note that in proceeding up the cone from direct to verbal experiences, the learning goes from concrete to abstract, and involves fewer senses with less-real experiences. The lower the experience is on the cone, the more involved the student, the more senses used, and the more real the experience.

General rule: Given cost, reality, and safety considerations, whenever possible, select learning experiences as far down on the cone as possible. *Make sure that the learning outcome is worth the time invested.*

At this point in the planning process it would be worthwhile to caution you that merely exposing students to different activities, no matter how exciting and dynamic they are, will not produce their desired results unless *the students know the purpose* of those activities (Nuthall & Alton-Lee, 1993; Nuthall, 1999).

The most important deliberations concerning the selection of overall instructional procedures (teaching strategies) are: "Which would be most suitable to meet the students' cognitive, cultural, and developmental needs, given the objective and its corresponding assessment?" "Will the students need more teacher direction?" Will some of the students be better off in a student-centered situation?" and "What learning experience choices will be offered?"

Just as students should be involved in suggesting goals and their assessments, students should also be involved in suggesting appropriate instructional procedures for attaining goals and meeting the assessments.

9. Resources and materials. The selection of appropriate corresponding materials is integral to the success of the unit. The materials must match the objectives, assessment, and instruction. When preparing a unit, teachers will frequently list only the textbook. But the textbook is far from the best resource, especially when it is the only resource. Primary sources are much more effective and make the learning experiences more related to the real (authentic) world.

Students must be actively engaged in learning, and must use many senses. Therefore, it is evident that the Dale (1969) cone of experience is useful as a guide for both instruction and in material selection.

Resources and materials that correspond to activities on the Cone of Experience can be placed into four general categories: technology, manipulatives, printed materials, and the community.

Technology. Students have rushed into the 21st century leaving schools stuck in the 20th century (Prensky, 2005/2006). In many respects, when it comes to technology, students have left teachers behind. Moreover, technology is changing so rapidly that by the time you read this, the information will likely not be up-to-date. Currently, technological resources include camcorders; overhead projectors; TV/VCRs; digital video disk (DVD) players, audio recorders; cameras; computers, and mobile smart phones.

Technology, especially computer technology, should be infused into the curriculum. Computer technology is a valuable resource for research, reinforcement, and enrichment. But as with all resources, it should complement and supplement the teacher's role and help tailor information for each learner's needs. *Technology should not be used for the sake of technology but should be used when it will be effective in implementing goals and objectives.*

Computer technology, with its access to text, sound, graphics, simulation, and video, has the potential to lead students to higher learning levels and engage them in active learning using multiple pathways. Of particular concern for teachers are programs such as PowerPoint™, which assists the teacher in preparing materials for overhead presentations, Blackboard Academic Suite™ which enables whole courses to be delivered on-line with constant communication between the students and teacher, and social media applications that allow students and teachers to interact with others anywhere in the world.

Interactive whiteboards (smartboards) are now being used to integrate digital information into teaching. These whiteboards enhance communication and engage students by making it possible for teachers to write notes; list student ideas; insert graphics; link to websites; cut, copy, and paste information from any application for display on the whiteboard; and save work for future use.

In a recent study it was reported that the use of whiteboards did not have any noted impact on children's test scores (Nightingale, 2006). This result may be attributed to the lack of appropriate training for teachers in the use of whiteboards and the fact that this technology allows lessons to flow too quickly without adequate time for developing student understanding. Yet, teachers in the study indicated that whiteboards increased motivation by keeping students engaged in interactive content.

eChalk designed its Online Learning Environment specifically for K–12. It offers a teacher-friendly communication tool that works with existing teaching practices. Among other activities eChalk allows teachers to save lesson plans, forms, resources, and materials. Students can submit homework, making it easier for teachers to manage assignments electronically. Teachers can share lessons, resources, and syllabi. Communication among all levels of school district personnel is more easily facilitated.

AlphaSmart is currently being seen more frequently in schools. It is a sturdy, portable computer accessory that allows students access to word processing. AlphaSmart shows text using a keyboard with a liquid crystal display (LCD).

The Internet, a network of other networks interconnected to millions of computers in all nations, has enormous potential in and out of the classroom. Besides e-mail, teachers can use mailing lists, discussion groups, chats, newsgroups, social networking sites, and forums to connect electronically with people and resources internationally.

Social media sites such as Facebook make it possible for students and teachers with common interests to interact worldwide. Forums are sections within an on-line service that provide information on a specific subject. The forum may include a library where various fields can be downloaded and may allow for a conference room.

The Internet's subset, the World Wide Web (WWW), provides for computer content to be accessed through an Internet browser. The WWW makes it possible for a specific website to be easily located and accessed from computers, tablet devices, and mobile smart phones with Internet access. Websites offer a valuable fund of information from government, industry, and different organizations that is available within seconds.

Teachers are cautioned to monitor websites used in the classroom carefully to ensure that they are appropriate for students. Marklein (2011) reported the results of a survey conducted by the National Cyber Security Alliance which concluded that ". . . teachers are ill-prepared to educate students on the basics of online safety, security and ethics, and more than a third of teachers receive no training in cyber security issues"(p. 10A).

Credible websites include the backing of credible organizations, the offering of varieties of activities, links to access additional information, and regular updates. Teachers can obtain safety guides on Internet use from numerous organizations such as World Kids located at http://www.worldkids.net/school/safety/internet/guidance.html.

In order to do research, students can also access *sources* of information, *not specific* information, from directories or search engines. These online tools help locate information based on the student's or teacher's requests. Common websites for these tools include: (http://www.bing.com); (http://www.ask.com); (http://www.google.com); (http://www.yahoo.com); and (http://www.dogpile.com).

Many teachers are now using handheld computers to enrich content by connecting with other teachers and sources. These computers assist teachers in providing their students with learning activities in all curriculum areas using technology that supports data analysis, thinking, and data retrieval (Staudt, 2005).

Students are also using laptops and smartphones to record their own stories along with videos they have made to create podcasts (audioblogs) that can be shared on a school's website as well as on the Internet. Students can listen to their own podcasts to self-correct content as well as speech, grammar, and delivery. Personal Digital Assistants (PDAs) can also aid students (and teachers) in keeping track of tasks, assignments, and other important information.

Smart phones, like Apple's iPhone, incorporate many advanced computer features including email; Internet access; calendars; text messaging; and social media applications. Most of these smart phones allow users to view educational videos, movies, and TV shows along with other media.

As much as technology solves problems, it also creates them. Internet plagiarism has become so widespread that companies have invested in developing plagiarism detection software. Educators continue to be challenged as technology makes other kinds of cheating easier. For example, students have been found to load class notes into handheld e-mail devices and try to read the notes during exams, or photograph test questions with cellphone cameras, transmit the questions to outside classmates, and receive answers back in text messages (Glater, 2006).

Moreover, teachers are increasingly worried about some aspects of technology. Freedman (2007) complains about competing with texting, video chatting, YouTube, and social media applications. He states that while older teachers view technology for information and communication, their younger students use laptops, cellphones, and BlackBerries for socializing and entertainment.

Technology overkill can also turn off talented young teachers where some measure of how effective they are is determined by how paperless they are (Welsh, 2008). He warns of the danger in using technology for the sake of technology not for what necessarily works to help students learn. Pushing a button or clicking a mouse allows too many students to go for the quick answer instead of taking the time to think.

Though you may have completed a course in technology as part of your teacher education program, just keeping up on the subject is an area that will need constant upgrading and professional development. Downey (2006) has identified six already occurring and future ed-tech trends. These include:

a. The leveling power of the World Wide Web whereby teachers themselves rather than solely professional producers and studios will be able to create and deliver to their students content in writing, audio files, or video clips. Internet sites such as YouTube allow anyone to post or watch photos, videos, or speeches;

b. Cloud computing in which a remote service will replace word processing applications such as Microsoft Word. Given the right kind of browser, a teacher will be able to access functions in the "cloud" *without* storing the application or data on his/her computer;

c. Service-oriented architecture, software which allows multiple processes to be gathered and organized without the need to purchase massive computing or storage hardware;

d. The Sharable Content Object Reference Model (SCORM) will allow teachers to share and reuse digital learning materials and adapt them to serve their own needs;

e. Telepresence, where videoconferencing anytime anywhere will be transformed into a virtual presence for all participants regardless of where they are located. This medium will impact school districts for management meetings and professional development;

f. 21st-century learning. A program has been developed by the Partnership for 21st Century Skills to prepare students to compete in a global innovative economy. Skills identified in this program cover: information and communication; thinking and problem-solving; interpersonal and self-direction; global awareness; financial, economic, and business; and civic literacy.

Stay tuned. Downey does make the point, however, that it is unlikely that anytime soon any of these technologies will replace an outstanding teacher or inspiring professor. Downey's sentiments are reinforced in the following:

Technology is just a tool. In terms of getting the kids working together and motivating them, the teacher is the most important.

Bill Gates

Manipulatives. Models, mockups, fraction pieces, counting sticks, and rocks, are some examples of hands-on materials students can work with to provide them with concrete experiences. Games/simulations can also be used effectively to reinforce learning or provide opportunities for discovery.

For example, the game New Town provides the opportunity for students to build a completely new town from acquiring the land to constructing homes, deciding what services must be offered and how to organize them. A detailed study indicated that age-old board games have assisted students from low-income families in achieving large long-lasting gains in math (Cavanagh, 2008).

Games can also be adapted for specific instructional objectives. Bingo can be adapted to match vocabulary words with definitions or reinforce basic math facts. For instance, if B 6 is called, anyone who has on a Bingo game card space a mathematical computation that equals 6 can cover the space. Examples of some computations that will yield this result are: $6 + 0$; $0 + 6$; $54 \div 9$; $1 + 1 + 1 + 3$; $10 - 4$; 3×2, 2×3, and $7 - 1$. Card games such as War can teach or reinforce greater than, less than, equal to, and counting.

Printed materials. Textbooks have value when they are *not* the sole means for teaching content but enrich, reinforce, and clarify meaning. Workbooks and worksheets can provide drill and practice once a concept is already learned, but remember that worksheets do not grow dendrites (Tate, 2003). Newspapers and magazines can provide timely as well as relevant instruction, sometimes as primary sources.

Catalogs such as the J. C. Penney catalog or other comparable home shopping materials can reinforce math and language arts concepts. Students can create simulated purchases which involve looking up items listed in alphabetical order; determining costs for several items; percentage discounts; shipping weights; measurements for clothing, carpeting, and completing forms.

Document-based questions, DBQs, already described in Chapter 3 as a means for assessment, can also be used for instruction. These documents are motivational because they represent brain-compatible primary sources for learning.

Regarding the use of materials in general, you should remember that if the teacher uses activities and materials that relate to the students' cultural backgrounds, the students respond more favorably.

The Community. Unless your school is in an extremely rural community, students will have access to libraries, banks, supermarkets, and other stores. These facilities frequently have important resources for field trips or for displaying authentic performance tasks or products created by students.

To illustrate, a student may come up with a new computer program for tying together several banking services. Students may have completed a nutrition project or a cost-effective shopping guide by comparing shopping lists from several different supermarket flyers. Field trips can be conducted to nurseries as part of studying plants, to the fire department while studying a unit on safety, or to a courthouse while studying law.

Parents are important community members who can offer enrichment and reinforcement. Many teachers have taken advantage of the parents' occupations to provide a different way to learn material, either as a motivating force in the beginning of a unit or as part of a culminating activity at the end. For example, a parent who is a dentist can be invited to demonstrate equipment or techniques that will stimulate curiosity at the beginning of a unit on health or tie together important points at the end. Parents with relevant occupations or interests can also mentor students on unit projects.

Parent involvement may not solely be academic. ". . . the types of relationships and encounters that are in place between teachers and parents can have a profound effect on student learning and growth (with) countless student transformations after reaching out to their families" (Mbadu, 2008).

It is imperative that materials and activities be previewed to ensure that they are appropriate for students' cognitive and developmental levels, match objectives, and are *not activities for the sake of activities*. Materials should be cost effective, simple to use, and, when feasible, brought to class by students. What student would not be excited about seeing *his/ her* cuddly toy, magazine, or model of a derrick being used by the teacher for instruction in the class? Remember that in accessing materials, you do not necessarily have to be creative, but you can be resourceful.

10. Correlations with other curriculum areas. Whether you are preparing a topic unit, or working on an integrated or thematic unit, it is productive for the contextual learning of your students to give some thought regarding how the content of your unit and other subjects are interrelated. Even though some of these correlations may be obvious to you, they may not become obvious to your students unless you consciously plan to make connections for them.

For example, studying "Methods of Warfare" is more closely related to science, history, and economics but can also include language arts, the arts, or mathematics. Language arts activities for this unit could incorporate: keeping diaries; writing letters of invitation to class activities, letters requesting information on the unit, or thank-you letters to resource people; writing a play; or writing a newsletter.

Arts activities might incorporate: organizing exhibits; constructing models of weapons; making overheads, slides, or videos; creating diagrams, charts, and maps; designing costumes or sets; writing war songs; painting murals; or constructing time lines.

Mathematics activities could comprise: measuring and purchasing materials for weapon or costume construction; computing word problems for distance, angle of projection, speed, or time; constructing a compass; determining longitude and latitude of sea targets.

11. Assessment/Summative Evaluation. At the end of the unit, assessments are collected to make a summative evaluation regarding how well the

students have achieved the unit objectives. Obviously, at the end it is too late to make changes, which is why formative evaluation is so important. The summative evaluation should be flexible by including a variety of methods and choices for demonstrating mastery.

Performance tasks and products, projects, portfolios and a final teacher-made test can be used to evaluate students. Performance tasks and products should be designed to be important, high-level, authentic, (something a student would have to confront in the world outside of school), and should demonstrate the achievement of not one but *all* the unit goals. Scoring rubrics should be constructed (with students, when possible) to provide an objective method of determining student accomplishments. "Share the culminating performance tasks and accompanying rubric(s) so students will know what will be expected and how their work will be judged [and] show models of student work on similar tasks so students can see what quality work looks like" (Tomlinson & McTighe (2006), p. 88).

During the summative evaluation, classes that used KWLH in the beginning of the unit to decide what they already *k*now and *w*ould like to know, can now describe the L part, what they have *l*earned and the H part, *h*ow they can find out more.

As already indicated repeatedly in your prior reading, depending on their stage of development, it is an effective practice to have students participate in constructing any evaluation (test) and scoring rubric(s). Students should have the scoring rubric *before* they embark on any project or task because the rubric is an important teaching as well as evaluative tool. And students should be offered the opportunity to choose activities for both instruction and evaluation according to their learning styles preferences and multiple intelligences (Tomlinson, 2001).

A most integral part of the evaluation process that must be reiterated is self-reflection on the part of the teacher. Even though assessment may have been continuous throughout the unit, s/he should consider at the end of the unit what was positive, what did not go as well, and how the unit planning and/or its implementation could have been improved. A critical component in gathering this information is *input from the students*.

Chapter Summary: Units provide an overall guideline for planning instruction over a several-week period thus providing a focus for instruction. Units generally contain several component parts that include: the common core state learning standard being addressed; a streamlined topic or theme based on that standard; an introduction; essential questions; content outline; benchmarks (goals) derived from the standard with accompanying scoring rubrics designed when appropriate with the students; assessment/formative evaluation; instructional activities, materials, and resources; and a summative evaluation.

Units should be implemented flexibly with particular consideration to the teacher's and students' continuous assessment of the results of instruction to determine whether the instruction by either or both needs adjustment to ensure that all achieve. This is one reason that assessment for formative evaluation should be planned right after planning the objectives. Students should be involved in adding their personal learning goals related to the topic, monitoring their progress, and in selecting learning activities and evaluation methods.

Assessments used in the summative evaluation should be collected from several sources including a teacher-constructed test and performance assessments. Performance assessments accompanied by scoring rubrics and classroom tests should be of a high caliber and include *all* the unit's goals. Teacher self-evaluation and input from students for improvement of the unit plan and its implementation must be part of the evaluation.

The Coaching Rubric for Unit Planning in Table 5.5 provides the criteria to plan successful units. With colleagues, use this rubric to indicate which criteria were implemented and which were not in the sample unit plan that follows.

SAMPLE UNIT PLAN

Improving Wellness with the Dietary Guidelines (Grades: 9–12)
Course: Gourmet Cooking
Unit Duration: 2 weeks

Patricia Donaldson
Family and Consumer Science Teacher
Clarkstown High School South
New City, NY

Introduction:

The Dietary Guidelines for Americans are designed to encourage lifelong healthy eating patterns that meet an individual's nutritional and caloric needs, promote health, support active lives, and help reduce the risk of chronic disease. This unit is designed for the interest level of high school students. Evidence based research has shown that improving dietary habits and increasing physical activity promotes health, reduces the occurrence of becoming

Table 5.5.   Coaching Rubric for Unit Planning (T for Implementation)

Criteria (Descriptors)	Performance Indicators (Examples)
INTRODUCTION	
The teacher	
performed a diagnosis of the students' prior knowledge	
identified the learning standard(s) on which content is based	
selected a topic/theme narrow enough to give the unit a focus	
described the nature and scope of the unit	
listed big ideas	
identified major (essential) questions	
indicated the relation of the unit to learners' lives	
capitalized on learners' interests	
introduced a stimulating initiating activity	
CONTENT OUTLINE	
listed topics and subtopics	
indicated an approximate time frame for each topic and subtopic	
prepared, displayed, and discussed an organizer (verbal/visual) for the content	
BENCHMARKS (GOALS)	
flowed logically from common state standard	
written to reflect deep understanding	
included those suggested by students	
communicated clearly and displayed in classroom	
presented in a way so that responsibility of class members to support each other and hold each other responsible for achieving goals was clear	

(Continued)

Table 5.5. Coaching Rubric For Unit Planning (T For Implementation) *(Continued)*

Criteria (Descriptors)	Performance Indicators (Examples)
offered corresponding scoring rubrics developed with students, when appropriate	
OBJECTIVES (PERFORMANCE, BEHAVIORAL, INSTRUCTIONAL)	
written correctly (observable, student oriented, results of instruction) and included an assessment statement	
covered several domains and domain levels	
led collectively to goal(s)	
ASSESSMENT/FORMATIVE EVALUATION	
matched objectives	
guided teacher instruction	
allowed periodically for student self-assessment of goals and self-adjustment of learning tactics	
INSTRUCTIONAL PROCEDURES	
matched assessments	
provided for the uniqueness of all learners (styles, genders, interests, multiple intelligences, cultural differences, cognitive and developmental levels)	
offered a variety of activities (field trip(s), simulations, technology, educational games, guest speakers, discussion groups, panels, committee work, role playing, drama, etc.)	
incorporated students' suggestions	
INSTRUCTIONAL MATERIALS	
included mainly hands-on activities	
incorporated largely primary sources	
demonstrated creativity and/or resourcefulness	
appealed to many senses	
ASSESSMENT/SUMMATIVE EVALUATION	

(Continued)

Table 5.5. *(Continued)*

Criteria (Descriptors)	Performance Indicators (Examples)
employed high-level performance tasks and/or products that demonstrated achievement of all goals	
offered corresponding scoring rubric(s) for performance tasks and/or products	
offered students choices	
included teacher self-evaluation and input from students	
Final paper and pencil test	
included all unit objectives reflecting time allotted to each	
reflected appropriate test construction practices for short answer and essay questions	
If a topic unit was used,	
connected concepts and activities with other curriculum areas	

overweight and obese and lowers an individuals risk of chronic diseases. The objective of this unit is to offer students nutritional guidance that will empower them to make informed, healthy decisions that will facilitate behavior chance and set the stage for enhanced lifelong wellness.

Content outline:
Improving Wellness with the Dietary Guidelines

CLASS	SESSIONS
A. Overview of unit—Pretest	1
B. Building Healthy Eating Patterns	2
Food guide pyramid	
Proper portion sizes	
Basic nutrients	
Moderation	
Interpreting food labels	
C. Balancing Calories to Manage Weight	1
D. Food and Nutrients to Increase	1
Increasing vegetables and fruit	

CLASS	SESSIONS

Increasing whole grains, milk and milk products
"At-risk nutrients"

E. Foods and Food Components to Reduce   2
Reducing dietary sugar, salt and refined grains
Reducing solid fats, saturated, trans fatty acids
and cholesterol
Effects of alcohol consumption

F. Lab activity   1

G. Helping Americans Make Healthy Choices   1

H. Evaluation of unit—post test and   1
self-evaluation

NYS Learning Standard #1: **Commencement Home Economics**

Students will use an understanding of the elements of good nutrition to plan appropriate diets for themselves and others. They will know and use the appropriate tools and technologies for safe and healthy food preparation.

Students:

3A—apply knowledge of food choices and menus to plan a balanced diet, use new technologies to plan and prepare nutritious meals for a variety of dietary needs

3B—adjust their own diet to accommodate changing levels of activity or to meet their nutritional needs throughout the life cycle

3C—identify ways to meet basic needs of all family members

3D—take reasoned action toward reaching personal health goals

Benchmarks:

• Relate the importance of each guideline to the students' own diet and lifestyle
• Describe the health concerns of added sugar, solid fats, trans-fatty acids, cholesterol, excessive sodium and refined grains
• Compare the relationship between body weight and overall health status
• Alter the students' eating habits to promote wellness
• Apply problem-solving skills to food and nutrition issues

Objectives: Students will be able to

• Describe the Dietary Guidelines for Americans and explain their importance to overall health status
• Provide examples of healthy eating patterns
• Estimate serving sizes by using common objects for comparison
• Compare food labels of various items to determine calories and nutrient density

- Correlate the relationship between body weight, food intake and physical activity
- Calculate and evaluate individual body mass index
- Plan a personal daily meal plan that includes the foods needed to meet the MyPyramid food group recommendations
- Justify the importance of choosing a diet low in solid fats, saturated fats, trans-fatty acids and cholesterol
- Document health-related benefits of eating less sodium
- Propose various dietary recommendations to reduce added sugar and sweetened beverages
- Alter a recipe to improve its nutritional value without compromising quality
- Influence others on the risks of alcohol consumption
- Analyze their current dietary habits and design a well-balanced diet plan utilizing the current dietary guidelines
- Analyze factors that alter one's nutritional needs and give examples of dietary modifications that promote wellness
- Discuss the benefits of routine physical activity

Assessment / Evaluation:

A. Pretest
B. De-briefing activity
C. Short paper – written analysis of own diet utilizing the 2010 Dietary Guidelines for Americans
D. Designing a five-day diet for another student of his/her choice in the class, taking into account the person's individual dietary/health needs, age, caloric level, weight, activity level, food likes and dislikes, and dietary habits). Students will share menu ideas with each other in small group discussions monitored by the instructor.
E. Oral presentation – rubric designed by students
F. Students will prepare a self-evaluation of unit: What did you learn from this unit? How will you alter your own dietary habits as a result of this learning experience? What topics from this unit would you like to learn more about?
G. Post test – questions constructed by both students and instructor

Instructional Procedures:

- Informal lecture
- Advance organizer
- Concept formation activity
- Large and small group discussions
- Concept attainment activity
- Written assignment

- Interactive game – questions created by students
- Graphic organizer
- Cooperative learning lab activity
- Oral presentation – format and presentation rubric designed by students

Instructional Materials and Resources:

A. Student handouts/worksheets
B. Web site: http://www.cnpp.usda.gov/DGAs2010-PolicyDocument.htm.
C. Web site: MyPyramid.gov
D. Reproducible mini-posters: USDA Team Nutrition
E. Projector
F. Laminated poster – Reading Food Labels Is a Healthy Habit
G. Visual aids (food models, food samples, food labels)
H. Food values of foods displayed in test tubes
I. Tri-fold display indicating nutrient content of popular teenage snack items

Correlations with Other Curriculum Areas:

- Nutrition and wellness issues correlate significantly with the health curriculum.
- Human nutrition, digestion and absorption of nutrients are integrated with biology.
- Students utilize math skills by calculating caloric values using numeric formulas.
- Written activities promote well-developed writing skills.
- Oral presentation segment assists students in their ability to speak before an audience.
- Different cultures' dietary habits reflect upon the health and longevity of their societies.
- Meets the commencement level NYSFACS Learning Standards for nutrition education .
- Meets District Wellness Policy goals and objectives for nutrition education.

ORAL PRESENTATION RUBRIC

Score of 18–20

- Presentation clearly indicates preparation in an organized manner with a beginning introduction, a body of knowledge, and logical conclusions and summary

- Appears confident, at ease, and makes excellent eye contact
- Presents in a clear voice and can be heard by all in the class
- Demonstrates enthusiasm and personal interest in the topic
- Shows little reliance on notes
- Actively engages all members of the group
- Thoroughly explains the process of creating the food product to the class (including how members of your group contributed to the final product)
- Utilizes proper cooking terminology and explanation of vocabulary
- Uses visual aids to highlight key points
- Explains if problems occurred during the preparation of the product how the group solved the problems
- Adequately fields questions
- Draws members of the class outside the group into presentation

Score of 16–18

- Presentation is generally as good as the one receiving an 18–20 but one/two elements are not as polished

Score of 15–16

- Presentation has generally attributes as those receiving an 18–20 but signs of disorganization are evident

Score below 15

- Speaker is difficult to hear, speaks at an inappropriate rate and shows little enthusiasm and interest in the topic
- Little organization apparent
- Heavy reliance on notes
- Presenter lacks understanding of central project theme and the ability to field questions

UNIT EXAM

Dietary Guidelines for Americans

Name:_____ Period:_____

Directions: Write T or F in the blank to indicate whether the statement is true or false. Correct false statements to make them true.

_____1. The average high school student should limit their daily saturated fat intake to about 60 percent.

_____2. A high protein meat substitute is dried beans.

_____3. Cooked vegetables generally provide more fiber than raw ones.

_____4. High School students should increase their intake of whole milk, and milk products such as cheese and yogurt.

_____5. Each of these counts as a single serving based on a 2000 calorie diet: 2–3 ounces of meat, 1 slice of whole grain bread, ½ cup of applesauce.

_____6. As a percent of total added calories, the major source of added sugar in the American diet comes from soda, energy drinks and sport drinks.

_____7. The average teenager should consume ¾ of total grains as refined grains per day.

_____8. Low fat dairy products are good sources of fiber.

_____9. Fresh fruits and vegetables are a good source of vitamins A and C.

_____10. The type of fat consumed is more important in influencing the risk of cardiovascular disease than the amount of fat in the diet.

_____11. Sodium is present in many foods and beverages, especially in processed foods, condiments, sauces, and pickled foods.

Fill in the blanks with the correct answers:

12. MyPyramid is based on the daily amounts of food using _____ calories per day

13. List four food items most people should eat more often? _____
    _____.

14. The daily amounts of foods and calories a person needs depends on gender, _____, and _____ _____.

15. Saturated fat comes primarily from _____food sources.

16. Ingredients are listed on a food label in order by weight from _____to _____.

17. List at least four food components most people should reduce?
    _____.

18. To maintain good health, eat a(an)_____ of foods.

19. It is recommended that most people consume less than _____ mg of cholesterol per day.

20. Current dietary intake of Americans has contributed to the _____ epidemic.

Multiple Choice: Write the letter of the best answer in the blank next to the number.

_____21. To reduce the amount of fat in the diet, (a) drink skim milk instead of whole milk (b) eat more grains and legumes (c) use low-fat dairy products (d) all of these.

_____22. Legumes are (a) foods high in cholesterol (b) dried beans and peas (c) osteoporosis (d) none of these.

_____23. The food having the most cholesterol is (a) egg yolk (b) rice (c) legumes (d) both a and c.

_____24. An example of a complex carbohydrate is (a) sugar (b) whole grain pasta (c) syrup (d) all of these.

_____25. Dietary fiber is (a) roughage in plant foods (b) cellulose (c) peels and skins of fruit , (d) all of these.

_____26. The best way to cook meats to reduce the fat is: (a) fry (b) deep-fat fry (c) broil (d) both a and b.

_____27. If soda has 40 grams of sugar in one serving, how many teaspoons of sugar does each serving contain? (a) 25 (b) 19 (c) 10 (d) 6

_____28. Dietary Approaches to Stop Hypertension (DASH) emphasizes:

(a) fruits and vegetables (b) low fat milk and milk products(c) reducing red and processed meats (d) reducing sodium(e) all of the above

_____29. To find the number of <u>fat</u> calories in food, multiply the number of fat grams by (a) 4 (b) 6 (c) 9 (d) 30

_____30. To help lower blood cholesterol you should: (a) choose foods high in soluble fiber (b) reduce the amount of saturated fat in the diet (c) avoid eggs all together (d) a and c

_____31. In order to maintain current weight, a person must: (a) devote time to sedentary activity (b) balance the food eaten with physical activity (c) check body fat distribution (d) have height and weight checked regularly by a health professional

_____32. Alcohol consumption increased the risk to develop: (a) cirrhosis of the liver (b) cancer of the throat and neck (c) heart disease (d) all of the above.

Essay – 30 points: Using full sentences summarize the correlation between the Dietary Guidelines for Americans and a healthy lifestyle. Explain how you will modify some of your lifestyle choices to reduce your risk of disease.

(*Source*: Reprinted by permission of Patricia Donaldson, the author.)

Chapter 6

Differentiating Instruction

RESPONSIVE TEACHING THROUGH DIFFERENTIATED INSTRUCTION

Before actually planning lessons based on your unit, you should remember that *pervasive* throughout your thinking during the lesson planning process should be ways to differentiate instruction. *Differentiated instruction* is responsive teaching embedded in the understanding of the varieties of student needs and how learning takes place.

Among other categories, students differ in cognitive ability; life experiences; gender; exceptionalities; interests; culture; language development; learning styles; engagement; and general readiness. Therefore, using the same instruction for all will not accommodate for these differences.

When learning a concept, in this case, differentiated instruction, it is important to understand what that concept is and what it is *not*. Differentiated instruction is not individualizing instruction for all; therefore, it is not judged by how many different types of instruction go on at the same time. It is not tweaking business as usual, such as offering simple assignments for the academically challenged and enrichment for the gifted. Differentiated instruction is not reactive in the sense that the teacher responds instructionally to assessments only after they occur. It is not grouping students homogeneously all the time.

Though differentiated instruction is rooted in assessment, the practice is proactive in that the teacher anticipates student instructional needs *before* instruction takes place, though adjustments may still be necessary as instruction occurs. Differentiated instruction is flexible and qualitative, offering different approaches rather than many. It is student-centered and dynamic, blending whole class, small group, and individualized instruction. There is a balance between curriculum requirements and student needs as well as between student choices and teacher selection of assignments.

Areas for differentiation include the content, the process/activities, and the product (assessment/evaluation). All three areas are based on student readiness, interests, and learning profile, and should focus on the essential knowledge, questions, and skills identified in the unit (Tomlinson 2001).

Content involves what the students should know, understand, and be able to do. Differentiation allows for teachers to adapt the content and how they give access to that content (Tomlinson 2001). Since we are in an age of standards, it is important to hold constant what the students are learning. But for students who are at lower skill readiness levels, it may be necessary to provide a progression of foundational skills at a challenging level of complexity to lead students to that content. It may also be necessary to provide that content with greater complexity to students who have already mastered it.

Process involves an activity that makes meaning of the information the student has received. "A worthwhile activity is one that asks students to use specific information and skills to come to understand an important idea or principle" (Tomlinson 2003, 5). This activity should allow the student to grapple with the information rather than merely reiterate it. Process is also one of the critical areas of culture that could lead to misunderstanding (Bennett 2007). Therefore, it is necessary that you offer choices to students regarding how they will learn.

A product is a work that demonstrates what the student knows, understands, and can do (Chapter 3) at the end of a long period of learning such as a unit. Students should be able to select from a range of options those that are challenging on the appropriate level to demonstrate learning.

Table 6.1 provides some examples for differentiating content, process, and product.

ENSURING APPROPRIATE DIFFERENTIATION FOR CULTURE, EXCEPTIONALITIES, AND GENDER

Culture

There is hardly a community, and therefore, a school in the nation that does not reflect student cultural diversity. Understanding students' cultures is important for teachers because this knowledge can lead to cultural sensitivity and thus improve communication between teachers and students.

Table 6.1. Differentiating Strategies for Student Readiness, Interest, and Learning Style

Content	Process	Product
• curriculum compacting (engaging students who have already mastered content being taught in more challenging material) • reteaching (in a different way) material for students who are having difficulty • providing texts and supplementary materials at varied reading levels • highlighting key sections of texts; providing outlines for taking notes • demonstrating skills after teaching them • preparing key vocabulary lists for reference • providing content on audiotapes and videotapes • using student questions to guide instruction • presenting material in audio, visual, and tactile-kinesthetic modes • employing examples based on student interests and learning styles • providing time for student reflection • organizing interest centers and a wide range of instructional materials • using reading buddies to explore text or supplemental materials • using examples and applications from representative cultures and both genders • teaching both from whole to part (for field-dependent learners) and part to whole (for field-independent learners)	• using tiered activities (those at different difficulty levels but covering the same goals) • varying the pacing of work • providing primary language materials for ESL learners • using activities that give multiple perspectives on content • using Jigsaw, a cooperative learning approach, so students can specialize in parts of a topic they find interesting • making tasks more specific for some and more open for others • providing resources at varied levels • conducting mini-workshops for students at varied skill levels • conducting activities that seek multiple perspectives on content • having students work in mixed and similar readiness work groups • having students work in mixed and similar interest groups • offering different ways to demonstrate learning • allowing students to participate in designing tasks • balancing whole class, small group, and individual work	• developing rubrics for success • offering auditory, visual, and tactile-kinesthetic options • assigning options that represent a range of student cultures • offering mini-workshops on finding information sources for developing products • using similar-readiness critique groups for advanced learners and mixed-readiness critique groups for emerging learners to provide feedback on product development • offering product options that are analytic/creative/pragmatic • encouraging students to show mastery of essential knowledge and skills in related topics of their interest • assisting students in finding mentors to guide product choice and development and pursue independent inquiries • allowing students to develop products independently or with a partner

(*Source:* From "Differentiation in Practice: A Resource Guide for Differentiating Curriculum" (6–9), by Carol Ann Tomlinson & Caroline Cunningham Eidson, Alexandria, VA: ASCD. © 2003 by ASCD. Reprinted with permission. from the Association for Supervision and Curriculum Development. Learn more about ASCD at www.ascd.org.)

Bennett (2007) gave a broad interpretation to culture by defining it in terms of customs and behavior patterns of a group. Different cultures, however, also represent different languages, races, religious affiliations, and social classes (Banks 2006).

It would be inefficient to try to learn everything about all cultural groups, especially since there is much diversity within the groups themselves. However, for you to plan instruction, it is incumbent upon you to learn as much as you can about the cultural groups within *your* class(es). Figure 6.1 provides some suggestions to help you.

Food	Mental processing and learning styles
Religion	Dress and appearance
Economics	Rewards and recognition
Politics	Social interaction
Family structure and values	Group vs. individual needs
Ways of communicating	Music
General attitudes and beliefs	Sense of self and space
Group norms	Time consciousness
Traditions/history	Attitude toward work

Figure 6.1. What You Should Know about the Cultures in Your Classroom

You will want to ensure that you are sensitive to all the different cultural groups represented in your classroom because cultural insensitivity could impede the progress of your students. In promoting an inclusive classroom community, all students should feel welcome, valued, and appreciated so that they will be able to participate in the educational process with the best chances for success.

In addition, to be a culturally responsive teacher you have to share time consistently, both inside and out of the classroom, building personal relationships with students whose skin colors are different from yours; use varieties of interactive and instructional strategies and interactive techniques such as demonstrating, rephrasing, explaining, using students' ideas, summarizing; using what you have learned about students' cultural backgrounds to link their prior knowledge to new information; and listen patiently and non-judgmentally to students' personal stories (Irvine 2003).

Some of the universally recommended suggestions in Figure 6.2 will help you show cultural respect for and sensitivity to your students.

Students with Limited English Proficiency

With cultural diversity comes linguistic diversity. Students from different cultures will frequently come to your class without English as their first language. It is common to have a large number of different languages

Develop a sense of common purpose in which all students respect and support each other

Display and use books that represent people with different skin colors

Display pictures of children of different hair colors, styles, and textures

Show pictures of people with different skin colors in positive terms and in many different occupations

Use music and literature from different countries of students represented

Celebrate holidays of cultures represented by the students in the class

Post common words in different languages represented

Discuss heroes of represented cultures

Use heterogeneous grouping

Use small group instruction

Allow no tolerance for disparaging ethnic/racial remarks

Figure 6.2. Classrooms That Encourage Cultural Respect and Sensitivity

represented in classes and even dialects within these languages. You should not assume that all students from foreign countries are not English-proficient.

However, many of these students will need help in standard English in order to succeed. This is particularly important because high school dropout rates have been linked to language deficiency (Brown 2006). Terminology regarding students who are limited English proficient (LEP) and English language learners (ELL) is often used to identify these students. Assistance is usually given by either removing them from class part of the day for instruction in their native language while providing instruction in English for the remainder of the day, or by placing students in relevant groups with a trained bilingual teacher.

You can assist your LEP students by

- Providing a rich context to which vocabulary can be connected in a meaningful way. For example, organizing a party for a cultural holiday associates terms you can use in that context such as day, special, cup, dish, fork, spoon, pass out, give, how many, more, cake, cookie, cut, to name just a few.
- Pairing LEP students with English-speaking students for some activities. Students at the same age level tend to communicate better with each other.
- Using simple language.
- Using gestures to convey meaning. "Raise your hand" should be accompanied by your raising your hand.
- Providing hands-on learning activities (Chapter 1).
- Using cooperative learning.

Sometimes teachers can become frustrated with all the information regarding how to provide instruction adequately for their students from different cultures. *The best way to address instruction for cultural diversity is to offer varieties of learning experiences and to allow students to choose among them.*

Exceptionalities

Not only must the teacher address instruction in the classroom for students from different cultures but also for those students with exceptionalities. Exceptionalities include gifted and talented students as well as students with disabilities. These exceptionalities represent approximately 15 percent of the school population—5 percent gifted and talented and the remaining 10 percent students with disabilities.

Gifted and Talented Students

The definition of gifted and talented students has changed over the years. There was a time when these students were described exclusively in cognitive terms such as IQ or achievement scores that were considerably above average. However, the definition has expanded to include creativity and task commitment (Renzulli and Reis 1991), allowing more students, especially those from minority groups, to partake in gifted programs.

In the name of equality, gifted students were neglected for many years. As a result of this neglect, over half of gifted students, in a survey conducted by Tomlinson-Keasey (1990), were not performing to their ability level. You should not allow the needs of this national resource to be unmet.

There are certain characteristics that can help you identify gifted students. They generally learn quickly and respond quickly; have large vocabularies and can manipulate language easily; possess good memories; can apply more easily what they learned; are creative across disciplines with unusual approaches to problem solving; have knowledge unattained by other students; can perceive relationships and demonstrate meaningful insights; are motivated and persistent in completing tasks (Renzulli and Reis 1991; Renzulli 2004). As already noted previously, gifted students are represented in all cultures and socioeconomic backgrounds.

When planning for gifted students in particular as well as for all students, the teacher should provide learning experiences that

- encourage independence,
- offer creative opportunities for developing projects or solving problems, and
- expose students to a high level of abstract thinking with less emphasis on facts.

Students with Disabilities

There are many categories of disability, each of which has the potential for interfering with the learning process. Though these disabilities are categorized specifically by each state, some general categories are described in Turnbull et al. (2002) and in Woolfolk (2004). These categories include the following:

Learning disabilities—reading, writing, speaking, listening, reasoning, or computational difficulties.

Attention deficit disorders (ADD)—inability to focus attention long enough to learn or complete a task.

Attention deficit hyperactivity disorders (ADHD)—difficulty remaining still long enough to pay attention and concentrate on work.

Speech/hearing disorders—difficulty (stuttering, articulating, inappropriate tone quality, pitch, or loudness, difficulty hearing in one or both ears) communicating with others.

Language disorders—problems expressing or comprehending language, or communicating by gestures, brief sentences or a few words.

Social/emotional/behavioral maladjustments—problems that interfere with the student's own personal development and in relating to others.

Mental retardation—mild to severe cognitive impairment.

Visual impairment/blindness—mild to complete vision loss.

Orthopedic impairment—a physical disability that interferes with movement or motor functions.

Non-congenital health impairments such as trauma injuries generally caused by accidents.

Autism—severe impairment in communicating, learning, and socialization.

Multiple disabilities. Some students exhibit combinations of the above, thereby increasing learning problems.

Several types of disabilities such as orthopedic impairments (general physical coordination) are sometimes recognizable. However, the teacher should be aware of clues that indicate potential problems in areas that are not as obvious. Smith and Luckasson (1995) and Hallahan and Kaufman (2003) have identified some common problems of students with learning disabilities.

These attributes may occur individually, in combination, and in lesser or greater degrees: distractibility; hyperactivity; poor coordination; speech impediments; hearing problems; social immaturity; problems with memory, language, and thinking; discrepancy between intelligence and achievement; and perceptual problems such as reversing numerals, letters, or words.

When a student shows *consistent* characteristics in any exceptionalities, you should document those characteristics and refer that student to a pre-assessment team who will, if necessary, refer that student to a special education team for evaluation. If their diagnosis confirms your suspicions (and remember that this holds true for a gifted and talented student as well as one with disabilities), then you will be assisted in designing appropriate instruction for that student through collaborative consultation with special educators and meetings with the school psychologist.

To provide adequate differentiated instruction for students with disabilities, Maniet-Bellerman (1992) has provided a specific list of examples of instructional strategies that should be used in the general classroom. Her strategies are still current today, but since Maniet-Bellerman made these suggestions, the Individuals with Disabilities Education Act (1997) replaced the term *handicap* with *disability*.

1. Present material on tape for students who cannot read successfully. . . .
2. Allow students to tape-record answers if writing is difficult or their handwriting is illegible.
3. Provide lots of visual reminders (pictures, maps, charts, graphs) for students who have trouble listening or attending.
4. Present handouts that are clear, legible, and uncrowded. . . .
5. Break directions and assignments into small steps. . . .
6. Give tests orally if the child has trouble with reading, spelling, or writing. . . .
7. Emphasize quality rather than quantity of writing.
8. Be consistent with directions, rules, discipline, and organization.
9. Arrange the class schedule so that the exceptional student does not miss important activities when he or she goes to the resource room.
10. Dispense encouragement freely but fairly. . . .
11. Discover the exceptional student's strengths and special interests. . . .
12. Carefully establish routines so that the student does not become further handicapped by the confusion of unclear expectations.
13. Arrange desks, tables, and chairs so every person can be easily seen and every word easily heard. . . .
14. . . . schedule difficult subjects when there are no outside noises. . . .
15. Provide carrels or screens—-an "office"—-for students who are easily distracted.
16. When checking students' work, check correct answers rather than incorrect answers. . . .
17. Allow the exceptional student to tape lectures or arrange for a classmate who writes neatly to use carbon paper. . . .
18. Correct deficient lighting, glare from windows, and light-blocking partitions.
19. Fit the furniture to the child. . . . (pp. 424–425).

An updated list of additional suggestions was offered by Hamel (2004).

- Use overhead projector or computer-enhanced image to enlarge materials.
- Allow hands-on experience of new materials when introducing a concept.
- Use computers for extra drill and practice.

- Limit the use of words not yet in the students' vocabulary (readiness level).
- Allow students to help plan their own learning and be a partner in the process.
- Vary the style of test items and provide accurate, complete study guides.
- Use short tests at frequent intervals (brief assignments and frequent review).
- Vary the style of test questions used.
- Wait at least five seconds . . . for students to process your questions (pp. 35–36).

Richard Lavoie pointed out that those who choose teaching as a profession are likely to have been successful in school and do not understand how it is to be learning disabled. Teachers can increase their empathy for these students by experiencing their daily Frustration, Anxiety, and Tension, FAT, as they view his video, "How Difficult Can This Be? The F. A. T. City Workshop" (Lavoie 1989). He also emphasized that treating students fairly does NOT mean treating them the same. Treating students fairly means providing them with what they need (Lavoie 2005a). Since there is a direct link between learning disorders and social incompetence, which leads to rejection and isolation, Lavoie (2005b) strongly recommends that teachers learn how to teach social skills.

Gender

Much of what is known about the way boys and girls are treated differently in the schools comes from the work of Sadker and Sadker (1994, 1997), and from a report of the American Association of University Women (1992). You should be aware of the results of the research so that you will implement instruction in your class in which boys and girls have equal expectations and opportunities for success. The research cited above has reported that girls are more frequently under-challenged and that *both male and female teachers* in general tended to treat boys and girls differently. Boys are

encouraged more than girls.
called on more often.
asked more higher level questions.
given more reinforcement for their responses, whether correct or not.
probed more often for their responses.
provided more instruction on independence.
in later years likely to surpass scores of girls on standardized tests in all areas, but especially in math and science, whereas girls in early years surpassed scores of boys in all areas.

On the other side of the coin, Sadker and Sadker (1994) found that boys are more likely to be misdiagnosed for learning problems, to fail, or become dropouts. Because boys tend to be more active, their behavior conflicts with the expectations of teachers, especially female teachers. Boys are more likely to receive lower grades, more likely to be punished, and are at greater risk for having accidents and for committing murder and/or suicide.

It should be noted that other studies found that boys are subject to greater inequities than girls in schools (Sommers 1996), that in some situations girls are given preferential treatment, and in other situations boys are given preferences (Lee, Chen, and Smerdon 1996).

Gurian (2001) criticized gender research that he contended has been conducted predominantly from a social point of view. He presented convincing biological research regarding brain-based differences between boys and girls.

These include tendency differences in ten areas researched over the past twenty years: deductive and inductive reasoning; abstract and concrete reasoning; use of language; logic and evidence; the likelihood of boredom; use of space; movement; sensitivity and group dynamics; use of symbolism; and use of learning teams. To accommodate these areas, Gurian (2001) has presented "ultimate" preschool through high school classrooms to help teachers maximize the differences for the benefit of both sexes.

What is becoming more disturbing is that Conlin (2003) has reported that there is a widening gulf in school, with boys trailing behind in every racial and ethnic group. She pointed out that boys are being surpassed by girls in national reading scores and in extracurricular activities. Conlin warned that in a global economy in which mental rather than physical prowess is valued, men could become losers.

Viadero (2006) has also reported that the gender gap is still shifting to boys and that this gap is universal. Of 41 nations tested, in all but one, girls outscored boys on a 2003 reading test administered to 15-year-olds. Additionally, from 1971–2001 in the United States, men went from being the majority of the nation's undergraduate college population to the minority with the trend holding in that direction.

This problem is of such concern that it is now being addressed by educators and therapists (Gurian and Stevens 2004, 2005) with school districts currently designing programs to address the needs of boys. In the classroom it has been a general recommendation that boys be given the opportunity to use physical movement and multimedia (videos, movies) in language arts activities and laptop computers for taking notes and writing papers (Baron-Cohen 2003; Gurian and Stevens 2005).

Specific suggestions for teaching *both* boys and girls in elementary school have been offered by Gurian and Stevens 2004). Their suggestions are summarized in Table 6.2.

Table 6.2. Teaching Boys and Girls in Elementary School

Boys	Girls
Limit verbal instructions to less than a minute	Use puzzles to promote perceptual learning
Because boys are generally behind in fine motor development when they enter school, use beadwork and other manipulatives	Because girls are generally behind in gross motor skills when they enter school, use physical games
Provide kinesthetic experiential lessons	Use manipulatives when teaching math
Incorporate male role models	Use working groups and teams to foster negotiation skills and leadership
Place bookshelves with books all around the room	Use cameras to photograph girls being successful at tasks
Allow healthy aggression	Promote science in a spatial medium by using water and sand tables
To increase his sense of attachment, personalize the desk, cubby, and coat rack	Encourage verbally the hidden energy of the quieter girls

(*Source*: "With Boys and Girls in Mind," by Michael Gurian & Kathy Stevens, 2004, Educational Leadership 62(3):21–26. © 2004 by ASCD. Reprinted with permission. Learn more about ASCD at www.ascd.org.)

As far as you are concerned, it is your responsibility to be cognizant of the tendency for treating boys and girls inequitably in different situations, and to ensure that you avoid any gender bias in your own classroom. You can do this by encouraging collaboration between boys and girls; eliminating children's self-imposed sexism; promoting math, science, and verbal achievement for both boys and girls; and most importantly, by offering choices of activities.

Universal Design for Learning (UDL)

To re-emphasize the need for planning the differentiation of instruction *before* actually preparing lessons, consider the information presented above in light of the Universal Design for Learning, UDL. About twenty-five years ago the Center for Applied Special Technology, CAST, was established to help students with disabilities gain access to the general education curriculum, with an emphasis on assistive technology. But by the early 1990s CAST realized that this emphasis was too narrow and shifted its focus to the general education curriculum. CAST advances the idea that students should above all conquer the learning process as they master knowledge and technologies needed in the twenty-first century. The result is their Universal Design for Learning, which has gained support in Congress.

UDL is a philosophy that promotes transforming the way lessons are taught by developing flexible lessons and materials to accommodate different learning styles. This concept evolved from applying accessibility such as closed-caption TV, curb cuts, and speakerphones geared originally for people with hearing and mobility disabilities which led to the realization that these accommodations have actually benefited everyone.

UDL is not a lesson package but a *variety of solutions* that transform the way lessons are developed and delivered. Instead of adjusting existing lesson plans for a variety of learners, teachers are being encouraged to be more aggressive in their original plan. UDL begins with the premise that the *curriculum,* not the student, has a disability. Curricula are disabled in who, what, and how they can teach.

To fix "disabled" curricula, use technology and other materials to make the curriculum more accessible in the first place, as opposed to using these materials for existing lessons so that after-the-fact adjustments will not be necessary. Rethink lessons and customize them for students with different needs.

UDL principles begin with individual differences and diversity, the challenge being not merely to differentiate instruction *but to do so effectively.* The teacher should structure lessons according to three main principles.

Principle I Provide multiple means of representation.
Principle II Provide multiple means of expression.
Principle III Provide multiple means of engagement.

A summary of the options under each principle is provided in Table 6.3.

You will note that the operative word in all of the principles is *options.* These options are not plans in themselves, but should be provided within the *original* plan regardless of what type of plan it is. CAST offers examples of options that are applicable in each of the sub-categories above.

For instance, in the first subcategory under Option 1, Customize the display of information, some options that would be available to accomplish this display could include the following perceptual features: size of the text or images; amplitude of speech or sound; contrast between background and text or image; color used for information or emphasis; speed or timing of video, animation, sound, or simulations; layout of visual or other elements.

Examples from each of the option subcategories in the above summary along with a full explanation of UDL can be obtained at http://www.cast.org/publications/UDLguidelines/version1.html.

An illustration regarding how UDL would work can be found in the approach to reading in Figure 6.3.

Table 6.3. **Universal Design for Learning**

Representation	Expression	Engagement
1. Provide options for perception that	4. Provide options for physical action in	7. Provide options for recruiting interest that
Customize the display of information Provide alternatives for auditory information Provide alternatives for visual information	The mode of physical response The means of navigation Assessing tools and assistive technologies	Increase individual choice and autonomy Enhance relevance, value, and authenticity Reduce threats and distractions
2. Provide options for language and symbols that	5. Provide options for expressive skills and fluency in the	8. Provide options for sustaining effort and persistence that
Define vocabulary and symbols Clarify syntax and structure Decode text and mathematical notation Promote cross-linguistic understanding Illustrate key concepts non-linguistically	Media for communication Tools for composition and problem solving Scaffolds for practice and performance	Heighten salience of goals and objectives Vary levels of challenge and support Foster collaboration and communication Increase mastery oriented feedback
3. Provide options for comprehension that	6. Provide options for executive functions that	9. Provide options for self-regulation that
Provide or activate background knowledge Highlight critical features, big ideas, and relationships Guide information processing Support memory and transfer	Guide effective goal setting Support planning and strategy development Facilitate managing information and resources Enhance capability for monitoring progress	Guide personal goal-setting and expectations Scaffold coping skills and strategies Develop self-assessment and reflection

Before distributing the bookmark, an outline of what the students must do when they write about a story they have read is presented verbally. Then, as a reminder and guide for the writing, the bookmark, which contains pictures corresponding to the different segments of the outline, is distributed.

The student can then cut out the elongated rectangle containing these pictures, put his/her name on the back, and use the rectangle as a bookmark that can be

Name _____   Date _____

	Title _____
	Characters _____
	Setting _____
	Kick off _____
	How did the characters feel? _____
	Then... _____
	Next... _____
	Finally... _____
	Tie Up _____
	How do the characters feel at the end? _____

Figure 6.3. *(Source:* Page reproduced from Reading Response Bookmarks and Graphic Organizers copyright © 2011 by Kimberly Blaise, published by Scholastic Inc. and used by permission.)

used for the rest of the year. The teacher can laminate the bookmark to preserve it. You will notice that using the visual helps *all* students remember what they have to do after reading a story, not just students with special needs.

As a teacher, you must examine *daily* the status of the learner with respect to the learning objectives in order to differentiate instruction for success (Tomlinson 2005). This daily examination has its greatest implications in lesson planning, a discussion of which follows in the next chapter.

Chapter Summary: Since students have varieties of needs, teachers must be flexible in meeting these needs by differentiating instruction. Planning the differentiation should come *before* instruction. Differentiation of the instruction includes the content, activities, and assessment, and is based on the student's readiness, interest, and learning profile.

Teachers need to be sensitive to their students' cultures and implement instruction that encourages cultural respect and offers students choices.

Teachers must also be sure to differentiate instruction for gifted students and those with disabilities. Gender equity in the classroom can be promoted by collaboration between boys and girls and by offering choices of activities.

The Universal Design for Learning emphasizes the need for teachers, when differentiating instruction, to present in their original plans multiple options for the following: representing information, having students express what they have learned, and engaging students in learning.

Chapter 7

Designing Optimal Lesson Plans

Chapter 5 reviewed content needed to plan units—instruction that provides an overall guide *over a period of time.* Chapter 6 emphasized the need to consider how to differentiate instruction *before* planning lessons. This chapter will review how to plan effective and thorough *daily* lessons. A lesson should develop one or several related objectives listed in the unit.

A carefully thought-out lesson plan increases teacher productivity and is the best way to meet the needs of *all* learners. This thought process must become a habit of mind. Just as there is not one way to plan a unit, there is not one way to plan a lesson.

Though it is not realistic or necessary that you implement all parts of the lesson plan outline all of the time (Hunter 1984), you must be aware that frequently omitting parts represents a *lost opportunity* for your students to learn. A commonly stated rule is that you should conduct each lesson as though you were being observed by your district's superintendent or your school principal.

As in the unit plan, you should put your lesson plan in writing to ensure that you have considered important elements and questions *before* the actual instruction takes place. This process will enhance the probability for student (and your attendant) success.

Your beliefs about how students learn will influence the approach you use in planning lessons. Jensen (2005) reminded teachers that there is no "perfect" or "best" way to teach and that over the centuries millions of students have learned successfully before the recent revolution in teaching and learning. Jensen does recommend, however, that you implement recent research by ensuring that students are engaged in multidisciplinary and authentic tasks; interactive exploratory instruction; real tasks not only during instruction but also during assessments; and collaborative work in heterogeneous groups.

In this chapter you will be exposed to the traditional and constructivist lesson plans. Regardless of the lesson plan used, it is important to remind you that ways to differentiate instruction should occur *before* the lesson planning actually takes place.

TRADITIONAL LESSON PLAN COMPONENTS

The traditional lesson plan is presented first because it is still the predominant format used in schools and because all other types of plans contain elements of the traditional lesson plan. In many school districts, teachers are required to submit written plans using some variation of this format a week in advance of instruction.

The lesson plan outline presented below is teacher-directed. The plan is based on the work of Hunter (1982) updated by her associate (Hunter 2004) to include more current research.

You should be aware of the fact that even though Madeline Hunter's work has been considered a twentieth-century relic, her model has been reaffirmed by recent brain research (Wolfe 2011). And researcher, Mike Schmoker (2011), has indicated that Hunter's planning model is the key to ensuring that all students learn necessary content and intellectual skills. He asserts that Hunter's basic model in addition to other essential educational practices can close the achievement gap in five years or fewer.

In this section you will examine all the elements in the traditional lesson plan as a whole. Then you will go back and review each part in detail.

Lesson Planning—An Overview

Figure 7.1 provides an outline of the traditional lesson plan format.

What to Include in Traditional Lesson Components

1. Analytic diagnosis and description of learners: Planning should be geared to your knowledge of the students. There must be constant purposeful and systematic planning in order to meet the needs of the varieties of students in your classroom, even if it is a homogeneous classroom or group.

    Though much more information about students comes as you teach, you should, at the very least when you begin working with them, have some understanding of each student's strengths and weaknesses. What is his/her cognitive level of functioning? What knowledge does the student already possess? How may gender affect learning? What attitudes and other affective considerations should you take into account?

---

 1. Analytic diagnosis and description of learners
 2. Learning standard
 3. Goal
 4. Objective
 5. Entry skills
 6. Anticipatory set
7A. Sequence of objectives 7B. Assessment of objectives 7C. Instructional strategies
 8. Materials
 9. Classroom organization
10. Modeling of content/skills
11. Guided practice activities
12. Closure
13. Independent practice activities
14. Evaluation of learning
15. Follow-up lesson
16. Other ways to teach lesson

Figure 7.1.   The Traditional Lesson Plan

For example, a person who is shy may need to work in a small group. Are there some student interests you could exploit? What psychomotor needs does the student have? Are there students with exceptionalities, including gifted exceptionalities? What different cultures are represented? Are any of the students non-English speaking? Unless you have a firm handle on each student, you will not know how to competently tailor and assess instructional needs.

You can gather this pertinent information by performing a diagnostic evaluation using the Student Diagnosis Checklist as a Guide to Instructional Planning presented in Chapter 3, Figure 3.3 which is presented again as Figure 7.2.

2. Learning standard: List the learning standard or standard combinations addressed in the lesson. This (these) standard(s) should be the same one(s) identified in your unit.

3. Goal: State the content or process goal/benchmark based on your unit or any other goal the class should achieve. Remember that the goal is a broad statement that will be achieved over the long term, not by the end of the lesson.

Goals do not have to be stated in behavioral (instructional, performance) terms. Students should be made aware of goals when you introduce the unit. The goal in the lesson should flow from your unit and, when appropriate, some of the goals should be those of the students. An

Name_____ Age/Grade_____

Standardized test results:

Achievement

Diagnostic

Aptitude

IQ

Other

Classroom test results:

Relevant family information:

General health:

Information from:

Parent/guardian meeting(s)

Prior teachers

Intelligence strength(s):

Verbal/linguistic

Logical/mathematical

Visual/spatial

Musical

Bodily/kinesthetic

Interpersonal

Intrapersonal

Naturalist

Learning preferences:

Cultural (Be careful to avoid stereotypes.)

Style

Field-dependent

Field-independent

Modality

Auditory

Figure 7.2.   Student Diagnosis Form as a Guide to Instructional Planning

---

Visual

Tactile/kinesthetic

Exceptionalities noted (if any):

Relevant information from:

Observation

Interview

Samples of student work

General strengths:

Weaknesses in need of remediation:

General prescription for student:

Figure 7.2. *(Continued)*

effective practice is that of reminding students of the particular goal they will be working toward in the lesson and what connection the goal has to their lives.

4. Objective(s): The objective is one selected from the unit and answers the question, "What will the students be able to *do* at the end of the lesson that will be *one step* toward demonstrating knowledge of the standard(s), benchmark(s), or other unit goal(s) you want to achieve?" The objective should be written in behavioral (instructional, performance) terms and should reflect the lesson topic.

Here again, as with the goal, you should connect the objective to the students' lives. More than one objective may be selected if they are closely related and realistically achievable within the time frame for the lesson.

Example of a goal and one objective that will lead to the goal:
Goal—Create costumes for the class play. (Note that this goal cannot be accomplished within the lesson but over the long term.)
Objective—Given a pattern, the student will be able to cut fabric according to the pattern (one objective achievable within a class period that will lead to the goal).
The objective is of particular importance in lesson planning. It will guide you in identifying the prerequisite knowledge (entry skills) the

students need to learn the new content, focus your teaching on the observable results that you will use to validate the acquisition of that new learning (formative evaluation), and direct you in deciding what instruction will best facilitate that learning. Even more important, sharing the objective with students will assist them in self-assessment FOR learning (Stiggins 2007).

5. Entry skills: The lesson you offer must be in context. You want to be aware of what the students can already do so that they will have a scaffold for the lesson. Listing their prerequisite skills in behavioral terms can help you be more accurate in determining what the students already know and can do. (Sometimes an experience like a field trip or a video will be sufficient for you to build a lesson.)

   The basic consideration is what experiential *readiness,* prior knowledge, or skills the students have so that they can absorb the objective of the lesson into schema (cognitive structures) already present. It is a frustrating experience and inefficient for the teacher and the student when a lesson does not build on prior knowledge. Some (or all) students may be lost and confused. The teacher then has to go back and teach (or re-teach) the prior knowledge before continuing with the planned objective.

7. Anticipatory set: Your students must be ready, willing, and able to receive the lesson (Ryan, Cooper, and Tauer 2008). As already stated, students must be prepared with prerequisite knowledge and/or experience that will serve as a foundation for the lesson. Since they are constantly being bombarded with competing stimuli, students will select those that are interesting and stay with those that are enjoyable.

   According to brain research, there is no learning without memory, and that memory depends on attention (Jensen 1998). So how do you get that attention? During the anticipatory set, you make students aware of and hooked into the objective. It is your opportunity to stimulate the students' curiosity.

   Brain research tells us that the brain can be primed, and if the students know (are primed with) the objective, the chances are that they will achieve it. And since the brain is always paying attention to something, the anticipatory set is your opportunity to concentrate the students' attention on the lesson by thwarting competing stimuli.

   The anticipatory set provides *motivation* for gaining this attention. Motivation, you will recall, introduces enough frustration to make the students want to go back into equilibrium, and the "going back into equilibrium" involves learning. " . . . significant learning is frequently accompanied or impelled by discomfort" (Joyce, Weil, and Calhoun 2004).

Students should be informed regarding why the objective is important and what it means to them personally. Assuming that the students can read, many teachers find that once the objective is elicited, an effective practice is writing it on the board or on a poster.

Displaying the objective helps keep the students focused on where they are heading and provides a link to eventually closing the lesson. In addition, as already mentioned, knowing the objective assists students in self-assessing.

Some teachers find it helpful to write the objective in the form of a question. "To calculate the area of a circle" would then become, "How can we calculate the area of a circle?" At the end of the lesson the students would then decide whether or not they could answer the question.

It is also important for you to know whether or not the students are aware of the objective. Just because you state it or one or more of the students can state the objective does not mean that everyone is aware of it. You will have a better handle on knowing how aware the students are of the objective if you have several students repeat the objective, not in parrot form but *in their own words*.

Example:

Teacher:	How many of you brought your lunch to school? (All hands go up.) What did you bring? Tom.
Tom:	Peanut butter and jelly.
Teacher:	(The teacher pats his belly.) One of my favorites. What about you, Henrietta?
Henrietta:	A tuna fish sandwich. (Some members of the class hold their noses, snicker, or say, "Yuk." The teacher ignores the behavior.)
Teacher:	Tuna is a very good source of protein, Henrietta. Whoever prepared that lunch is smart and must really care about you. And what do you have for lunch, George?
George:	A ham sandwich.
Teacher:	Also a great source of protein. Well, class, I brought my lunch today, too. (Teacher places his lunch box on the desk.) What do you think is in my lunch box? Frank.
Frank:	Soup and crackers.
Teacher:	Maybe. What do you think, Johnny?
Johnny:	A Big Mac.
Teacher:	It's possible. And you, Sheila?
Sheila:	Chicken nuggets . . . or a hot dog. But, but then the hot dog would be cold. (The class laughs.)

> Teacher: Good guesses, but in my lunch box is *another* lunch box.
>   (The students all look at each other with puzzled faces (discomfort level), obviously having been thrown off balance. The teacher opens his lunch box. The students look with anticipation. In the lunch box is a lima bean. The teacher places the lima bean on his desk.) So what do you think we are going to learn today? (There is a long pause as the teacher observes the still crinkled faces.) Debbie.
> Debbie: How . . . how or why a lima bean is a lunch box?
> Teacher: Excellent, Debbie. Now who can say that in another way? Jerry.
> Jerry: How a lunch box and a lima bean are the same.
> Teacher: Great, Jerry. Give us another way of saying this. Paul.
> Paul: What makes a lima bean like lunch.

Note that in the example the teacher did not tell the students at the beginning what the objective of the lesson was. *The objective flowed from the anticipatory set*—what the teacher did to stimulate curiosity so that the students would want to know the objective—how the lunch box and lima bean were alike.

Some teachers just state the objective at the beginning. For example, a teacher might say, "Today we're going to learn about a lima bean" or, given a different lesson, "Today we are going to learn how sounds are produced." Merely stating the purpose of the lesson is *much less efficient* than throwing the students a little off balance in the beginning with the anticipatory set and letting the objective derive from that set.

Another way to get student attention is by introducing a problem whose solution is made possible only by the achievement of the lesson objective. In this type of situation, the learning becomes more meaningful because there is a *reason* to learn something (Hunter 2004).

Example:

> Teacher: Mrs. Shiller just informed me that our class mothers raised $476 in our bake sale to buy a carpet for our classroom. But before we can buy that carpet, we first have to decide how much we need to cover the floor. And to do this we have to learn how to measure area." Unless the students can measure area (solve the problem by achieving the lesson objective), the class cannot buy the carpet (the reason for the learning).

Time spent on the anticipatory set should be relatively short, leaving the largest portion of lesson time to accomplishing the objective.

7A. Sequence of objectives: At this point the students should be curious to find the answer to the question raised in the anticipatory set and thus achieve the objective. Now what? For you to decide what step is next in determining the assessment and instructional process, and therefore, how you will continue with the lesson, you have to analyze the lesson objective to determine *if* sequence is important. If it is, you have to break up the lesson objective into smaller objectives that will lead to it.

Example: Lesson objective—the student will be able to describe the digestive process.

That is what the students will do at the *end* of the lesson. How do you get to that final stage? There are intervening steps, a sequence of smaller objectives also written in behavioral terms that will lead the students to describing the digestive process. You have to arrange the content so that it makes sense to the learner, especially for field-dependent learners (Chapter 1).

In order for students to be able to describe the digestive process, they have to be able to

1. explain the function of digestion
2. identify the organs in the digestive system
3. locate the organs in the digestive system
4. describe the function of each organ
5. trace different food particles through the digestive system

When you read these five objectives, you will note that they sequentially and collectively describe the digestive process—the lesson objective. A student who cannot identify the organs will not be able to describe their function. A student who cannot locate the organs will not be able to trace food through them.

Writing these smaller intermittent objectives is often a difficult process for teachers. It takes practice. But the identification of these objectives tells you where to begin after the anticipatory set, with an assessment and an input (instructional) activity that will, as in the above example, assist the students in being able to explain the function of digestion.

Identification of smaller intermittent objectives will help you assess the attainment of these objectives as the students proceed and, therefore, whether or not you or they need to adjust instruction along the way. Also, having a clear idea of the sequence of instruction, when sequence is necessary, avoids the problem of sometimes "losing" the students when a *critical* step in the learning process is omitted.

7B. Assessment of objectives: It is the instinct of teachers, once they determine objectives, to "teach" by immediately delving into ways of
achieving them. After all, "teaching" is the goal for which teachers
were educated. But it has long been a criticism that too much education
is concerned with input, not results.

Often teachers (and students) are constantly "doing things" but the
students are not learning. This situation is similar to the police department's implementing different policies to fight crime, after which the
crime rate is still high. You must keep your eye on the target—student
learning. Decide first how you will assess each intermittent objective
to assist you in knowing whether or not instruction should continue,
or whether or not you have to take a different track (Wiggins and
McTighe 2005).

Using again the above digestion example, you should decide for
each intermittent objective how you will know whether or not the students are "getting it." Students might explain the function of digestion
by simply restating it, or by giving an example. They may identify and
locate the organs by filling their names on a diagram. Frequently, the
same assessment can cover more than one objective.

What is NOT productive in assessment is asking questions like,
"Does everybody understand?," "Do you all agree?," "All right?," or
"Okay?" If you really want to know if the students understand, *ask
questions about the content.*

Assessment may occur by an informal method such as simple observation or it may be having the students identify organ parts on a model,
draw their own diagram, name the organs on a diagram you provide,
place the parts of a model together, or any other assessment that makes
sense. You could also use hand signals to assess. "Raise your right hand
if the pyloric valve comes *before* the stomach, and your left hand if the
pyloric valve comes *after.*" You will note how quickly students signal
and which signals are correct and which are incorrect. Students who
look at others' hands before raising theirs will indicate uncertainty.

You can offer self-correcting materials for students to use and, when
applicable, have peers check each other. Always keep the students
involved in and responsible for their own assessment (Stiggins 2005).
Identifying the assessment(s) for the objectives ensures that your students, not you, will be covering the curriculum.

7C. Instructional strategies (learning experiences): In selecting instructional
strategies, also referred to as input, there are a myriad of possibilities.
This decision becomes more complex given your need to provide

instructional options for different student readiness, interests, and learning profiles.

Before you continue reading, keep in mind that objectives are the *re-sults* of instruction. Once you have decided the main objective, the intermittent objectives that will lead to it, and how each will be assessed, you will be in a better position to decide the most effective learning experiences the students should have in order to meet each assessment. To help you decide, ask the questions that follow.

QUESTIONS TO ASK IN SELECTING INSTRUCTIONAL ACTIVITIES

Q1. Does the objective involve semantic knowledge, that which is concerned with meaning? If so, is the meaning

a concept—a category that groups similar things such as a noun, vertebrate, or government,
a principle—a generalization that states relationships between two or among several concepts, such as a rule or a law like "i before e except after c," or
an attitude, such as respect for the culture of others?

Q2. Does the objective involve procedural knowledge, that which is intended to develop the performance of a task or skill? If so, is the skill

cognitive (a mathematical computation),
social (exhibiting positive behavior to others who are different),
or physical (setting up and using a microscope)?

Q3. Does the objective involve a combination of the above?

When you are clear regarding the purpose of the objective, you can select the most appropriate strategy or combinations of strategies. Many suggestions were offered in Chapter 6, accommodated by the Universal Design for Learning options of representation, expression, and engagement (Table 6.3). Some other corresponding strategies are categorized in Table 7.1. You are already familiar with many of them. (If you are unfamiliar with implementing concept attainment, concept formation, the advance organizer, or mastery learning, see Pagliaro 2011.)

You will note that several strategies such as problem solving and discovery are listed in several columns and can cover different learning outcomes. Your challenge here is keeping the students' attention,

Table 7.1. Instructional Strategies and their Learning Outcomes

Concepts/Principles	Skills	Attitudes/Social Development
Lectures	Drill and practice	Role playing
Debates	Computer-assisted	Dramas
Panels	instruction	Cooperative learning
Videos	Modeling	Discussions
Guest speakers	Demonstrations	Videos
Discovery	Games/simulations	Problem solving
Internet research	Independent study	Games/simulations
Concept attainment		Debates
Concept formation		Case studies
Advance organizers		Discovery
Mastery		
Learning/contracts		
Cooperative learning		
Learning activity centers		
Case studies		
Problem solving		
Demonstrations		
Dramas		
Discussions		
Games/simulations		
Independent study		

and keeping them meaningfully engaged. (A comprehensive review of engaged learning has been conducted by the North Central Regional Educational Laboratory. You can access this information at http://www.ncrel.org/sdrs/engaged.htm.)

To reiterate, regarding the instructional strategy, " . . . the most effective instruction is that which addresses multiple modalities: instruction where students get to hear, see, touch, and discuss . . . there is no one best way" (Hunter 2004, 7).

Sometimes each intermittent objective, assessment, and learning experience (input, strategy) needs a one-to-one correspondence. In other cases the same assessment and learning experience can cover several objectives.

As indicated previously, knowledge of your students is particularly crucial in making learning experience decisions. It is becoming a nationwide trend to distinguish between accommodations and modifications, two distinctions with a difference (Beech and Barnitt 2001).

Accommodations are the ways we differentiate instruction. They are changes in the way students are taught, the assignments they are eventually given after the lesson, and the way students are assessed/

evaluated. In the lesson there is an accommodation for different learning styles, multiple intelligences, cultural preferences, and genders. Even though there may be differences in methods, groupings, assignments, and evaluations, when accommodations are necessary, there is *no change* in the objectives covered.

Students themselves can frequently offer suggestions regarding accommodations needed. Learners with Individualized Educational Programs, also referred to as Individualized Educational Plans, IEPs, usually have the necessary accommodations identified in the program (plan).

As in the Universal Design for Learning, you will find that specific suggestions for accommodating students with disabilities represent effective teaching for *all* students. Once again, some *general* suggestions for *accommodating* students are as follows:

Keep in contact with specialists in exceptional education so that you can seek their input, when necessary.

Make an effort to identify student strengths and use them in both instruction and assessment.

Plan visual, auditory, and tactile/kinesthetic activities in both instruction and assessment. Keep expectations high but reasonable.

Plan lessons and all supportive activities with a high level of structure.

Show by your own behavior the proper attitudes and methods of interacting with exceptional students that the other students should emulate. (Adapted from Kellough 2003).

Modifications are actual *changes in the content* (objectives) taught. These may include objectives for partial requirement completions, alternate curriculum goals, and different diplomas. Some of your students may actually need modifications. These students are most frequently those who are significantly below age/grade level.

Modifications are those adaptations (changes) that are made to curriculum, instruction, classroom set-up, or assessment. Therefore, they change the instruction level, the course content, and the performance criteria (Castagnera et al. 1998). If modifications are warranted by any of your students, the IEP committee (Child Study Team) and the parent must be involved in the changes and they must become part of the IEP.

To summarize, accommodations change *how* instruction is delivered: modifications change *what* is taught.

8. Materials. After you decide what instructional strategies you will use, identify the matching materials you and the students will need. Make sure the materials are meaningful to the students, are as concrete and multi-sensory as possible, engaging the students actively in hands-on learning whenever appropriate. Remember that the hands are the most important organ of the brain and that, whenever possible, primary sources should be used (Jensen 1998).

9. Classroom organization. Will the students be arranged for whole class, small group, individualized instruction, or a combination of these patterns? The selection should be based on students' needs in achieving the objective. More details on grouping will be presented later in this chapter.

10. Modeling of skills: The teacher ensures that the content or directions presented are clear by providing examples and/or demonstrations. The modeling you select depends on the learning outcome (lesson objective). Does it involve a concept or set of concepts, or a skill? Concepts are modeled by providing examples and/or products (samples). When offering examples and products, select those that connect to the students' experiences. Skills are best modeled by demonstrations. For solving a problem or applying a skill (process), you can also model by thinking out loud.

11. Guided practice: During guided practice the new material is reinforced. If the objective involves movement such as bending a piece of glass, then drill or rote rehearsal is in order. Rote rehearsal involves practicing the material over and over again in the same way.

    But since most of school learning involves semantic knowledge, or meaning, elaborative rehearsal is necessary. Elaborative rehearsal involves practicing the material in different ways to strengthen connections and deepen understanding—an expansion of behavior theory through brain research. Moreover, you may recall from Chapter 1 that research conducted by Nuthall (1999) concluded that content should be learned in *four different ways.*

    There are many options available for elaborative rehearsal: repeating the material in varied ways; teaching the material to someone else; drawing a picture of the content; writing what was learned; working with a partner or group to explain the content and/or discuss applications of the content; playing a game; applying the objective, to name a few. Always remember that the ways of rehearsing should be personalized.

12. Closure: During closure the lesson content is tied together. It should be clear in your mind how this will be done. Will it be summarized by the students? Will they explain how the content was personally meaningful? Will the students draw conclusions? Closure is an appropriate time to go back to the displayed objective of the lesson to determine if the students can *perform* the objective. If the objective was displayed in the form of a question, can the students *answer* the question?

   Using the same examples of lesson objectives presented earlier in this chapter, students could explain how a lima bean is like a lunch box, or describe the digestive process. They could do this orally, write in their journals, or perform any other activity which demonstrates knowledge of the objective.

13. Independent practice: Remember that most original learning is forgotten within the first 24 hours (Chapter 1). Therefore, during independent practice, understanding is deepened further as the teacher provides additional reinforcement the students do on their own. It may be a homework assignment, constructing a different diagram from one used in the lesson, arranging the content in a different way, or practicing on worksheets. It cannot be overemphasized that homework, just as any other assignment or activity, should be *meaningful,* not busy work.

14. Evaluation of learning. What will each learner do at the end of the lesson to demonstrate achievement of the lesson objective? This summative evaluation could include a quiz, the construction of a model, the writing of a coherent paragraph, playing a game, completing a worksheet, or any other activity relevant to demonstrating mastery of the objective.

    Though you should have considered what instructional accommodations/ modifications were necessary during the lesson by addressing the needs described in the diagnosis of your students, you should revisit this issue when you have completed the evaluation of the lesson. If the objective(s) was (were) not achieved by any student, ask yourself if you provided appropriate content, assessment, learning experiences, and materials for that student. Be sure to also ask the students who did not achieve the objective(s) the same questions.

    Did you change (with caution) the objective for a student who was *significantly* behind in entry skills for the lesson, or offer a series of basic preparatory skills as a foundation for students who did not have the entry skills for the lesson? On the basis of the evaluation, what should you do *now* to ensure the success of any student who did not achieve the lesson objective? And keeping in mind the student's responsibility for his/her own learning, what should that student do now to adjust his/her learning tactic(s) (Popham 2008)?

15. Follow-up lesson: Once the students have mastered the lesson objective, what will be the next objective they should learn? Communicating this information in advance gives students a sense of purpose and anticipation and could serve as part of the anticipatory set for the subsequent lesson.

16. Other way(s) to teach the lesson: Teachers must be flexible to switch gears, when necessary, as a result of constantly assessing learning during the lesson. In addition, teachers should make it a *regular procedure* to consider different ways to present the same content.

Marzano and his colleagues (2001, 2005) researched the most effective strategies that promote student achievement. These strategies *can occur at any appropriate point in the lesson and beyond.* As you read through them, consider in which lesson component they could be applied. They are arranged in order of their effect, beginning with the greatest: identifying similarities and differences; summarizing and note taking; reinforcing effort and providing recognition; homework and practice; using nonlinguistic representations; cooperative learning; setting objectives and providing feedback; generating and testing hypotheses; and questions, cues, and advance organizers.

THE CONSTRUCTIVIST LESSON PLAN

To round out your knowledge regarding lesson planning, it would be valuable for you to consider how to implement a constructivist lesson plan. As you read in Chapter 1, constructivists are concerned with how students make meaning of the world. According to constructivists, since all students' experiences are unique, students make meaning differently. For example, if all your colleagues read about constructivism and were then asked to explain it, the answers would reflect their own meaning of the term.

Constructivists assume that:

knowledge is constructed *physically* when students are actively involved;

knowledge is constructed *symbolically* when students make their own representations of action;

knowledge is constructed *socially* when students express the way they make meaning to others;

knowledge is constructed theoretically when learners attempt to explain what they do not fully understand (Gagnon and Collay 2006).

Constructivists see methodological differences between their teaching and the traditional model already presented. In the constructivist model, the teacher is a guide/facilitator who assists students in generating their own knowledge. There is less of a focus on teacher-directed structured experiences based on goals and objectives arranged in a hierarchy. Instead, students collaborate with the teacher and peers on projects that involve hands-on activities and the creation of products, thus developing higher and lower skills simultaneously.

Measurement of goals and objectives is replaced by student growth, which is determined by improved ability before and after the projects in both knowledge and skills and in the ability to work both independently and collaboratively. Students are provided with choices of performance tests and products accompanied by scoring rubrics.

In summary, constructivists focus on *general* problem solving and research skills as opposed to specific skills/objectives. More group than individual work is involved, with students exploring open-ended questions, doing research, and developing portfolios (Roblyer 2002; Fosnot 2005; Gagnon and Collay 2006.)

You should note that even though there are general differences between traditional and constructivist methods, it is *not* unusual for traditional teachers to incorporate the constructivist strategies perspective on learning, constructivist lessons promoting questions, exploring plausible answers, and developing authentic products.

How are the above methods put into a workable format? Rather than offering a plan for teaching, constructivists offer a design for learning (Gagnon and Collay 2006). Their design contains six components, with assessment as an integral step overseeing all of them. These components are Situation; Groupings; Bridge; Questions; Exhibit; and Reflections. Table 7.2 serves as a guide to designing constructivist lessons.

Though other constructivists have offered their own lesson plans (Roblyer 2002; Fosnot 2005), the basic concepts included in the plans are similar.

It has been argued recently that though meaning and understanding are constructed by individual learners through their different experiences, abilities, and interests, the teacher has an essential role in assisting students in constructing that meaning (Tomlinson and McTighe 2006). They encourage teachers to offer a balance between giving students opportunities to make meaning of essential knowledge and offering direct instruction that will assist students in constructing that meaning. Tomlinson and McTighe (2006, 85–86) offer a quote from cognitive psychology to support their point of view.

Table 7.2. Constructivist Learning Design

Assessment	Questions to Consider	Implementation	
Situation	What do you expect the students to do and how will they make their own meaning? What situation will you arrange for the students to explain?	Describe the situation as a problem solving process, answering questions, creating metaphors, making decisions, drawing conclusions, or setting goals	Design situation on the basis of student knowledge (needs, learning preferences, and interests)
Groupings	How will you group students and materials to correspond to the situation you have arranged?	Group students as teams, whole class, or as individuals Group materials needed for the situation for physically modeling, numerically describing, graphically representing, or reflectively writing students' individual or collective experience	Design a process for grouping on the basis of student needs and available materials
Bridge	How will you connect prior and new knowledge?	Solve a simple problem, conduct a group discussion, use a game or simulation, brainstorm	Design an assessment based on what the students already know as a bridge to what they are expected to learn
Questions	What questions will you ask to introduce the situation and keep thinking going? What questions do you anticipate students will ask?	Ask questions to set up the bridge, and then ask questions to keep the students thinking independently	Design questions to assess students' comprehension of concepts, skills, and attitudes
Exhibit	How will you show student explanations for others to understand?	Write card descriptions, draw a visual or physical representation, role play or act out, videotape, audiotape, or photograph	Design an exhibit for students to document what they know and submit the document for assessment by others
Reflections	How will students explain their process of thinking about the situation?	Have students express feelings, images, internal dialog, what attitudes, concepts and skills they already had, which they wanted to know, and what they learned, especially what they learned that they will not forget	Arrange reflections on student achievement and their internal processes for self-assessment

(Source: Adapted from Gagnon and Collay (2006) by permission of Sage Publications Inc. Books.)

A common misperception regarding "constructivist" theories of knowing is that teachers should never tell students anything directly but instead should allow them to construct knowledge for themselves. This perspective confuses a theory of pedagogy (teaching) with a theory of knowing. There are times, usually after people have first grappled with issues on their own, that "teaching by telling" might work extremely well (Bransford, Brown, and Cocking 2000, 11).

OTHER CONSIDERATIONS IN PLANNING AND DELIVERING LESSONS

Several other factors will influence the success of your instruction. Effective questioning skills have a significant impact on instruction (Pagliaro 2011a). Your enthusiasm determines whether or not the students will be "fired up." The pacing of the lesson is also critical. If the lesson is too fast, too slow, or has intermittent slowdowns, the momentum of the lesson can be lost and students may become disruptive. Time-on-task with minimal interruptions is also significant to a lesson's success. And how you manage classroom routines and materials will also affect your instruction (Pagliaro 2011b).

GROUPING FOR INSTRUCTION

One of the decisions you will have to make as part of lesson planning involves grouping your students for instruction. Grouping makes it easier to differentiate instruction that will provide for the cognitive, social, and developmental needs of students. Grouping also increases motivation because it provides a better medium for the teacher to stimulate and challenge students.

Grouping methods depend on several factors. Are you in a self-contained classroom? Is your classroom instruction departmentalized? What are the curricular and instructional needs of your students?

Different strategies need different types of classroom arrangements. Regardless of strategy, these arrangements may be presented in three categories: large group instruction (whole class), small group instruction, and individualized instruction. Remember that none of these is mutually exclusive. You will often see combinations of these approaches used in the classroom.

In general, strategies where the teacher has most of the control usually involve whole class arrangements, and strategies that give the students more of the control involve small group or individualized instruction. The most critical factors in deciding which approach to use are those that will most adequately meet the needs of the students, and that will have the greatest effect on student achievement (cognitive, affective, and psychomotor).

Large Group Instruction

Large group instruction, also known as whole class instruction, is used quite frequently. The teacher usually presents the same content, instructional activities, materials, and evaluation to the entire class, generally gearing all of these processes to the "average" learner. Instruction is often structured so that the teacher can provide time at the end of the formal presentation of the lesson to work individually or in small groups with students who need reinforcement or enrichment.

Large group instruction is useful for lectures, demonstrations, discussions, or for gathering students for general class concerns, for the sharing of ideas and resources, or for establishing rules and routines. Even though the teacher is in control in large group instruction, it is also a suitable structure for having students share some of the work they have done in conjunction with the content presented in class. For example, reports; debates; projects; performance tasks and products; portfolios; panels; trials; and brainstorming are some whole class activities that can round out content.

While whole class instruction may be effective in teaching specific procedures and skills, the skills may tend to be taught at the expense of higher cognitive learning. When teaching large groups, it is difficult to keep high achievers challenged, low achievers on target, and to receive and provide adequate feedback.

If you begin your year with whole class instruction, you will be able to determine what adjustments in grouping are necessary by implementing the diagnostic procedures you examined in Chapter 3.

Small Group Instruction

It has been reported consistently that when President George W. Bush asked his wife, Laura, if she would support his going into politics, she responded that she would go along only if she did not have to make a speech in front of a group. The feeling Mrs. Bush expressed is very common, because it is a well-known fact that one of the greatest fears people have is speaking in front of a large group.

Using small groups tends to alleviate this fear in students. And if you return to the key questions that should guide your decision about which type of classroom arrangement to use, namely, "Which will meet students' needs?"

and "Which will help students attain specific objectives?," the small group may provide the best match.

Small groups provide certain benefits. They offer a greater opportunity for students to

- be more actively involved in the learning process;
- be in a safer environment to express themselves or try out new ideas and activities;
- develop social skills;
- explore interests;
- learn new content or review content at a more appropriate level;
- be matched according to learning style;
- exercise more control over their own learning;
- monitor each other's work; and
- reinforce life skills such as sharing responsibilities and negotiating strategies.

Small groups allow the teacher to match the pace of instruction more appropriately for each student, gear content to age and developmental level, and supervise work more easily.

Before continuing a discussion of group work, be constantly aware that your students' future success in work, academics, or life in general depends on *self-reliance*. For students to be successful in group or any other work, you must teach them what resources are available for information, how to find and use these resources, and how to take notes, when necessary. Successful people know how to access information.

When students need help, they should first check their resources (texts, the Internet, other students in the group or class) because your tendency, as a member of a caring profession, may be to give help too quickly. If you do this without having students first use available resources, you will enable their self-defeating (dependency) behavior. This type of behavior can also be facilitated by classmates who should give assistance only after a student has initially tried to acquire information on his/her own (Ginsburg 2011).

Types of Small Groups

Peer tutoring. When implementing peer tutoring, students teach each other, most frequently, but not necessarily, in pairs. Peer tutoring may occur between or among students of different ages or grades, referred to as cross-age tutoring, or within the same class.

Using peers to help each other has many positive results. Peers relate better to each other than they do to adults. Peers are often "on the same wave length," thus better able to communicate academic content to each other. Tutors themselves clarify knowledge and gain greater depth when they teach the content to others. Peer tutoring gives the teacher more freedom to work with other groups. New students, academically-challenged students, or non-English speaking students can be better assimilated into the class beginning with peers.

Think-pair-share. In this technique, two students paired together, also known as dyads, are given a concept. They discuss the concept, share ideas about it with each other, then with the class as a whole. The most effective use of this technique is to ascertain what students know, have experienced, or think they know about a topic so that misconceptions can be diagnosed before the topic is introduced.

When appropriate, the teacher may also ask the students to put the ideas they came up with in writing before they are presented to the class. If the writing element is added, the technique is referred to as think-*write*-pair-share.

Cooperative learning. Cooperative learning is a specific and structured small group strategy. This strategy usually follows whole class instruction.

Formal lesson. The teacher may present a formal lesson adapted to the needs of a particular group.

Activities Appropriate for Small Groups

Some of the activities that could be used in large groups are also suitable for small groups. Relevant activities mentioned earlier in this chapter are brainstorming, reports, projects, role-playing, or the sharing of performance tasks, products, and portfolios.

Other small group activities include the following:

Fish bowl. This method is particularly effective for having a student explain an idea or point of view. As s/he is communicating his/her point of view, this student sits in one of two chairs facing each other placed in the middle of a circle formed by the rest of the group.

The group must concentrate on what the student is saying. If another student wants to participate in sharing ideas about the first student's ideas, s/he sits in the other chair, and the two have a discussion as the rest of the group listens. Any other student who wishes to participate must wait for the discussion to end, at which time the second chair is vacated and the next student occupies it to continue the discussion.

Buzz session. The buzz session can communicate new content, correct misconceptions, or state or clarify a position. Students are encouraged to express their opinions in an environment where there are no opportunities for them to be ridiculed for their ideas and where there are no right or wrong opinions or answers.

Round table. Students are given the opportunity to discuss content or problems either among themselves or with others observing. Even though there are advantages to using small group instruction, note that there are also disadvantages (McCaslin and Good 1996).

- Students often perceive that they are actually learning because they are enjoying the *process* of learning.
- Students can reinforce misunderstandings rather than correct them.
- Socializing with each other may take precedence over achievement.
- Learning can be passive and incorrect as a student depends on the group leader who is considered by some as a substitute for the teacher.
- Differences in status may be reinforced. Less capable students may think they cannot learn without group support. Non-participants may not contribute as the group progresses without them.

Group Size

The number of students in each group depends upon the purpose for organizing the group, but a general recommendation is that the group should have no more than six members. Too large a group has many of the same disadvantages as those of whole class instruction.

It is also recommended that the teacher have no more than three groups operating at any one time. Each group requires *special planning and monitoring* which could become overwhelming and unmanageable when too many groups are involved.

Roles within Groups

Whatever the grouping arrangement selected, roles should be changed periodically so that no one person takes over and all share responsibilities. Shifting roles adds to the growth of all group members and provides insights into ways each member can be more cooperative. The teacher should monitor the roles undertaken to ensure that the role is understood and implemented properly. If necessary, the teacher should model the role for the student. Then the students should practice the roles before actually implementing them.

The *group guide* makes sure that all members understand goals and directions so that the group keeps on target.

The *supply coordinator* checks that supplies and materials are available when needed. This person is also responsible for distributing and collecting materials.

The *secretary* notes the activities and achievements of all group members and ensures that a time schedule is followed (Lang and Evans 2006).

The *assessment coordinator* constantly examines the progress of both the entire group and of each member individually and, as a result, subsequently suggests adjustments that may be necessary to ensure that group goals are achieved.

Using small groups may be more effective to accommodate the needs of diverse learners. Students who do not have mastery over English, those who are new to the school, students who need to develop friendships, or are from cultures where they do not speak up will do better in the beginning in small groups. Academically-challenged students will also benefit by participating in small groups as long as there are high enough expectations and frequent movement into different groups so that these students are not stigmatized.

INDIVIDUALIZED (INDEPENDENT) INSTRUCTION

Students can work independently for a variety of reasons. These may relate to learning style, or to the need for drill, practice, review, make-up work, or enrichment. When an assignment or activity is tailor-made for a student, s/he will be more inclined to be motivated and responsible for delivering.

Some individualized learning activities include: working at the computer (CAI), working at a learning station (learning activity center), and implementing a learning contract or self-instructional package (mastery learning). If you are not familiar with setting up a learning activity center or implementing a learning contract that contains a self-instructional packet, see Pagliaro 2011.

Research on Class Size

Berns 2011 should be the last in this series of references. The research on class size continues to be inconclusive and conflicting (EdNews 2008; Henry 2008, Jacobson 2008; Mathews 2008; Toppo 2008; Viadero 2008; Berns 2011). The major benefit of small classes seems to be an improved atmosphere (Kelderman 2004). Keep in mind that Bloom (1984) cautioned teachers, *and it cannot be repeated too frequently,* that regardless of the class arrangement or size, the most significant factors that affect student learning are teacher performance and time on task. Bloom's recommendation has been verified by 40 years of research conducted by Eric Hanushek, as reported by Berns (2011).

A report by Cotton (2000) concluded that class size reduction is productive only when the teacher uses effective teaching practices. Her research was further supported by Darling-Hammond and Youngs (2002), who found that gains in student achievement were less influenced by class size and composition than by the assigned teacher. And Kelderman (2004) suggested that an effective teacher with 30 students will improve student achievement more than an ineffective teacher with a class of 18.

More important, however, than class size is that recent research has shown that student achievement is raised when students in the class or group are *closer in age* (Wang 2011).

Chapter Summary: Daily lesson plans develop one of the objectives (or closely related objectives) identified in the unit plan. Teacher productivity is improved by carefully thought-out lesson planning. Differentiating instruction for student needs should be an essential component of the thought process.

In general, two overall approaches are used in planning lessons: the traditional and the constructivist. Both approaches have elements that are common and those that are different. Regardless of the type of plan, instructional implementation should incorporate hands-on, authentic, and personalized experiences with choices available to students.

The Universal Design for Learning, UDL, encourages curricular and instructional choices that teachers should consider *before* actually planning lessons so that re-planning is not necessary. These curricular options include those for representation, expression, and engagement.

Instruction can take place in whole class, small group, and individualized settings as well as in combinations of the three. Each setting has advantages and disadvantages.

Results of class size research connecting with student achievement are inconclusive. What is known, however, is that regardless of class size, teacher performance has the most effect on student achievement.

Read first the traditional lesson plan which follows, "Liquid Measurement," and then the script of its actual implementation. Use Table 7.3, the Coaching Rubric for Lesson Planning and Implementation, to perform an analysis of that plan. Which rubric criteria were implemented and which were not? What are the positive aspects of this lesson? What suggestions would you give the teacher to improve the instruction? How would you plan the original instruction using UDL guidelines? Share your ideas with your colleagues.

Re-write the lesson plan to teach the same concepts using a constructivist approach. To guide you, use Table 7.4, the Coaching Rubric for a Constructivist Lesson Plan, which is presented after the traditional lesson plan script.

Table 7.3. Coaching Rubric for Lesson Planning and Implementation

Criteria (Descriptors)	Performance Indicators (Examples)
The teacher	
analyzed and described students' needs	
GOAL	
flowed from unit's identified standard/ benchmark	
OBJECTIVE(S)	
stated appropriately (observable, outcome-based, student-oriented)	
flowed from goal	
ENTRY SKILLS	
expressed in behavioral (performance) terms	
ANTICIPATORY SET	
provided an interesting and engaging hook	
connected content to prior learning	
led into lesson objective that was restated by several students in their own words	
The teacher,	
displayed objective	
explained how objective was connected to students' lives	
SEQUENCE OF OBJECTIVES	
written in behavioral (performance) terms	
listed in sequential order, when sequence was important	
ASSESSMENT	
expressed clearly for each objective (though one assessment may cover several objectives)	
CORRESPONDING INSTRUCTIONAL STRATEGIES	
matched the sequence of objectives and assessment	
employed several senses	
involved students with hands-on activities	
provided differentiated options	

(Continued)

Table 7.3. *(Continued)*

Criteria (Descriptors)	Performance Indicators (Examples)
MATERIALS	
included multisensory experiences	
connected to students' lives	
included primary sources, when possible	
CLASSROOM ORGANIZATION	
met most appropriately the lesson objective and needs of students	
MODELING	
The teacher	
demonstrated the skills (if the objective was a skill)	
provided examples or products (if the objective was a concept or set of concepts)	
GUIDED PRACTICE reinforced objective by re-teaching it in several different ways	
CLOSURE demonstrated that the students could PERFORM the objective	
INDEPENDENT PRACTICE provided activities that were meaningful to and engaging for students	
EVALUATION OF LEARNING measured the attainment of the lesson objective for each student	
FOLLOW-UP LESSON communicated to class	

TRADITIONAL LESSON PLAN: LIQUID MEASUREMENT, 4TH GRADE

Analytic description of pupils:	Twenty-three students, most on grade level. Six low achievers, four high achievers, an even distribution of auditory, visual, and tactile-kinesthetic learners. Six Latino students (two with LEP). Seven African-American students. Two Asian-American students. Eight Caucasian students.

Learning Standard:	Understands the basic measures perimeter, area, volume, capacity, mass, angle, and circumference, Level II, Grades 3–5 (Kendall and Marzano 1997)
Goal:	To develop the understanding and correct use of volume measurement
Objective(s):	The students will be able to state the relationship among cups, pints, and quarts and identify the abbreviations for each.
Entry skills:	The students are able to discriminate between greater than and less than
Classroom organization:	Whole class
Anticipatory set:	Discussing the students' experiences in a grocery store or supermarket to lead into the importance of liquid measurement
Sequence of objectives:	1. distinguish among cups, pints, and quarts
	2. label cups, pints, and quarts
	3. state that 2 cups equal 1 pint
	4. state that 2 pints equal 1 quart
	5. state that 4 cups equal 1 quart
Assessment:	Objectives 1–2 Observation
	Objectives 3–5 Responses of students after discovery of relationships. Oral quiz before continuing

Corresponding learning experiences:

Objective 1:	students physically separate the cups from the pints from the quarts
Objective 2:	students place the correct label card in front of the corresponding group
Objective 3:	students pour cherry soda from pint container into cups
Objective 4:	students pour orange juice from quart container into pint containers
Objective 5:	students pour tomato juice from quart container into cups
Materials:	Standard transparent measuring cup, pint and quart pitchers, various examples of standard liquid measures (cups, milk cartons, ice cream containers, mayonnaise jars, orange juice containers labeled cup, pint, and quart), water, vegetable coloring, paper cut-outs representing cups, pints, and quarts, laces, worksheets
Modeling of skills:	How to play the game and performing the first example on the worksheet
Guided practice activities:	Playing a game using representative material. Several students chosen to place over their necks a lace attached to one paper cutout of cups, pints, or

quarts. Another student places over the neck a lace attached to a paper cutout of the equal sign. These students come to the front of the room. The teacher puts several expressions on board followed by the equal sign. For each expression a different student in the class is assigned as "it" and arranges the students in the front wearing the symbols so that the symbols on both sides of the equal sign will make a "living" equation followed by a completion of the expressions on the board to form a written equation, and then the same equation using abbreviations.

Closure:	Students go back to objective displayed on board and several of them state the relationship among cups, pints, and quarts without referring to equations still on board.
Independent practice activities:	Worksheet
Evaluation of learning:	Answers to questions. Success in completing worksheet
Instructional accommodation/ modification:	Lower achievers—reminder in worksheet, pictures in worksheet, role playing as cups, pints, quarts, and equal sign. Higher achievers—state relationships after pouring activities, challenge question in worksheet. Visual learners—different vegetable colors to represent cherry soda, orange and tomato juice, seeing paper cutouts in game and pictures in worksheet. Auditory learners—listening to questions and answers in development of relationships and in feedback. Tactile-kinesthetic—pouring liquids. No instructional modifications necessary.
Follow-up lesson:	Making pink lemonade
Other ways to teach modification:	Setting up learning activity centers for individualized instruction or working in small groups using the same materials

Traditional Lesson Plan Implementation

Teacher:	Boys and girls, how many of you have ever gone to a grocery store or supermarket? (All hands go up.)
Teacher:	That's great, what did you buy?
	(Students begin to name what they bought. Whenever a liquid is mentioned, the teacher lists it on the board.)
Teacher:	(Points to list) How are all these items that you bought the same? George.
George:	They're all liquids.

Teacher:	That's right, George. (Teacher writes the title "Liquids" above the list.) And because we have all bought liquids, it is important for you to know how to measure liquids. So what are we going to learn today? Marilyn.
Marilyn:	How to measure liquids.
Teacher:	And, Marilyn, why is it important that we know how to measure liquids?
Marilyn:	Because we've all bought them.
Teacher:	Thank you, Marilyn. And in particular all of you should know how some of the measures we use—cups, pints, and quarts—are related to each other, and since they're sometimes written on the containers as abbreviations, and we're studying abbreviations in language arts, we'll identify those abbreviations also. (Teacher writes on the board, Objective: To state how cups, pints, and quarts are related and to state their abbreviations.) I want several of you to restate the objective in your own words. Luis.
Luis:	How are liquids measured?
Teacher:	Excellent, Luis, but be more specific.
Luis:	How are cups, pints, and quarts related?
Teacher:	Great, Luis. Now who can tell us our objective in another way? Inez.
Inez:	We're going to find out how to measure liquids we buy, especially cups, pints, and quarts, and find out what their abbreviations are.
Teacher:	Very good. (Teacher then proceeds to place on a demonstration table an assortment of different liquid containers.) I need a volunteer to come up and take all the largest containers and put them on the side to form a group. (Everyone volunteers.) Regina. (Regina comes to the front of the room, examines the containers, and places the largest ones to the side.)
Teacher:	Thank you, Regina. Now I need someone else to find the smallest containers and put them on the opposite side. (All, including Regina, volunteer.) Tyrone. (Tyrone pulls the small containers out of the remaining pile and moves them to the side of the demonstration table opposite from where the largest are placed.) Good job, Tyrone. Now all we have left are the medium size containers in the center. (Teacher pushes the medium size containers together, then points to each relevant group.) Small, medium, large. (Teacher takes out labels. She holds up the quart label.) Who can put this label in front of the correct group? (Most students raise hands.) Mimi. But before you put the label in front of the group, how will you decide? (Mimi looks at all the groups, pauses for a moment.)
Mimi:	I'm not sure. Maybe it's written on the containers?
Teacher:	Fine, go ahead and read the print. (Mimi reads the print on each container. She then places the quart label in front of the largest group.
Teacher:	What can you tell us about the quarts, Mimi?
Mimi:	They're the largest.

Teacher:	Good work. Now who can put this label in front of the correct group? (Teacher holds up the cup label. Most hands go up.) Vinny. (Vinny checks the last two groups and places the label in front of the group of smallest containers.) Did all the containers say cups?
Vinny:	Yes.
Teacher:	Thank you, Vinny. Tell me class, what label do you think I have left that will go in front of the medium size group? Viola.
Viola:	The pints?
Teacher:	You don't seem so sure. Come up and check. (Viola checks the print on the containers in the remaining group in the middle.)
Viola:	I was right. They're pints. (Teacher hands Viola the last label and she places it in front of the medium size group of containers.)
Teacher:	Take some time to look at these groups again. When you are sure you know the difference among the cups, pints, and quarts, raise your hand. (One by one all hands are up. Who can summarize what we just did? Consuela.
Consuela:	We put labels in front of the groups.
Teacher:	You're right. Which group has the smallest containers?
Consuela:	Cups.
Teacher:	The medium size?
Consuela:	Pints.
Teacher:	And what can we say about the quarts?
Consuela:	They're the biggest.
Teacher:	You were really paying attention, Consuela, thanks. (Teacher holds up a transparent pint pitcher and two cups filled with red liquid.) Suppose I offered you cherry soda in either this pint container or in these two cups. Which would you take? Darren.
Darren:	I'd take the two cups.
Teacher:	Why?
Darren:	It's more. (Several hands wave furiously. Teacher calls on a student whose hand is not up.) Frank.
Frank:	I think the taller one, the pints, is larger.
Teacher:	How many agree with Frank? (Three hands are raised.)
Frank:	Wait a minute, I think they might both be the same.
Teacher:	Let's find out. Come up, Frank. (Teacher has Frank pour the two cherry soda cups into the quart container which the two cups fill.) What did you find out?
Frank:	I was right. They're the same.
Teacher:	So what's the relationship between cups and pints?
Frank:	Two cups is the same as a pint.
Teacher:	Nice going, Frank. (Teacher writes under the objective the equation, 2 cups = 1 pint on the board, then writes directly underneath 2 c. = 1 pt.) (Goes back to Darren) Darren, would you still take two cups?
Darren:	Guess it doesn't matter; they're the same.
Teacher:	You're right, Darren. Let's all say this together. (She points to the first equation. The class repeats, 2 cups = 1 pint.) Close your eyes

and make a picture in your mind of what Frank just did. (Teacher gives the class some time to make a mental picture.) With your eyes still closed, raise your hand when you can tell me the equation. (Teacher waits. Soon all hands are up.) Anita.

Anita: 2 cups = 1 pint.

Teacher: Say it another way, Yen.

Yen: 1 pint is the same as 2 cups.

Teacher: Wow, that's great. Now suppose, class, you asked the grocer for a quart of orange juice and he didn't have a quart container and gave you two pints instead. Thumbs up if you think he did the right thing. (Slowly, most thumbs are up. Some students look around to see if the other students are holding thumbs up or down.)

Teacher: Let's find out. (Teacher calls on a student whose thumb was not up.) Come up, Rich. (Teacher has Rich pour two orange-colored pint containers into the quart container.) Well, Rich?

Rich: They're the same amount. (Teacher writes on board under the other equations, ___ pints = ___ quarts and asks Rich to fill in the equation. When he writes 2 in the first blank and 1 in the second, the teacher erases the 's' in the word quarts and then rewrites the same equation underneath using abbreviations.)

Teacher: Thanks, Rich. Close your eyes, everyone, and keep in mind what Rich just did. When you remember his equation, thumbs up. (When all thumbs are up, teacher calls six children to the front of the room and gives each a cup. She then holds up a quart pitcher filled with a red liquid.) Suppose this quart pitcher contains a quart of tomato juice. How many children will get a cup of tomato juice? (Students estimate. Some say six, some say five, others, four. Then the teacher calls a student to pour the red liquid out of the quart container into the cups.) How many cups could you fill with the quart pitcher, Ginny?

Ginny: Four.

Teacher: Tell me that as an equation.

Ginny: A quart equals four cups.

Teacher: Say it another way.

Ginny: 4 cups equal a quart. (Teacher writes under the equations already listed, 4 cups = 1 quart, then writes underneath the same equation using abbreviations.) For the last time, make a mental picture of what Ginny did. Then close your eyes and thumbs up when you remember the equation. (Most thumbs go up.) Alan.

Alan: 4 cups equal 1 quart.

Teacher: Correct. I want all of you to look at the equations on the board and see if there are any you don't understand. (The teacher waits.) Let's find out. (Teacher then proceeds to walk around the room asking the following questions calling on different students.)
           How many pints in a quart?
           How many cups in a quart?

How many cups in a pint?

One quart equals how many cups?

One pint equals how many cups?

One quart equals how many pints?

Two quarts equals how many pints?

You seem to know the liquid measures very well, but I want you to close your eyes and think of what we just did. When you believe you can visualize what we did to find our relationships, then make sure you know what they are. I'll give you enough time. (Teacher waits.) Let's play a game. (The teacher calls on nine students. To four of them she hands out cup symbols with laces they place around their necks. Two more students place quart symbols, and two others place pint symbols around their necks. One student wears the equal sign around his neck. The teacher lines the students on the side of the room. While they are moving to the side, the teacher erases the equations on the board, leaving the lesson objective visible. The teacher writes on the board 2 pt. = ___qt(s). and calls on a seated student to be "it." That student must rearrange the students wearing the symbols to make the equation correct. Then that student completes the written equation on the board. Several other students are selected to be "it." Other equations the teacher writes are:

____ cups = 1 pt.

____ pt(s) = 2 cups

1 qt. = ____ pt(s).)

Teacher: You all performed very well today. So let's go back to our objective. (Teacher points to it.) Read it please, Beverly.

Beverly: To state how cups, pints, and quarts are related and to state their abbreviations.

Teacher: O.K. Can you give me one way that pints and quarts are related, Beverly?

Beverly: Uh, two pints equals one quart.

Teacher: Correct, and who can tell me how cups and pints are related? Jeff.

Jeff: Two cups equal one pint.

Teacher: Very good. How about cups and quarts? Jeff.

Jeff: Four cups equals one quart.

Teacher: Great, Jeff. Let's now go to the abbreviations. What is the abbreviation for cups? Lucille.

Lucille: c

Teacher: And what always follows the abbreviation?

Lucille: Sorry, c period.

Teacher: Fine, and what is the abbreviation for pints? Shelly.

Shelly: Pt period.

Teacher: Right, Shelly, so why don't you call on someone who has not had a chance to answer yet to tell us what the last abbreviation is, quarts. (Shelly calls on Jack.)

Jack: Qt period.

Teacher: Congratulations to all of you for learning the objective. (Teacher distributes worksheet, Figure 7.3.) Since you all did so well, tomorrow we'll use what we learned today to make pink lemonade and some other drinks you might like. Just bring in your recipes. Begin working on your worksheet. If you finish it before lunch, continue working on building your vocabulary game. If you don't finish the worksheet before lunch, complete the worksheet for homework.

Name_____

Liquid Measurement

Remember: 2 cups (c.) = 1 pint (pt.)
2 pints (pt.) = 1 quart (qt.)
4 cups (c.) = 1 quart (qt.)

Look at the pictures. Fill in the blanks.

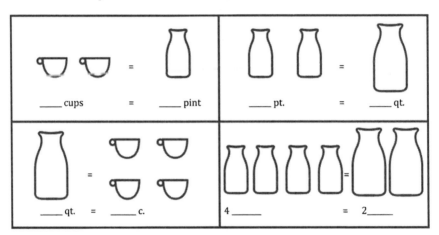

_____ cups   =   _____ pint

_____ pt.   =   _____ qt.

_____ qt.   =   _____ c.

4 _____   =   2 _____

Fill in the blank spaces.
1. 2 c. = _____
2. 2 _____ = 1 qt.
3. 4 c. = _____ qt.
4. 2 cups + 1 cup = _____ cups
5. 1 pint + 1 cup = _____ cups

Challenge (Use abbreviations.)
1. Mrs. Wilson poured 8 cups of tomato juice for her family. Is this more or less than a pint? _____
2. Joan drinks 1 qt. of milk a day. How many pt. would that be? _____
3. Eddie's mother bought 8 pt. of sour cream. How many qt. would that be? _____
4. 1 c. = _____pt.

Figure 7.3.

Table 7.4.   Coaching Rubric for a Constructivist Lesson Plan

Criteria (Descriptors)	*Performance Indicators (Examples)*
The teacher	
diagnosed student needs (readiness, interest, learning style)	
reflected on what students should be able to do (content, skills, attitudes)	
reflected on how students would make meaning of the content, skills, attitudes	
designed a situation (problem) based on student needs	
designed a process for grouping students according to needs and available materials	
planned a bridge based on what students already know to connect with new knowledge they should learn (content, skills, attitudes)	
planned questions to set up the bridge	
planned questions to assess students' comprehension of what they were expected to learn	
designed an exhibit (product) to document what the students learned	
allowed students to explain their products to the class	

References

INTRODUCTION

Haycock, K. 1998. Good teaching matters . . . a lot. *Thinking K–16,* 3(2):1–14.

Joyce, B., and B. Showers, 2002. *Student achievement through staff development.* 3rd ed. Alexandria, VA: Association for Supervision and Curriculum Development.

Lavoie, R. 2005a. *Beyond F.A.T. city: A look back, a look ahead.* Alexandria, VA: PBS Video.

Lavoie, R. 2005b. *It's so much work to be your friend: Helping the child with learning disabilities find social success.* New York: Touchstone/Simon and Schuster.

Marzano, R. 2003. *What works in schools.* Alexandria, VA: Association for Supervision and Curriculum Development.

Marzano, R. 2007. *The art and science of teaching: A comprehensive framework for effective instruction.* Alexandria, VA: Association for Supervision and Curriculum Development.

National Commission on Teaching and America's Future. 1996. *What matters most: Teaching for America's future.* New York: Carnegie Foundation.

Pappano, L. 2011. Using research to predict great teachers. *Harvard Education Letter* 27 (May/June):3.

Pipho, C. 1998. The value-added side of standards. *Phi Delta Kappan* (January): 341–42.

Popham, W. J. 2008. *Transformative assessment.* Alexandria, VA: Association for Supervision and Curriculum Development.

Popham, W. J. 2011. *Transformative assessment in action: An inside look at applying the process.* Alexandria, VA: Association for Supervision and Curriculum Development.

Sanders, W., and J. Rivers. 1996. *Cumulative and residual effects of teachers on future student academic achievement.* Research progress report. Knoxville: University of Tennessee Value-Added Research and Assessment Center.

Silver, H., R. Strong, and M. Perini. 2007. *The strategic teacher: Selecting the right research-based strategy for every lesson.* Alexandria, VA: Association for Supervision and Curriculum Development.

Stiggins, R. 2005. *Student-involved assessment FOR learning.* Fourth ed. Upper Saddle River, NJ: Pearson/Merrill Prentice Hall.

Tomlinson, C., and J. McTighe. 2006. *Integrating differentiated instruction and understanding by design.* Alexandria, VA: Association for Supervision and Curriculum Development.

Viadero, D. 2009. Top-notch teachers found to affect peers. *Education Week.* (September 1) 26(3):1, 12.

Wiggins, G. 2005. *Educative assessment.* Second ed. Alexandria, VA: Association for Supervision and Curriculum Development.

Wiggins, G., and J. McTighe. 2005. *Understanding by design.* Second ed. Prentice Hall.

Wiggins, G., and J. McTighe.. 2011. *The understanding by design guide to creating high-quality units.* Alexandria, VA: Association for Supervision and Curriculum Development.

Wright, S., S. Horn, and W. Sanders. 1997. Teacher and classroom context effects on student achievement: Implications for teacher evaluation. *Journal of Personnel Evaluation in Education* 11:57–67.

CHAPTER 1 LEARNING THEORY: A FOUNDATION FOR IMPLEMENTING ALL CURRICULUM AND INSTRUCTION

Airasian, P. W., and M. E. Walsh. 1997. Cautions for classroom constructivists. *Education Digest* (April): 62–68.

Armstrong, T. 2000. *Multiple intelligences in the classroom.* Second ed. Alexandria, VA: Association for Supervision and Curriculum Development.

Ausubel, D. P. 1963. *The psychology of meaningful verbal learning.* New York: Grune and Stratton.

Brandt, R. 1998. *Powerful learning.* Alexandria, VA: Association for Supervision and Curriculum Development.

Bransford, J., A. Brown, and R. Cocking, eds. 2000. *How people learn: Brain, mind, experience, and school.* Washington, DC: National Academy Press.

Breaden, M. 2008. Researchers examine importance of learning from 'explaining'. *Education Week* (January 30) 27(21):5.

Brophy, J.E. 1988. *On motivating students.* In Talks to teachers, ed. D. Berliner and B. Rosenshine, 201–245. New York: Random House.

Bruner, J.S. 1966. *Toward a theory of instruction.* New York: Norton.

Caine, R.N., and G. Caine. 1994. *Making connections: Teaching and the human brain.* Menlo Park, CA: Addison Wesley.

Checkley, K. 1997. The first seven . . . and the eighth: A conversation with Howard Gardner. *Educational Leadership* (September) 55(1): 8–13.

Covington, M. V. 1992. *Making the grade: A self-worth perspective on motivation and school reform.* New York: Cambridge University Press.

Covington, M.V., and C. L. Omelich. 1987. "I knew it cold before the exam": A test of the anxiety-blockage hypothesis. *Journal of Educational Psychology* 79: 393–400.

Cruickshank, D., D. B. Jenkins, and K. Metcalf. 2003. *The art of teaching.* Third ed. Boston: McGraw-Hill.

Csikszentmihalyi, M. 1990. *Flow: The psychology of optimal experience.* New York: Harper and Row.

Deci, E.L., and R. M. Ryan. 1985. *Intrinsic motivation and self-determination in human behavior.* New York: Plenum.

Diamond, M. 1997. *The brain, the mind, and the classroom.* Audiotape #296282. Alexandria, VA: Association for Supervision and Curriculum Development.

Diamond, M., and J. Hopson. 1998. *Magic trees of the mind: How to nurture your child's intelligence, creativity, and healthy emotions from birth through adolescence.* New York: Dutton.

Dweck, C. 2010. Mind-sets and equitable education. *Principal Leadership* (January): 26–29.

Eisner, E. W. 1998. *The kinds of schools we need: Personal essays.* Portsmouth, NH: Heinemann.

Elawar, M.C., and L. Corno. 1985. A factorial experiment in teachers' written feedback on student homework: Changing teacher behavior a little rather than a lot. *Journal of Educational Psychology* 77:162–173.

Ellis, A. 2001. *Research on educational innovations.* Third ed. Larchmont, NY: Eye on Education.

Erwin, J. 2004. *The classroom of choice: Giving students what they need and getting what you want.* Alexandria, VA: Association for Supervision and Curriculum Development.

Ewy, C. 2003. *Teaching with visual frameworks.* Thousand Oaks, CA: Corwin Press.

Foote, C. J., P. J. Vermette, and C. F. Battaglia. 2001. *Constructivist strategies: Meeting standards and engaging adolescent minds.* Larchmont, NY: Eye on Education.

Franklin, J. 2005. Mental mileage: How teachers are putting brain research to use. *Education Update* (June) 47:6. Association for Supervision and Curriculum Development.

Gagne, R. M. 1977. *The conditions of learning* . Third ed.. New York: Holt, Rinehart, and Winston.

Gallagher, K. 2010. Why I will not teach to the test. *Education Week* (November 17) 30(12):29, 36.

Gardner, H. 1999. *Intelligence reframed: Multiple intelligences for the twenty-first century.* New York: Basic Books.

Gardner, H. 1998. A multiplicity of intelligences. *Scientific American Presents,* 9(4): 18–23.

Gardner, H. 1995. Reflections on multiple intelligences: Myths and messages. *Phi Delta Kappan* (November) 77(3):202–209.

Gergen, K. J. 1994. *Realities and relationships: Soundings in social construction.* Cambridge, MA: Harvard University Press.

Gergen, K. J. 1985. The social constructionist movement in modern psychology. *American Psychologist* 40:266–275.

Green, F. L. 1999. Brain and learning research: Implications for meeting the needs of diverse learners. *Education* 119:4.

Hyerle, D. 1996. *Visual tools for constructing knowledge.* Alexandria, VA: Association for Supervision and Curriculum Development.

Jensen, E. 1998. *Teaching with the brain in mind.* Alexandria, VA: Association for Supervision and Curriculum Development.

Jensen, E. 2005. *Teaching with the brain in mind.* Second ed. Alexandria, VA: Association for Supervision and Curriculum Development.

LeDoux, J. 1996. *The emotional brain: The mysterious underpinnings of emotional life.* New York: Simon and Schuster.

Marzano, R. 2002. *Research-based strategies for increasing student achievement.* Audiotape #203062. Alexandria, VA: Association for Supervision and Curriculum Development.

Marzano, R. 2003. *What works in schools.* Alexandria, VA: Association for Supervision and Curriculum Development.

Marzano, R. 2007. *The art and science of teaching: A comprehensive framework for effective instruction.* Alexandria, VA: Association for Supervision and Curriculum Development.

Marzano, R., D. Paynter, and J. Doty, 2003. *The pathfinder project: Exploring the power of one: Teacher's manual.* Conifer, CO: Pathfinder.

Mumford, M. D., D. P. Costanza, W. A. Baughman. V. Threlfall, and E. A. Fleishman. 1994. Influence of abilities on performance during practice: Effects of massed and distributed practice. *Journal of Educational Psychology* 86:134–144.

Nuthall, G. 1999. The way students learn: Acquiring knowledge from an integrated science and social studies unit. *Elementary School Journal* 99(4):303–341.

Oakes, J., and Lipton, M. 2003. *Teaching to change the world,* Second ed. New York: McGraw-Hill.

Palincsar, A. S. 1998. Social constructivist perspectives on teaching and learning. In *Annual Review of Psychology,* ed. J. T. Spence, J. M. Darley, and D. J. Foss, 345–375. Palo Alto, CA: Annual Reviews.

Phillips, D. 1997. How, why, what, when, and where: Perspectives on constructivism and education. *Issues in Education: Contributions from Educational Psychology* 3: 151–194.

Riding, R. J., and S. G. Rayner. 1998. *Cognitive styles and learning strategies: Understanding style differences in learning behaviour.* London: David Fulton.

Rosenthal, R., and L. Jacobson. 1968. *Pygmalion in the classroom.* New York: Holt, Rinehart, and Winston.

Salomon, G., and D. Perkins. 1989. Rocky roads to transfer: Rethinking mechanisms of a neglected phenomenon. *Educational Psychologist* 24:113–142.

Silver, H., R. Strong, and M. Perini. 2000. *So each may learn: Integrating learning styles and multiple intelligences.* Alexandria, VA: Association for Supervision and Curriculum Development.

Sousa, D. 2001. *How the brain learns.* Second ed. Thousand Oaks, CA: Corwin Press.

Sousa, D. 2006. *How the brain learns.* Third ed. Thousand Oaks, CA: Corwin Press.

Stansbury, M. 2008. 'Learning' replaces 'teaching'. eSchool News (March 21).

Sternberg, R. 1990. *Metaphors of mind: Conceptions of the nature of intelligence.* New York: Cambridge University Press.

Sternberg R., and J. Kaufman.1998. Human abilities. In *Annual Review of Psychology,* ed. J. T. Spence, J. M. Darley, and D. J. Foss, 479–502. Palo Alto, CA: Annual Reviews.

Sylwester, R. 2000. *A biological brain in a cultural classroom: Applying biological research to classroom management.* Thousand Oaks, CA: Corwin Press.

Tate, M. 2003. *Engage the brain: Graphic organizers and other visual strategies.* Thousand Oaks, CA: Corwin Press.

Weiss, R. 2007. Gestures convey message: Learning in progress. *The Washington Post* (August 6),A06.

Wolfe, P. 2001a. Brain research: Fad or foundation? Audiotape #201099. Alexandria, VA: Association for Supervision and Curriculum Development.

Wolfe, P. 2001b. *Brain matters: Translating research into classroom practice.* Alexandria, VA: Association for Supervision and Curriculum Development.

Woolfolk, A. 2008. *Educational psychology.* Tenth ed. Boston: Pearson Education.

CHAPTER 2 IMPLEMENTING CURRICULUM AND INSTRUCTIONAL PLANNING SKILLS

Brookhart, S. M. 2004. *Grading.* Upper Saddle River, NJ: Pearson Education.

Danielson, C. 2007. *Enhancing professional practice: A framework for teaching.* 2nd ed. Alexandria, VA: Association for Supervision and Curriculum Development.

Danielson, C. 2006. *Teacher leadership that strengthens professional practice.* Alexandria, VA: Association for Supervision and Curriculum Development.

Danielson, C., and L. Abrutyn. 1997. *An introduction to using portfolios in the classroom.* Alexandria, VA: Association for Supervision and Curriculum Development.

Danielson, C., and T. McGreal. 2000. *Teacher evaluation to enhance professional practice.* Alexandria, VA: Association for Supervision and Curriculum Development.

Delpit, L. 1995. *Other people's children: Cultural conflict in the classroom.* New York: The New Press.

Good, T., and J. Brophy. 1974. Changing teacher and student behavior: An empirical investigation. *Journal of Educational Psychology* 66:390–405.

Hook, C., and B. Rosenshine. 1979. Accuracy of teacher reports of their classroom behavior. *Review of Educational Research* 49: 1–12.

Joyce, B., and B. Showers. 1995. *Student achievement through staff development.* Second ed. New York: Longman.

Joyce, B, and B. Showers. 2002. *Student achievement through staff development.* Third ed. Alexandria, VA: Association for Supervision and Curriculum Development.

Lazear, D. 1998. *The rubrics way: Using MI to assess understanding.* Tuscon, AZ: Zephyr Press.

Pianta, R. 2007. Measure actual classroom teaching. *Education Week* (Nov 6): http://www.edweek.org/ew/articles/2007/11/07/11pianta.

Reiman, A., and L. Thies-Sprinthall. 1998. *Mentoring and supervision for teacher development.* New York: Longman.

Sadker, M., and Sadker, D. 1994. *Failing at fairness: How America's schools cheat girls.* New York: Scribner.

Welch, J. 2000. *GE strategy and performance . . . as reported to share owners 1980 to 2000.* Fairfield, CT: GE Corporation.

Wiggins, G. 1998. *Educative assessment: Designing assessments to inform and improve student performance.* San Francisco: Jossey-Bass.

Wiggins, G. 2005. *Educative assessment.* Second ed. Alexandria, VA: Association for Supervision and Curriculum Development.

Wolfe, P. 2001, *Brain matters: Translating research into classroom practice.* Alexandria, VA: Association for Supervision and Curriculum Development.

CHAPTER 3 ASSESSMENT/EVALUATION OF LEARNING

Airasian, P. 1994. **Classroom management.** Second ed. New York: McGraw-Hill.

Bangert-Drowns, R., J. Kulik, and C. Kulik. 1991. Effects of frequent classroom testing. *Journal of Educational Research* 85: 88–99.

Carr, J. and D. Harris. 2001. *Succeeding with standards: Linking curriculum, assessment, and action planning.* Alexandria, VA: Association for Supervision and Curriculum Development. pp. 15–18. Colorado Springs, CO: PEAK Parent Center, Inc.

Danielson, C., and L. Abrutyn. 1997. *An introduction to using portfolios in the classroom.* Alexandria, VA: Association for Supervision and Curriculum Development.

Fadel, C., M. Honey, and S. Pasnik. 2007. Assessment in the age of innovation. *Education Week* 26(38) (May 23): 34, 40.

Ferlazzo, L. 2011. My students help assess my teaching. (January 11): www.edweek.org. Guskey, T. R. 1996. Reporting on student learning: Lessons from the past—Prescriptions for the future. In Communicating student learning; 1996 ASCD Yearbook, ed. T. R. Guskey, 13–24. Alexandria, VA: Association for Supervision and Curriculum Development.

Kendall, J. S. 2011. and Marzano, R. 1997. *Content knowledge: A compendium of standards and benchmarks for K–12 education.* Online ed. Retrieved from http://www.mcrel.org/standards-benchmarks/.

Kika, F., T. McLaughlin, and J. Dixon. 1992. Effects of frequent testing of secondary algebra students. *Journal of Educational Research* 85:159–162.

Marzano, R. J. 2000. *Transforming classroom grading.* Alexandria, VA: Association for Supervision and Curriculum Development.

Marzano, R. J. 2006. *Classroom assessment and grading that work.* Alexandria, VA: Association for Supervision and Curriculum Development.

Meyer, C. A. 1992. What's the difference between authentic and performance assessment? *Educational Leadership* 49 (May):39–40.

Mitchell, R. 1992. *Testing for learning: How new approaches to evaluation can improve American schools.* New York: The Free Press.

Popham, W. J. 2007. Accountability tests' instructional insensitivity: The time bomb ticketh. *Education Week* (November 13)*:* http://www.edweek.org/ew/articles/2007/11/14/12popham

Popham, W. J. 2008. *Transformative assessment.* Alexandria, VA: Association for Supervision and Curriculum Development.

Popham, W.J. 2011. *Transformative assessment in action: An inside look at applying the process.* Alexandria, VA: Association for Supervision and Curriculum Development.

Ryan, C. 1994. *Authentic assessment.* Westminster, CA.: Teacher Created Materials.

Stiggins, R. 2002. Assessment crisis: The absence of assessment FOR learning. *Phi Delta Kappan* 83(10):758–765.

Stiggins, R. 2005. *Student-involved assessment FOR learning.* Fourth ed. Upper Saddle River, NJ: Pearson/Merrill Prentice Hall.

Stiggins, R. 2007. Assessment through the student's eyes. *Educational Leadership* 64(8) (May):22–26.

Taggert, G. L., S. J. Phifer, J. Nixon, and M. Wood. 1998. *Rubrics: A handbook for construction and use.* Lancaster, PA: Technomic.

Tomlinson, C., and C. Eidson, 2003. *Differentiating in practice: A resource guide for differentiating curriculum, K–5.* Alexandria,VA: Association for Supervision and Curriculum Development.

Tomlinson, C., and J. McTighe, 2006. *Integrating differentiated instruction and understanding by design.* Alexandria, VA: Association for Supervision and Curriculum Development.

Wiggins, G. 1998. *Educative assessment: Designing assessments to inform and improve student performance.* San Francisco: Jossey-Bass.

Wiggins, G. 2005. *Educative assessment.* Second ed. Alexandria, VA: Association for Supervision and Curriculum Development.

Wiggins, G., and J. McTighe, 1998. *Understanding by design.* Alexandria, VA: Association for Supervision and Curriculum Development.

Wiggins, G., and J. McTighe, 2005. *Understanding by design.* Second ed. Prentice Hall.

Wilcox, J. 2006. Less teaching, more assessing. *Education Update* 48(3) (February). Alexandria, VA: Association for Supervision and Curriculum Development.

CHAPTER 4 REVIEWING UNIT
AND LESSON PLANNING BASICS

Allen, R. 2009. Has the time come for national standards? *ASCD Infobrief* 15(2).

Anderson, L. W., D. R. Krathwohl, P. W. Airasian, K. A. Cruikshank, R. E. Mayer, P. R. Pintrich, J. Raths, and M. C. Wittrock. 2001. *A taxonomy for learning, teaching, and assessing: A revision of Bloom's taxonomy of educational objectives.* New York:Longman.

Bloom, B., M. Englehart, E. Furst, W. Hill, and D. Krathwohl. 1956. *Taxonomy of educational objectives: The classification of educational goals Handbook I, Cognitive domain.* New York: McKay.

Buchen, I. H. 2004. The rise of the 'parentariat'. *Education Week* 24(6):31.

Caine, R. N., and G. Caine. 1994. *Making connections: Teaching and the human brain.* Second ed. Menlo Park, CA: Addison-Wesley.

Carr, J. F., and D. E. Harris. 2001. *Succeeding with standards: Linking curriculum, assessment, and action planning.* Alexandria, VA: Association for Supervision and Curriculum Development.

Cavanagh, S. 2006. Network sponsors worldwide sharing of curricula. *Education Week* 25(22) (February 8):10.

Ciurczak, E. 2011. Officials in 48 states are working to develop standardized tests that are aligned with common core standards. *The Hattiesburg American* (April 26): hattiesburgamerican.com

Cotton, K. 2000. *The schooling practices that matter most.* Alexandria, VA: Association for Supervision and Curriculum Development.

Cummings, C. 2000. *Winning strategies for classroom management.* Alexandria, VA: Association for Supervision and Curriculum Development.

Dillon, S. 2011. Bipartisan group backs common school curriculum. *The New York Times* (March 7):A12.

Frisby, B. and M. Martin,. 2010. Instructor-student and student-student rapport in the classroom. *Communication Education* 59(2) (April):146–164.

Gewertz, C. 2008. States press ahead on 'twenty-first-century skills'. *Education Week* (28) 8 (October): 15, 21, 23.

Glatthorn, A. 1999. *Performance standards and authentic learning.* Larchmont, NY: Eye on Education.

Gronlund, N. 2004. *Writing instructional objectives for teaching and assessment.,* 7th ed. Upper Saddle River, NJ: Pearson.

Harrow, A. J. 1977. *Taxonomy of the psychomotor domain.* New York: Longman.

Jacobs, H. 1997. *Mapping the big picture: Integrating curriculum and assessment K–12.* Alexandria, VA: Association for Supervision and Curriculum Development.

Jacobs, H., and A. Johnson, 2009. *The curriculum mapping planner: Templates, tools, and resources for effective professional development.* Alexandria, VA: Association for Supervision and Curriculum Development.

Jacobs, H., ed. 2010. *Curriculum 21: Essential Education for a Changing World.* Alexandria, VA: Association for Supervision and Curriculum Development.

Jensen, E. 2005. *Teaching with the brain in mind.* Second ed. Alexandria, VA: Association for Supervision and Curriculum Development.

Kendall, J. S., and R. J. Marzano. 1997. *Content knowledge: A compendium of standards and benchmarks for K–12 education.* Second ed. Alexandria, VA: Association for Supervision and Curriculum Development.

Kohn, A. 2000. *Beyond the standards movement: Defending quality education in an age of test scores.* Videotape. Port Chester, NY: National Professional Resources.

Krathwohl, D., B. Bloom, and B. Masia, 1964. *Taxonomy of educational objectives: The classification of educational goals, Handbook II, Affective domain.* New York: McKay.

Lavin, M. 2011. Elementary, my dears: The relationship between motivation and learning. *San Mateo County Times* (May 29):3–4.

Mager, R. F. 1997. *Preparing instructional objectives: A critical tool in the development of effective instruction.* Third ed. Atlanta: Center for Effective Performance.

Mager, R. F. 1984. *Preparing instructional objectives.* Second ed. Belmont, CA: David S. Lake.

Marzano, R. J. 2001. *Designing a new taxonomy of educational objectives.* Thousand Oaks, CA: Corwin Press.

Marzano, R. J. 2003. *What works in schools: Translating research into action.* Alexandria, VA: Association for Supervision and Curriculum Development.

Marzano, R. J., and J. S. Kendall, 2007. *The new taxonomy of educational objectives.* 2nd ed. Thousand Oaks, CA: Corwin Press.

Oakes, J., and M. Lipton, 2003. *Teaching to change the world.* Second ed. New York: Mc Graw-Hill.

Reynolds, D., and C. Teddlie, 2000. The process of school effectiveness. In *The International Handbook of School Effectiveness Research,* ed. C. Teddlie and D. Reynolds, 134–159. New York: Falmer Press.

Secretary's Commission on Achieving Necessary Skills. 1991. *What work requires of schools: A SCANS report for America 2000.* U.S. Department of Labor.

Sylwester, R. 2000. *A biological brain in a cultural classroom: Applying biological research to classroom management.* Thousand Oaks, CA: Corwin Press.

Tucker, M. S., and J. B. Codding,. 1998. *Standards for our schools: How to set them, measure them, and reach them.* San Francisco: Jossey-Bass.

U.S. Department of Education. 1994. *Strong families, strong schools: Building community partnerships for learning.* Washington, DC: Author.

Zuckerbrod, N. 2007. Study examines public, private schools. (October 10):Boston.com.

CHAPTER 5 MAXIMIZING UNIT PLANNING FOR STUDENT ACHIEVEMENT

ben Shea, N. 2002. *Great quotes to inspire great teachers.* Thousand Oaks, CA: Corwin Press.

Bloom, B., J. Hastings, and G. Madaus. 1971. *Handbook on formative and summative evaluation of student learning.* New York: McGraw-Hill.

Brooks, J., and M. Brooks. 1999. *In search of understanding: The case for constructivist classrooms.* Alexandria, VA: Association for Supervision and Curriculum Development.

Cavanagh, S. Playing games in classroom helping pupils grasp math. *Education Week* (2008, April 29):http://www.edweek.org/ew/articles/2008/04/30/35games.

Cotton, K. 2000. *The schooling practices that matter most.* Alexandria, VA: Association for Supervision and Curriculum Development.

Covey, S. 2004. *The 8th habit: From effectiveness to greatness.* New York: Free Press.

Cummings, C. 2000. *Winning strategies for classroom management.* Alexandria, VA: Association for Supervision and Curriculum Development.

Dale, E. 1969. *Audio-visual methods in teaching.* New York: Holt, Rinehart, and Winston.

Downey, G. Six ed-tech trends to watch in 2007. (December 2006) eSchool Newsonline.

Ewy, C. 2003. *Teaching with visual frameworks.* Thousand Oaks, CA: Corwin Press.

Fogarty, R. 1999. *How to raise test scores.* Arlington Heights, IL: Skylight.

Freedman, S. 2007. *New class(room) war: Teacher vs. technology. The New York Times* (November 7):6.

Glater, J. D. 2006. Colleges chase as cheats shift to higher tech. *The New York Times* (May 18):8–9.

Hyerle, D. 1996. *Visual tools for constructing knowledge.* Alexandria, VA: Association for Supervision and Curriculum Development.

Hyerle, D., ed. 2004. *Student successes with thinking maps.* Thousand Oaks, CA: Corwin Press.

Jacobs, H. 1997. *Mapping the big picture: Integrating curriculum and assessment, K–12.* Alexandria, VA: Association for Supervision and Curriculum Development.

Jensen, E. 2005. *Teaching with the brain in mind.* Second ed. Alexandria, VA: Association for Supervision and Curriculum Development.

Kellough, R., and J. Carjuzaa, 2006. *Teaching in the middle and secondary school.,* Eighth ed. Upper Saddle River, NJ: Pearson/Merrill Prentice Hall.

Kendall, J. S., and R. J. Marzano.. 1997. *Content knowledge: A compendium of standards and benchmarks for K-12 education.* Second ed. Alexandria, VA: Association for Supervision and Curriculum Development.

Marklein, M. 2011. Study: Teachers lack training in online issues. *The Journal News* (May 4): 10A.

Marzano, R. J. 2007. *The art and science of teaching: A comprehensive framework for effective instruction.* Alexandria, VA: Association for Supervision and Curriculum Development.

Marzano, R. J. 2002. *Research-based strategies for increasing student achievement.* Audiotape #203062. Alexandria, VA: Association for Supervision and Curriculum Development.

Marzano, R. J. 2003. *What works in schools: Translating research into action.* Alexandria, VA: Association for Supervision and Curriculum Development.

Mbadu, D. 2008. The power of parent-teacher relationships. *Teacher Magazine* (March 26): http://www.teachermagazine.org/tm/section/first-person.2008/03/26/mbadu_first_web.h19.httm.

McTighe, J., and G. Wiggins, 2004. *Understanding by design: Professional development workbook.* Alexandria, VA: Association for Supervision and Curriculum Development.

Nightingale, J. 2006. Whiteboards under the microscope. *Education Guardian* (June 20): 2–3.

Nuthall, G. 1999. The way students learn: Acquiring knowledge from an integrated science and social studies unit. *The Elementary School Journal* 99(4):303–341.

Nuthall, G., and A. Alton-Lee, 1993. Predicting learning from student experience of teaching: A theory of student knowledge construction in classrooms. *American Educational Research Journal* 30(4):799–840.

Popham, W. J. 2008. *Transformative assessment.* Alexandria, VA: Association for Supervision and Curriculum Development.

Popham, W. J. 2011. *Transformative assessment in action: An inside look at applying the process.* Alexandria, VA: Association for Supervision and Curriculum Development.

Prensky, M. 2005/2006. Listen to the natives. *Educational Leadership* 63(4) (December/January): 8–13.

Staudt. C. 2005. *Changing how we teach and learn with handheld computers.* Thousand Oaks, CA: Corwin Press.

Steiny, J. 2010. Teaching kids to learn the most from their mistakes. *The Providence Journal* (December 20) www.projo.com/education/juliasteiny/content/Education_ Watch_12_.

Tate, M. L. 2003. *Worksheets don't grow dendrites: Instructional strategies that engage the brain.* Thousand Oaks, CA.: Corwin Press.

Tomlinson, C. 2001. *How to differentiate instruction in mixed-ability classrooms.* Second ed. Alexandria, VA: Association for Supervision and Curriculum Development.

Tomlinson, C., and J. McTighe. 2006. *Integrating differentiated instruction and understanding by design.* Alexandria, VA: Association for Supervision and Curriculum Development.

Udelhofen, S. 2006. Writing essential questions. In Curriculum mapping workshop: Integrating assessment data and standards into curriculum maps, K–12. Rye, NY: The Center for Curriculum Mapping.

Welsh, P. 2008. A school that's too high on gizmos. *The Washington Post* (February 10): B01.

Wiggins, G. 1996. Anchoring assessment with exemplars: Why students and teachers need models. *Gifted Child Quarterly,* 40(2) (Spring): 66–69.

Wiggins G. 1998. *Sophisticated and naïve vs. right and wrong: How to teach and assess for intellectual progress.* Audiotape # 298303. Alexandria, VA: Association for Supervision and Curriculum Development.

Wiggins, G., and J. McTighe. 1998. *Understanding by design.* Alexandria, VA: Association for Supervision and Curriculum Development.

Wiggins, G., and J. McTighe. 2011. *The understanding by design guide to creating high-quality units.* Alexandria, VA: Association for Supervision and Curriculum Development.

CHAPTER 6 DIFFERENTIATING INSTRUCTION

American Association of University Women. 1992. How schools short-change girls: *The AAUW Report.* Washington, DC: AAUW Educational Foundation. Author.

Banks, J. 2006. *Cultural diversity and education: Foundations, curriculum and teaching.* Fifth ed. Boston: Allyn and Bacon.

Baron-Cohen, S. 2003. *The essential difference: The truth about the male and female brain.* New York: Basic Books.

Bennett, C. I. 2007. *Comprehensive multicultural education: Theory and practice.* Sixth ed. Boston: Allyn and Bacon/Longman.

Brown, L. 2006.. Dropout, failure rates linked to language. *The Toronto Star* (June 23):7–8.

Conlin, M. 2003.. The new gender gap. *Business Week* (May 26):74–82.

Gurian, M. 2001. *Boys and girls learn differently.* San Francisco: Jossey-Bass.

Gurian, M., and K. Stevens. 2004. With boys and girls in mind. *Educational Leadership* 62 (9) (November):21–26.

Gurian, M., and K. Stevens. 2005. *The minds of boys: Saving our sons from falling behind in school and life.* San Francisco: Jossey-Bass.

Hallahan, D. R., and J. M. Kaufman. 2003. *Exceptional learners: Introduction to special education.* Ninth ed. Boston: Allyn and Bacon.

Hamel, A. 2004. Inclusion strategies that work. *Music Educators Journal* 90(5):33–37.

Irvine, J. 2003. *Educating teachers for diversity: Seeing with a cultural eye.* New York: Teachers College Press.

Lavoie, R. 1989. *How difficult can this be? The F.A.T. city workshop.* Alexandria, VA: PBS Video.

Lavoie, R. 2005a. *Beyond F.A.T. city: A look back, a look ahead.* Alexandria, VA: PBS Video.

Lavoie, R. 2005b. *It's so much work to be your friend: Helping the child with learning disabilities find social success.* New York: Touchstone/Simon and Schuster.

Lee, V. E., X. Chen, and B. A. Smerdon. 1996. *The influence of school climate on gender differences in the achievement and engagement of young adolescents.* Washington, DC: American Association of University Women.

Maniet-Bellerman, P. 1992. Mainstreaming children with learning disabilities: A guide to accompany "L. D." does NOT mean learning dumb! In *Educational psychology and classroom practice: A partnership,* ed. R. R. McCown and P. Roop. Boston: Allyn and Bacon.

Renzulli, J. S., ed. 2004. *Identification of students for gifted and talented programs.* Thousand Oaks, CA: Corwin Press.

Renzulli, J. S., and S. M. Reis.1991. The schoolwide enrichment model; A comprehensive plan for the development of creative productivity. In *Handbook of Gifted Education,* ed.N. Colangelo and G. Davis, 111–141. Boston: Allyn and Bacon.

Sadker, M., and D. Sadker. 1997. *Teachers, schools, and society.* New York: McGraw-Hill.

Sadker, M., and D. Sadker,1994. *Failing at fairness: How America's schools cheat girls.* New York: Scribner.

Smith, D. D., and R. Luckasson.1995. *Introduction to special education.* Boston: Allyn and Bacon.

Sommers, C. H. 1996. Where the boys are. *Education Week* (June 12):1, 9.

Tomlinson, C. 2001. *How to differentiate instruction in mixed-ability classrooms.* Second ed. Alexandria, VA: Association for Supervision and Curriculum Development.

Tomlinson, C. 2003. In Wiggins, G., J. McTighe, and C. Tomlinson. *Understanding by design and differentiated instruction: Partners in classroom success.* Audiotape #503281. Alexandria, VA: Association for Supervision and Curriculum Development.

Tomlinson, C. 2005. Traveling the road to differentiation in staff development. *Journal of Staff Development* 26 (4) (Fall):8–12.

Tomlinson, C., and C. Eidson. 2003. *Differentiation in practice: A resource guide for differentiating curriculum, grades 5–9.* Alexandria, VA: Association for Supervision and Curriculum Development.

Tomlinson-Keasey, C. 1990. Developing our intellectual resources for the twenty-first century: Educating the gifted. *Journal of Educational Psychology* 82: 399–403.

Turnbull, R., A. Turnbull, M. Shank, S. Smith, and D. Leal, 2002. *Exceptional lives: Special education in today's schools.* Upper Saddle River, NJ: Merrill Prentice-Hall.

Viadero, D. 2006. Concern over gender gap shifting to boys. *Education Week* (March 15): 1, 16–17.

Woolfolk, A. 2004. *Educational psychology.* Ninth ed. Boston: Allyn and Bacon.

CHAPTER 7 DESIGNING OPTIMAL LESSON PLANS

Beech, M., and V. Barnitt. 2001. *Dealing with differences: Strategies that work.* Audiotape #201174. Alexandria, VA: Association for Supervision and Curriculum Development.

Berns, D. 2011. Amid crowds, some students are left behind. *Las Vegas Sun* 1.

Bloom, B. S. 1984. The two sigma problem: The search for methods of group instruction as effective as one-to-one tutoring. *Educational Researcher* 34 (July):4–16.

Bransford, J., A. Brown, and R. Cocking, eds. 2000. *How people learn: Brain, mind, experience, and school.* Washington, DC: National Academy Press.

Castagnera, E., D. Fisher, K. Rodifer, and C. Sax. 1998. *Tools for tailoring individual supports.* In Deciding what to teach and how to teach it: Connecting students through curriculum and instruction, Author, 15–18. Colorado Springs, CO: PEAK Parent Center, Inc.

Cotton, K. 2000. *The schooling practices that matter most.* Alexandria, VA: Association for Supervision and Curriculum Development.

Darling-Hammond, L., and P. Youngs. 2002. Defining "highly qualified" teachers: What does scientifically-based research actually tell us? *Educational Researcher* 31(9): 13–25.

EdNews. 2008. Smaller classes not enough to reduce achievement gap. *Northwestern News* (February 28). Copy of report at http://www.journals.uchicago.edu/toc/est/current.

Fosnot, C. 2005. *Constructivism: Theory, perspective, and practice.* Second ed. New York: Teachers College Press.

Gagnon , G, and M. Collay. 2006. *Constructivist learning design: Key questions for teaching to standards.* Thousand Oaks, CA: Corwin Press.

Henry, J. 2008. Study finds big classes bad for less-able pupils. Telegraph Media Group Ltd. Telegraph (March 24). UK: www.telegraph.co.uk.

Hunter, M. 1982. *Mastery teaching.* El Segundo, CA: TIP Publications.

Hunter, M. 1984. *Knowing, teaching, and supervising.* In Using what we know about teaching, ed. P. Hosford, 169–192. Alexandria, VA: Association for Supervision and Curriculum Development.

Hunter, R. 2004. *Madeline Hunter's mastery teaching: Increasing instructional effectiveness in elementary and secondary schools.* Updated ed. Thousand Oaks, CA: Corwin Press.

Jacobson, L. 2008. Class-size reductions seen of limited help on achievement gap. *Education Week* 27(25) (February 27): 9.

Jensen, E. 1998. *Teaching with the brain in mind.* Alexandria, VA: Association for Supervision and Curriculum Development.

Jensen, E. 2005. *Teaching with the brain in mind.* Second ed. Alexandria, VA: Association for Supervision and Curriculum Development.

Joyce, B., and M. Weil, with E. Calhoun. 2004. *Models of teaching.* Seventh ed. Boston: Pearson.

Kelderman, E. 2004. Class size squeeze: When Florida voters approved an amendment to reduce class sizes, did they know all the ramifications? *State Legislatures* 30(5): 28–30.

Kellough, R. 2003. *A resource guide for teaching K–12.* Fourth ed. Upper Saddle River, NJ: Merrill Prentice Hall.

Kendall, J. S., and R. J. Marzano. 1997. *Content knowledge: A compendium of Standards and Benchmarks for K–12 Education.* Alexandria, VA: Association for Supervision and Curriculum Development.

Lang, H., and D. Evans. 2006. *Models, strategies, and methods for effective teaching.* Boston: Pearson.

Marzano, R., D. Pickering, and J. Pollock. 2001. *Classroom instruction that works: Research-based strategies for increasing student achievement.* Alexandria, VA: Association for Supervision and Curriculum Development.

Marzano, R., J. Norford, D. Paynter, D. Pickering, and B. Gaddy. 2005. *A handbook for classroom instruction that works.* Upper Saddle River, NJ: Merrill/Prentice Hall.

Matthews, J. 2008. Smaller classes don't close learning gap, study finds. *The Washington Post* (March 10), B02.

McCaslin, M. M., and T. L. Good. 1996. *Listening in classrooms.* New York: HarperCollins.

Nuthall, G. 1999. The way students learn: Acquiring knowledge from an integrated science and social studies unit. *The Elementary School Journal* 99(4): 303–341.

Pagliaro, M. 2011. *Differentiating instruction: Matching strategies with objectives.* Lanham, MD: Rowman & Littlefield Education.

Pagliaro, M. 2011a. *Exemplary classroom questioning: Practices to promote thinking and learning.* Lanham, MD: Rowman & Littlefield Education.

Pagliaro, M. 2011b. *Educator or bully? Managing the twenty-first-century classroom.* Lanham, MD: Rowman & Littlefield Education.

Popham, W. J. 2008. *Transformative assessment.* Alexandria, VA: Association for Supervision and Curriculum Development.

Roblyer, M. 2002. *Integrating educational technology into teaching.* Third ed. Upper Saddle River, NJ: Prentice Hall.

Ryan, K., J. Cooper, and S. Tauer. 2008. *Teaching for student learning: Becoming a master teacher.* Boston: Houghton Mifflin.

Schmoker, M. 2011. *Focus: Elevating the essentials to radically improve student learning.* Alexandria, VA: Association for Supervision and Curriculum Development.

Stiggins, R. 2005. *Student-involved assessment for learning.* Fourth ed. Upper Saddle River, NJ: Prentice Hall.

Stiggins, R. 2007. Assessment through the student's eyes. *Educational Leadership* 64(8) (May):22–26.

Tomlinson, C., and J. McTighe. 2006. *Integrating differentiated instruction and understanding by design.* Alexandria, VA: Association for Supervision and Curriculum Development.

Toppo, G. 2008. Size alone makes small classes better for kids. *USAToday* (March 24): www.usatoday.com.

Viadero, D. 2008. Student engagement found to rise as class size falls. *Education Week* (March 25): http://www.edweek.org/ew/articles/2008/03/25/29.

Wang, L. 2011. Shrinking classroom age variance raises student achievement: Evidence from developing countries. Policy Research Working Paper 5527 (January). The World Bank Development Research Group.

Wiggins, G., and J. McTighe. 2005. *Understanding by design.* Expanded second ed. Alexandria, VA: Association for Supervision and Curriculum Development.

Wolfe, P. 2011. Neuroscience reaffirms Madeline Hunter's model. *ASCD Express* 6(8).

About the Author

Marie Pagliaro is currently a professional development consultant. She was a full professor and Director of the Teacher Education Division at Dominican College, Chair of the Education Department at Marymount College, a supervisor of student teachers at Lehman College of the City University of New York, and Chair of the Science Department and teacher of chemistry, general science, and mathematics in the Yonkers Public Schools. She received her Ph.D. in Curriculum and Teaching from Fordham University.